amazing
Grace

The Official Autobiography

BRENDAN GRACE
with Tara King

BLACKWATER PRESS

Editor: Adam Brophy

Design and Layout: Liz White Designs

ISBN 978-0-9563541-1-2

© Blackwater Press, 2009

BWP Ltd., 1 Great Denmark Street, Dublin 1.

Printed in the Republic of Ireland.

The author would like to thank the following for giving their kind permission to reproduce photographs: Collins Photos, Dave Cullen, Frank Gavin, Brenda Fingleton, Brian Keane, Frank Knell, Maxwell's Photo Agency, Mike Mulcaire, Liam Quigley and Frank Savage.

While every effort has been made to contact copyright holders, we may have failed to contact some. Blackwater Press will be happy to come to some arrangement with these should they wish to contact us.

Contents

Foreword

Songs are magic carpets and there is no better man to ride a magic carpet than Brendan Grace ... so I wrote him a song! His ever mischievous friend Bottler played a vital part in that song's story when he stole a rose from a flower dealer's stall in Dublin's Moore Street for Brendan to give to the beautiful girl that the song was all about ... Ringsend Rose! The song was a hit and Brendan wooed the fair damsel leaving me out in the cold ... some friend he turned out to be. But sure I am only joking ... they were the rare old times!

Brendan Grace is still a friend of mine and is also one of the finest performing artistes of the modern era in Irish theatre. His fine vocal renditions of our favourite songs blending seamlessly with his amazing comedic talents make Brendan a man for all seasons. Full theatres and standing ovations are standard at Brendan Grace concerts and long may it continue. He still sings my songs but I have still not forgiven him for him stealing Ringsend Rose from me all those years ago!

This book is really a great read and a page turning, lighthearted insight into the life of a very special Irish performing artiste. Generous of spirit, totally professional, respectful of fellow artistes and a man always ready to laugh at life at all times ... that's Brendan Grace! Bottler tells me he has never changed one bit in all the years so maybe it is time I wrote him another song ... and joined him on the magic carpet? As we search for another Ringsend Rose!

Pete St John

one

I can recall a few occasions where I was driving along thinking Brendan was asleep in the back of the van when in fact he was quietly looking for a piece of paper to set alight and place down beside me. Next thing, all I would see is this piece of paper going up in flames beside me while Brendan would be in stitches laughing in the back. He was always a practical joker like that.

Brian Keane – manager and "other wife"

Scuttin'

Way back before French met Saunders, (but thankfully not so long back that it was before Laurel met Hardy) I was hitting the stage as a comic mime artist. I was 14 years of age and a one night stint does not a mime artist make, but even so, my one time novelty act went down well with the crowd in Dalkey's Khyber Pass Hotel. Sure how could they not laugh at a chubby young Jackeen miming his heart out to a Johnny McEvoy tape followed by a Spike Jones comedy track?

The reaction from the crowd obviously ignited something dormant inside me because prior to that night, I had never really given serious thought to a performing career, let alone one in comedy. Looking back however, I can see that I had always been drawn to centre stage. As with everything, there were a few obstacles along the way, but I always believed that from every negative stemmed a positive. Maybe this was why my father nicknamed me his super optimist. Somehow though, my belief was always proven right. To give you an example, I was once run over by an army ambulance, which resulted in the Minister for Defence, Charlie Haughey, buying my parents their first house and me a car. So you see, there was more light shed than blood shed! That's a story for another chapter though.

My childhood was divided between my grandmother's house in Crumlin and our flat in the Coombe. Prior to giving birth to yours truly, my poor mother, Christina, had no idea what to expect. I know they say that about all expectant mothers, but my mother literally hadn't a clue what lay ahead of her. She had no idea what the labour process entailed never mind the actual birth. In fact, my mother used to think that once you got married, you only had to sleep with your husband the one time and the babies would just automatically arrive in the years that followed.

When I was about five years of age, my mother gave birth to a daughter who was later christened Bríd. Our Coombe abode only contained one single bedroom with a bucket for a toilet, which meant I had to share a bed with my parents. How they created a child with me stuck beside them, I will never figure out. After Bríd was born, I was immediately fascinated by her. I showed her to absolutely everyone and anyone as she lay in her pram. There wasn't enough space in our small flat for a cot so Bríd's bed was a drawer. The drawer would be taken out of the chest every night, placed on two chairs and laden with blankets. Sadly Bríd only survived six weeks. She had gastroenteritis, which at the time was a common enough killer amongst young kids. I have always found it strange however that while I can vividly remember showing Bríd to people and explaining, as five year olds do, that she was my new sister, I honestly cannot remember what she looked like. I also have no recollection of her death. I'm sure my mother broke it to me by telling me she was an angel but if she did, I unfortunately have no memory of it.

When I was around eight years of age and living with my grandmother in Crumlin, Phil Lynott was living at the other end of the same street. Coincidentally, he too was living with his grandmother. Even though all the kids on that street got on very well together as friends, I can't really recall any of us ever actually knowing Phil's name. We only ever knew him by his nickname "Blackie". Phil was the only black kid in the area, so we christened him with a particularly blunt pet name. While needless to say it would be frowned upon today, back then it wasn't meant as a derogatory name or a racist insult. If anything, it was a term of endearment. Years later when we were both established in our careers, we shared a few drinks in Neary's Pub near the Gaiety Theatre. We were chatting away about music and I mentioned an idea I had for a witty rap song which would be sung by Bottler. That's when Phil told me about his studio in London and invited me to stay at his house while we recorded the song over a few days.

We only saw each other occasionally, but we had a mutual respect and liking for each other. In fact Phil had long been a fan of my act due to his fascination with the character of Bottler. When I made the trip to London to begin work on our rap venture, he kicked off the shenanigans by bringing me to a very famous London club, Stringfellows to be precise. By this stage Phil was hugely famous, so much so that he even had to have a bodyguard accompany him to the club. On the night in question, I was dressed in a pin stripe suit and tie while Phil was dressed in his distinctive Phil Lynott style. Unfortunately, the bouncers in the club took one look at me in my suit and jumped to the conclusion that I was a cop. Phil told me afterwards that they had actually taken him aside and asked why he had brought the cops into the club with him. We shared a good laugh about it but even though his spirits were up at the time, medically he didn't appear to be a well man. He just seemed like someone who was out of sorts health wise. When it came to the music however, he didn't falter. The moment we stepped inside his studio, he was immediately on the keyboard experimenting with the various sound effects. He had also brought in a couple of musicians to play on the track as well. We got down to work and created the basis of a song which, as far as I can remember, was a rap version of "Whiskey in the Jar" as performed by Bottler. It was an amazing experience. Not many have the honour of saying they collaborated with Phil Lynott but when I look back, I don't think I actually appreciated the significance of it at the time. The song was very much in its infancy; in fact we hadn't even created a title for the track and to this day I have no idea where the recording is. Musicians and record companies don't generally discard such material, so it may be lying in a vault or a basement somewhere. On the other hand, the recording was in such an unfinished state that salvaging it probably isn't even a possibility. We didn't have a format, we were simply experimenting and brainstorming various ideas.

Shortly after that collaboration however, Phil's health deteriorated even further and he became quite ill. Looking back now, I still can't quite believe his death was imminent. While he seemed slightly unwell, he definitely didn't seem like a man who was in the final weeks of his life.

I heard the news of his passing being announced on the RTÉ Radio news and to say I was shocked is an understatement. The man, like his mother Philomena, was an absolute gem. I knew him when he was a kid in Crumlin and an adult in showbusiness, and I can honestly say that throughout those periods of his short life, he was one in a million.

We all did mad things as young kids, however my friends and I could probably lay claim to being slightly more extreme than most. Potential consequences weren't even considered if it got in the way of us having a laugh. One of the games in which we regularly participated was called "scuttin". This involved sneaking up behind a lorry that had stopped at traffic lights, climbing onto its back door and holding on as it took off. Needless to say, a firm grip was the only requirement for this game as letting go was not an option until the lorry had stopped. A school friend of mine actually lost his leg through scuttin' on a Guinness truck. Remarkably, not even the fear of enduring a similar fate could stop us from scuttin'.

Another activity in which we used to indulge quite a lot was the game of holding onto a lorry while on our bikes. Usually it was seen as a way of getting a lift up a steep hill, but on one particular day an anxious thirst for devilment prompted me to hold onto a fire brigade truck that had pulled up at Sally's Bridge on the canal. Looking back, I'd say it was going at a speed of around sixty miles an hour. But when you're eight years of age and hanging onto the back door with one hand while on a bicycle, it might as well have been a young Eddie Irvine behind the steering wheel. Moments of childhood madness like that are those I tend to blame on my inner-Bottler.

The streets we were usually scuttin' through were always filled with various Dublin characters. Individuals whom, I have no doubt, the readers of this book will remember as fondly as I do.

One such man was known simply as Bang Bang.

Bang Bang, who was in his fifties and almost legally blind, would hop onto a bus, point at someone with his large house key, and say: "Bang bang." The person on the receiving end would be expected to fall down and play dead. However, if Bang Bang happened to point at a country person who was up in Dublin for the day, the poor thing was left bewildered by what had just happened. Bang Bang endeared himself to everyone and bus drivers loved having him on their bus. He was the only person I knew at that time who could get a bus to stop for him absolutely anywhere. As well known as he was, I don't think anyone ever found out his actual name or where he lived.

Another character familiar to many was Paddy Byrne. Paddy owned a donkey named Nelly, but the poor creature was always referred to as simply Paddy Byrne's ass. Paddy was known for collecting leftover food, known as slop, from people's houses and pouring it into barrels which he would then sell to pig farms as feed. Even today I find it amazing that there were actual farms in Dublin city centre back then. On and off over the years, my friends and I would help Paddy collect the slop. Likewise when he would have the cart filled with turf, we'd lend a hand. How Nelly's legs didn't give way, I will never know.

To this day, I can still see in my mind's eye the vision of Paddy and Nelly struggling to make it over Sally's Bridge in Crumlin. Nelly's hooves continually slipped as she tried to pull the heavy cart of turf attached. Traffic would be held up behind her. However, fortunately for Paddy, that particular route was used by the number 81 bus. Seeing the commotion, the bus driver would drive up behind the donkey and cart and push it on gently until it was over the hump of the bridge. You would never see anything like it today, but then there were so many innocent things like that which I only came to appreciate in later years.

If you think the idea of a donkey and cart being pushed on by a large double decker bus in the middle of Dublin City sounds off the wall, then try imagining a horse pulling a large cart carrying a double bed, a wooden wardrobe, a chest of three drawers and a table and four chairs across the city! This was exactly the scene back in 1959 when the Graces set about moving from their one-bedroom flat in the Coombe to a luxury pad in Echlin Street. The new flat was known as an "artisan dwelling". At the time, we thought it was really lavish. The reality however was that it was located so close to Guinness brewery that I often joke I was reared on the smell of the hops. The new flat had two bedrooms, a living room, a scullery (nowadays known as a kitchen) and it was located on the fourth floor of the building. I can still see us walking into the church on James Street for mass very shortly after we arrived so as to meet our new neighbours. Mass was sacred. I once attended a mass in St James Street Church where the priest deliberately stopped a ceremony after one particular woman walked in. He publicly singled her out and asked her to leave, all because she wasn't wearing a hat or a scarf on her head. I think she returned with a hankie on her head. Even though I was very young, I was shocked by what had happened.

Personally, I loved the Latin mass and its absence is one that annoys me. For some, a Latin mass would conjure the impression of tedium and dreariness, but for me, it held a certain mystique. You know how a scent can trigger memories? Well for me, the scent of incense immediately inspires memories of the old Latin masses. After attending a few of them, you would actually begin to understand certain sayings that were used in the ceremony. Being unable to understand the language of the mass didn't frustrate me in the slightest. After all, there were parts of the English mass that might as well have been in Latin for all the understanding I had of it. I practically knew the Hail Mary backwards when I was a child, but that in no way meant I understood it. As far as I was concerned, the word "womb" was a funny way of saying the word "room". There were various prayers we were made learn off by heart but we hadn't a clue what they meant, so in that sense the Latin mass was about as understandable as the English version.

The one thing I did understand about the mass however was that, regardless of the language it was performed in, you showed respect. If you were seen getting restless, a clip around the ear would soon sort you out. This sense of respect certainly survived into my adulthood and, as a result, I still bless myself when I pass a graveyard, a grotto or a church. I also make a point of genuflecting properly when entering the pew at mass. When I say properly, I mean your knee has to hit the floor. Then again, I'm the first to admit that I'm one of the dinosaurs from a bygone era. Looking back, it's sometimes difficult to believe the extent to which we were a nation of innocent Catholics. For example, I can remember my mother approaching the priest and asking him if he would bless her candles again. She had attended the blessing of the candles in the church the previous night but she hadn't realised at the time that her candles were still in their wrapping while the blessing was taking place. She genuinely believed the blessing wouldn't be able to make its way through the wrapping to the candles. The priest reassured her that the previous blessing would work but, sensing her concern, he went ahead and blessed them again.

My father, Seamus, on the other hand was a man who enjoyed the blessing of a good pint. One of his good friends, Jim O'Reilly, has often told me that I'm the second funniest man to come out of Ireland; he is adamant my father was the funniest. He's right too. Me Da was renowned for his humour, his pranks, and in particular his captivating ability as a *seanchai*. Jim and his wife Peggy lived on the third floor of the Echlin Street flats around the same time as ourselves. Every night without fail, as me Da made his way home from the pub, he would always call in to see Jim and Peggy. It's fair to say they would usually hear him before he even knocked on the door as his walk home was never complete without him singing at the top of his voice. When inside the O'Reilly's flat, me Da would almost always eat a boiled potato with them and for some reason, it seemed to have a calming effect on him. Visiting the O'Reilly's became almost a ritual. The two families were very close though. My sister Marie and the O'Reilly's daughter Collette were inseparable as there was only a few months in age difference between them. Marie was born in August of 1961 while Collette arrived in February of 1962. I have a very vivid memory of the two days in question. On the day Collette was born, a Morris Minor car pulled up outside the Echlin Street flat complex while we were outside playing. A man emerged from it carrying a leather case and one of the neighbours told us that he was the doctor who was bringing the baby to Peggy. Peggy's daughter Rita was one of the kids out playing that day and someone told her that the new baby was inside the doctor's bag. For a shockingly long time afterwards my friends and I genuinely believed that the leather bag the doctor was carrying that day had the baby inside it. As far as we were concerned, women never "had" babies, they "got" them. After Peggy "got" Colette, my mother brought me in to the O'Reilly's flat to see the new addition to the Echlin Street family. Peggy has since told me that when I saw her newborn, the first thing I asked my mother was if she could buy me one as well. Ma agreed and she kept her promise too! I didn't know it at the time, but she was already three months pregnant! Six months later, I was presented with Marie.

I was ten years of age when Marie was born. When she was brought home from the hospital, I felt concerned. I think I was worried that if my first baby sister had returned to God, would the second one do the same? My mother never looked at Bríd's passing as a "loss" exactly. Instead she felt she had gained a new baby. Ma always saw Marie as a reincarnation of Bríd and she firmly believed this until her dying day. Her belief wasn't without reason either. When Marie was a baby, she had the same little mole in the same part of her body as Bríd had. To my mother, that alone was a message from God that Bríd had been sent back.

Marie and Collette were close friends from as far back as I can remember. Marie would regularly stay over at Jim and Peggy's and Collette likewise would stay at ours. Tragically, Collette's life was cut far too short in 1980 when she was killed at a pedestrian crossing in Tallaght. Me Da was working with the ambulance service at the time and he always said it was with the grace of God that he had not been on duty the day Collette had been killed. He knew that if he had attended the scene of Collette's accident, it would have absolutely destroyed him. Marie and Collette were so close that Collette was almost like another daughter to him. It was the same with Marie and the O'Reillys. I'll never forget Marie's devastation when the news was broken to her. She was absolutely inconsolable and never came to terms with the loss of beautiful young Colette.

In writing this book, I met up with Jim and Peggy to muse over memories of our Echlin Street days. During our chat, Peggy recalled for me the day my mother arrived into their flat giving out like bejaysus about me. It seems we had been on the bus when she told me to go to the shop and buy some eggs. On this particular occasion, my mother was wearing an expensive fur coat she had received from my aunt Wyn who was a well-known model in Ireland at the time. In those days, eggs were sold cheaper if they were damaged, and apparently as I went to get off the bus I roared back in front of the whole bus: "Ma, d'ya want me to get ya the good ones or the cracked ones?" My poor mother was standing there in her long fancy coat absolutely mortified that her son was asking if he should buy damaged food.

It was Jim O'Reilly who encouraged me at 14 years of age to perform in the Khyber Pass Hotel in Dalkey, as I mentioned earlier. The Spike Jones track I used that night possessed a particularly contagious laugh so I saw it as an ideal source of entertainment for a mime act. Another song, which is equally as amusing, is "The Laughing Policeman". Almost once every three months Ronan Collins receives a request to play that particular song on his radio show. It's happened so often now that each time before playing it, he'll say: "I know bloody well who sent in this request!"

In a small way, I was always surrounded by an atmosphere of showbiz. Jim O'Reilly was a big participant in the acting and staging of the pantomime in the local Parochial Hall while Peggy was one of the finest singers in 1960's Dublin. She even used to sing professionally under the name Peggy Kavanagh. It was at the wedding of their daughter Rita that I first performed my Father of the Bride act. I wanted to test the reaction to this new routine I had created so I decided to try it out on Rita's wedding audience. Thankfully it went down a storm because if it hadn't, who knows if the Father of the Bride would have ended up staggering through as many venues as he did in the years afterwards. Not many people know this but Father of the Bride is actually a combination of the various traits possessed by the actor Brendan Caldwell, the comedian Bob Newhart and my father. While my father was a drinking man, he was in no way a violent drunk. Like the character he partly inspired, he would stagger and sing. The most damage he would do on a night was rouse people from their sleep with his singing of "Up the Furry Mountain". I'd say anyone who lived in those flats at the time will remember many a night when they could hear Seamus Grace from the moment he walked around the corner on James Street. The solemn hush of the street was always broken the moment he was in the vicinity with a few drinks inside him.

His downfall was whiskey. Once he had polished off a few glasses, he became Jack the lad. Sometimes he was so drunk that he and my mother would row, which would end with her walking out. It could be two or three in the morning when it would happen, but she would always take Marie and me with her, usually to stay with her mother. Me Da never once in his life lifted a hand to her, but the drink made him loud and his drunken stupor was something she detested with a passion. With Marie's pram in tow, and having to carry it down three flights of stairs, the three of us would walk from James Street all the way out to Crumlin which would take about forty minutes. The place was so safe back then that walking the route late at night never gave anyone cause for concern.

Ma would usually end up feeling sorry for him however and return after a few days. On some occasions though, it wasn't long before we were walking out again. Sometimes I would even run out to the phone box across the street and dial 999 to try to get a guard to help my drunken Da. On one occasion, the famous guard Lugs Brannigan arrived out. Lugs, a pure gentleman, was renowned for always taking the side of the wife who was getting a hard time from the husband. He was a big, solid man and I can still picture him stepping into our small flat and calling my father a drunken bowsy. At one point, he even threatened to lock him up if he didn't pipe down and go to bed. Drunk and all as my father was, words got through to him that night. On other occasions, I would call my uncle John, who was my mother's brother. He would collect us in the car but, before leaving, he would throw a few harsh words in the direction of my father. The following day, my father would be a totally different man – very quiet and incredibly remorseful. It was like Jekyll and Hyde. Me Da wouldn't remember just how drunk he had been but when he would wake to find his wife and kids gone, it wouldn't take him long to guess.

Despite this one flaw however, he was still the most popular man with people. In fairness to him, he made the effort several times to draw a line under his drinking. He even took the pledge on a couple of occasions. He would go through the whole process of kneeling down before a priest while the relevant prayers were said. He would then emerge from the church filled with the zeal of the newly reformed. Unfortunately however, he only ever managed to keep the alcohol away from his lips for a few weeks before he was back to square one again. I see now just how difficult it must have been for him, particularly as his job in O'Reilly's Bar on Hawkins Street meant he was continuously surrounded by drink.

Whatever about his love of a few jars, his love for his kids beat it by a mile. Both he and my mother were excellent providers. I never went around in my bare feet and there was always food on the table. If anything, they went the extra mile to give Marie and me a happy childhood. When I was around ten years of age, my father used to bring local kids to the Wellington Monument and regale them with stories. He was an avid *seanchaí* and would always have his listeners entranced. Due to Da's working hours as a barman, he would often be free during the day so he would sometimes take myself and about a dozen of my friends to the Phoenix Park. He would then sit us all down on the Wellington Monument to tell us a tale, usually one from the country; stories about fairies, leprechauns, things like that. For some reason, the weather was always warm – summers were summers back then. He would take the route down by Stephen's Hospital and Kingsbridge Station and even that was an adventure for us because we would be able to see the trains up close, which was a novelty at the time.

After that, me Da would bring us to the shop and treat us to crisps, ice cream and bottles of minerals. The Wellington Monument holds many good memories like that but there is one memory in particular of which I am not so fond. When I was around eleven years of age, I got this notion into me to climb up as high as I could on the Wellington Monument. Unfortunately however, my spontaneity lacked foresight and it was only when I was up there that I realised I had no idea how to get down. Completely stranded, I gave my friends a good laugh although I can't say the fire brigade that was called to rescue me found it funny.

Another place for devilment and acting the maggot was the farm attached to my father's home house in Dunlavin, county Wicklow. We always travelled there for the summer holidays, but the main trip was at Christmas. The journey to Dunlavin always began on Christmas morning and consisted of a long bus ride to Analacky Cross. I remember two things about that journey that you would never see today – Marie's pram would always be tied to the roof of the bus while up at the front of the bus there would be about ten cardboard boxes full of day-old chicks ready for delivery to people along the route.

One Christmas Eve, just hours before our trip to Dunlavin, Peggy answered the door to my mother who was in a slight state of panic. Me Da was a very popular barman and every Christmas punters reflected their gratitude for his year-round humour and good company with a token of good will, usually in the form of a naggin of whiskey. We were supposed to be heading off to Dunlavin the following morning but Ma feared that Da's consumption of his "tokens of good will" that night would result in us being late for our trip. Peggy, who was heavily pregnant at the time, decided on a ruse to disarm me Da of the whiskey gifts upon his arrival home.

Sure enough, they soon heard him navigating his way to our flat; the echo of the glass bottles clanging together in his pockets almost as loud as his singing. As he made his way up the concrete stairs, Peggy approached him and told him she had a toothache. Whiskey was Da's cure for everything so, as expected, he took a bottle from his pocket and told her to knock it back. Ten minutes later, Peggy approached him again. Da, who was fluthered to say the least, greeted her as though it were the first time he had seen her all day. Repeating her tooth problem, she was quickly handed another bottle of whiskey to cure the ache. This process went on and on until Peggy had secured every naggin of whiskey from his pockets.

The following morning, me Da was up and about all bright eyed with no trace of a hangover. Peggy, who was on her way to six o'clock mass called by to wish us a happy Christmas before we left for Dunlavin. After some banter, me Da said to her, "Jaysus Peggy d'you know what happened me last night? I had a couple of bottles of whiskey and the effin' taxi man must have robbed me." I honestly don't think he ever found out that the bottles were behind the chair in Peggy's flat all along.

Over the years, my mother acquired a number of tricks when it came to making alcohol disappear. me Da sometimes had in his possession a small bottle of whiskey known as the Baby Power. It contained just over a glass of whiskey. When he wasn't looking, Ma would empty the bottle and replace the whiskey with cold tea thinking he wouldn't notice. There were times all right when me Da had enough consumed that he genuinely wouldn't notice his drink tasting more like a Barry's tea than a Paddy's whiskey, but in saying that there were also occasions when he would cop what she had done. I have to admit, Christmas usually witnessed these tricks go into overdrive!

Anyway, upon our arrival at Analacky Cross we were usually collected by either my cousin Tim or my uncle Eamon who would arrive on the horse and cart. If for some reason they were late, we would just begin the three-mile walk to the house because along the way someone would always stop and offer us a lift on their horse and cart.

I must have been a bit of an entertainer even back when I was a kid because from the age of six my cousins were always excited about meeting me. I suppose they saw me as a young Dublin Jackeen who always seemed to find himself stuck on the roof of some shed or knee deep in pond water. I have many memories of those times but one that I wish I could forget is the memory of killing a baby chick when I was too young to have common sense. I looked into the shed and saw all the chickens running around and for some reason decided to roll a tyre towards them to make them scatter. They all did except for one and the bloody tyre went over him. I was absolutely devastated at the time. I still don't know how I managed to roll the tyre because, God knows, I was barely the height of it.

Following the Christmas dinner in Dunlavin, there was always a singsong. "Softly Softly" must have been my party piece because it's all I can remember ever singing for the family. I would confidently stand and sing to the room, the chair my stage, the dresser my backdrop! Afterwards, everyone else would take it in turns to sing. Apart from the singsong, the one thing that still stands out in my mind about that time was having to say the Rosary every single night before going to bed. There was never a night when it wasn't said. The very notion was unthinkable.

I'm very fortunate that I still possess a crystal clear recollection of that particular time of my life. One of my most vivid memories from those years is of me sitting in the Radio Éireann building on Dublin's Henry Street, having a cup of tea and a laugh with Pat Kenny. He wasn't a presenter then, nor was I a comedian. We were both teenage messenger boys. Not many people actually know that Pat and I have been friends since our early teens. I don't know if Pat himself at that age harboured any ideas of breaking into broadcasting, but I know, for me, showbusiness couldn't have been further away from my mind. I can see how over time this changed drastically and I ended up developing a hankering for the limelight.

I lay the blame primarily at the door of my aunt, Wyn Myler, who was a famous fashion model in 1950's Ireland. Wyn was, and still is, strikingly beautiful, and through her career in showbusiness, was able to expose me to little luxuries I would never have otherwise experienced at that time. Things like going for an Indian or a Chinese meal, going to the cinema and having popcorn, shopping for new clothes, these were all the type of things that Wyn would arrange for us to do together. I think she saw me as a living doll for her to dress. A chubby doll, but a doll nonetheless. Unlike Wyn however, I couldn't exactly entertain the option of making a living from the modelling route.

Funnily enough, it wasn't the places she would take me to that I found the most interesting. What intrigued me was the public reaction to her. Being in her company was indescribable. Taxi drivers would beep the horn at her as she was walking down the street, strangers would not only turn and stare at her, but they would know exactly who they were looking at - Wyn Myler.

I think witnessing what Wyn experienced on a daily basis encouraged my showbusiness gene. It made me hungry to become a recognisable public figure. The potential earnings from a career in the entertainment industry was never a motivation for me; I was purely attracted to the idea of someone stopping in their tracks and remarking: "Jaysus, that's yer man Brendan Grace!"

Looking back now I can see how, over a period of time, various incidents combined together fuelled my appetite for this kind of attention. For instance, I was in Roches Stores on Henry Street one day and witnessed the reaction to Tommy Byrne from the Wolfe Tones as he progressed down the escalator. The man was only in to do some shopping with his wife yet the reaction his presence alone commanded was something I still to this day find phenomenal. Likewise, the reaction to Joe Dolan. The very first time I saw Joe, I was in my early teens and I looked on at him in awe. Joe was running as fast as he could from the door of the RDS towards the door of his car in order to try and escape the mass of lovestruck women who were chasing him. It was pure hysteria.

I don't know if Wyn recognised something in me that seemed eager for that kind of centre stage attention, but even so, she made a whole other world available to me. As a result of that and a variety of other factors, I craved a life in the limelight. Little did I know then that a subsequent return to the school uniform would provide me with my wish. The boy Bottler actually began as a violent gurrier, but somehow he turned into this lovable rogue.

Channelling the character of Bottler as an adult was never a difficult job as I only had to draw from my experience as a mischievous nipper. One of my more innocent crimes back then involved me standing on the wall outside my grandmother's house in Crumlin with my trousers down around my ankles, mooning the buses that passed. This continued until one day, a bus driver decided to stop and inform my grandmother of the disturbing view her grandson was providing his passengers with. Needless to say, I was in her bad books for a while after that.

It's probably hard to imagine, but there were orchards near Dublin's South Circular Road back then. What's definitely not hard to imagine is my friends and I robbing them! We even had our own little system in place as well. Someone could climb up and collect the loot while another person would be the lookout. Of course, I would never be on climbing duty because I was a fat young lad. Instead I would catch the apples as they were thrown down by my accomplice. Usually we would be chased by the owner and if we were caught, which we often were, a kicking ensued.

Everyone had bangers when they were kids. You would be saving up for ages to buy them and once you had them, it was just a matter of choosing the doors of the flats you would slip them through. You would only get away with it a few times though because sooner or later your backside would be on the receiving end of yet another kicking. You would think with all the kickings we got, we would have learned our lesson, but as I said earlier, consequences were never considered if it meant a laugh being potentially hampered.

Wyn and my grandmother reared me as much as my parents did. I often spent a good deal of time in their house because they had facilities like a bath. A shower was unheard of, back then it would have been classed as exotic. They also had a refrigerator which I would often raid. I used to regularly relieve the fridge of a few tins of fruit cocktail. To disguise my little theft, after polishing off the whole tin I would throw the empty can over the wall and think no more of it. Out of sight, out of mind. This routine continued for months until one day my uncle happened to look over the wall and discovered the mountain of empty fruit cocktail cans. Immediately after that, a lock was installed on the fridge and my days of fruit cocktails were well and truly over.

two

*All my fondest childhood memories are from Christmas because my
parents would really get into the spirit of it. The things they would
do! I remember one year we awoke on Christmas morning to what
I now know was the sound of my Dad throwing bricks on the roof.
At the time however, Mum told us not to leave our rooms as Santa
was still on the roof! It was the best. In retrospect, I suspect a few
too many drinks the night before had perhaps delayed the normal
routine but it made for a great Christmas morning and as always
my parents were troopers!*

Bradley Grace

An Honest Fib

It was always very easy to convince people, including potential employers,
that I was older than my 13 years. For a start, I was a big young lad and
if that didn't work, well I just showed them the birth certificate I had
carefully forged.

The idea to "adjust" my birth certificate came about after I started working
as a messenger boy for Browne & Nolan's book suppliers in Dublin. Even to
get that job I had to lie and say I was 16, but luckily for me they took me
on my word. Unfortunately, when it came to obtaining a motorbike license,
government officials needed more than just my word, they needed proof. At the

time, Browne & Nolan's sold a special type of ointment that removed ink, and it was upon finding this ointment that my forgery idea was born. Carefully, I applied it over my date of birth and waited for it to completely dry before then changing it to suit my motorcycling needs. If that document is anything to go by, I'm now technically 63.

Working for Browne & Nolan's was an interesting time. I was given a parcel one day to deliver to the theatre actor Micheál Mac Liammhóir in Earlsfort House. I instantly recognised the name but at the time I didn't appreciate just how great a man he was. When I arrived at Mac Liammhóir's house with the book, the first thing I noticed as he answered the door was that he was wearing make up. He was also donning a silk smoking jacket – it was the first time I had ever seen one. Mac Liammhóir's entire appearance was the epitome of old style showbusiness. The man possessed a certain eccentricity about him that was entirely unique at the time. Upon taking the delivery, he invited me inside and sat me down while he carefully cut away the parcelling around the book. I would give absolutely anything to know the name of that book. It intrigues me to know what reading material he had selected. Following some small talk, he handed me a tip of two shillings. In those days a tip of any amount wasn't the done thing, but a tip of that amount was unimaginable. His kindness was extreme. Mac Liammhóir's name actually arose many years later in a conversation with Maureen Potter. By this time however the great man himself had long since passed away. Maureen had seen my show one night in Clontarf Castle and while we were enjoying a few drinks after the show, she looked at me and said, "Mac Liammhóir would have loved to have seen your act." That's when I stunned her with the story of our brief meeting.

While I got to know Maureen quite well, I never had the opportunity to speak to her panto partner Jimmy O'Dea. I did, however, once see him in a shop on Parliament Street near the Olympia while I was out on one of my messenger boy rounds. He walked into the shop and asked for a pack of twenty Players and a newspaper. Even though I was only a teenager at the time, I was towering over him as he was incredibly small in stature. I distinctly recall the elegance he possessed. Wearing a hat, an overcoat and gloves, he had a natural air and poise about him. Jimmy went on to star in my all-time favourite movie *Darby O'Gill and The Little People* and I always regret not having had the courage to ask him for an autograph in the shop that day.

Of all the things I could have bought with my first week's wages from Browne & Nolan's, I chose to spend it on a globe; the kind that lit up. I was fascinated by travel and of particular interest to me was the map of Ireland. My favourite subject at school was geography and at one stage I badly wanted to be a van driver or a salesman, anything that would allow me to tour around Ireland. I only viewed it as an interest; in no way did I realise at the time that my entire life would one day revolve around travelling. I suppose in a way, the travelling began when I was 15 years of age, just after I left the Christian Brothers.

My reliable birth certificate forgery not only secured me a bike license, it also helped get me work in England. I got a job as barman in The Bull and Star pub. The Hynes agency on Dublin's O'Connell Street was known for sourcing jobs in England for barmen and nurses so I sought out her help. I remember my mother crying her eyes out before I left. She thought my move to England was the end of me. At that time, going to England was seen in the same light as going to America. I didn't get the boat over however, I actually travelled by plane. It was my first time on an aircraft and the ticket set me back exactly six pounds and ten shillings. In 1966, six pounds and ten shillings was a significant amount of money. Would you believe, after all these years, I still have the ticket stub from that very flight! It's ironic to think that back when we didn't have the money and needed to emigrate, our plane tickets out of here cost a small fortune. These days they can be bought on-line for a cent.

After I arrived at Heathrow, I had to take two buses: one from the airport and then a second one to Putney Bridge. I got off to a less-than-desirable start however. The fare was four pence, but I only had a penny and what was known as a thrupenny bit, which was a three penny piece. I gave the money to the bus conductor and after taking one look at it, he threw me off the bus. The penny was an Irish penny, not an English one. Even though it was still legal tender and nearly all establishments would still take it from a customer, he refused outright. That was literally all the money I had to my name, so I ended up having to walk quite a long distance to my new lodging with a large suitcase in tow. After that bad start, you would think my circumstances would improve, however not so. I hated being away from home and in the end, I only lasted three weeks. My misery was short-lived as my aunt Wyn arrived over to release me from my grief and take me home. I simply told my boss that I wouldn't be in for work because I had the flu, and with that, I hightailed it back home.

I might have looked like a big lad, but underneath it all, I was still a homesick young boy. You know, for as long as I can remember, I have always hated the term "a fine lad" or worse again, "stout". The word "stout" in particular always bothered me. People used to often make remarks about me being "a fine lad" either to my mother or to myself, but I always knew even at a young age, it was just another way of saying: "Jaysus, he's a bit of a fat young lad!"

Whenever I hear the term "a fine lad" though, it brings back memories of a comment made to me by a nun at the very first dance I went to. Back then a school dance was nicknamed "the hop", and when I was about 13 years of age I attended one for the first time. This particular "hop" was being held in the convent on Basin Lane and as it was run by the nuns, needless to say there was no close dancing. I was always very conscious of being the chubby red faced boy. After all it wasn't exactly the stereotype of a lady magnet! When I went to pay the entry fee of about one shilling, the nun collecting the money said to me, "Oh well, aren't you a fine lad. You look like a responsible person. Maybe you will do the door for us?" Straight away, I was commandeered and placed in what was effectively the role of a bouncer. To think the first time I attended a dance, I never even saw the dance floor never mind get an actual dance!

School for me however was abandoned at 13 years of age. Back then, it was more in your line to go out and get a job and help supplement the family income. I attended the James Street Christian Brothers and I have to admit, I liked them. That's not to say there weren't occasions when I abhorred them. There was one time when I was asked the Catechism question "Who made the world?" that I replied, "God, sir." With that I was given a hiding and asked the question a second time. Again I gave the same answer because I genuinely could not see what was wrong with it. No sooner had I uttered the words when

I found myself on the receiving end of yet another beating. It seems the answer was not "God, sir", but rather "God made the world, sir."

On occasions like that it was difficult to like school. But there was one particular teacher called Danny Finn who rarely tried to impede my classroom humour. He knew I was a bit of a clown, and if he were alive today he wouldn't be at all surprised by my choice of career. Any time teachers turned their backs, I would get up and do things, pulling faces and the like. I was caught a few times and the consequence might be a belt or two from the teacher, but to me it was always worth it if what I had done made the class laugh. Mr Flynn allowed me to be funny. There was something about his nature that appeared to give the thumbs up to my style of wit, and on occasion, a kick up the backside if I pushed it too far. I always had a persistent inclination towards transforming something ordinary into something funny. Combine this with an anxiousness to be centre of attention and what you are left with is a downright stubborn refusal to be ignored! 192582

Academically, I was very bright. I was one of a few who had won a seat in the scholarship class in the Christian Brothers. As a young, restless teenager however, I had other things than school lessons on my mind. As a result, my concentration went out the window and needless to say, my schooling days soon went with them.

I certainly didn't suffer as a result of having departed the classroom in my early teens. I had good role models and looking back I seemed to constantly absorb the different mannerisms and traits that made them popular, witty people overall.

Joseph Molloy was one such individual. A few years older than me, he ran a grocery shop on James Street along with his mother. Joseph was a right character. He was always very endearing to his customers and he possessed a beautiful sense of reverence for his older customers in particular. It was through Joseph that I developed a love of miniature metal cars and trucks known as Corgi toys. At the time, they were hugely popular in general but Joseph and I were particularly big fans. I went on to become a member of the Corgi models club, based in Swansea in Wales. It was a fan club for car enthusiasts. I entered every competition running in the club at the time, and on two occasions I was the winner. One of the prizes was a fabulous articulated circus truck while the other was a beautiful fire brigade. The quality of these toys was like nothing else at the time. My aunt Wyn sometimes generously added to my collection and even at the time, she warned me to take good care of them as one day they would be valuable. She was right. They are now collectors' items. I'm raging that I didn't take her advice. I gave them to my two girls when they were younger and they pulled them asunder.

Getting back to the Molloys however, Joseph was the eldest in his family and because of this rank, he held the responsibility for running the shop. At the time, there was a system in place called "the bill". It was the equivalent of buying on credit. If a customer didn't have the money to pay for the groceries on the day, either Joseph or Mrs Molloy would list the items and the customer could pay for them later. One day, my mother's bill ran a little over what she could afford. It was no big deal at the time, but to my mother it was a huge issue. She was a proud lady and the thought of owing money was one she loathed. I think the sum of what she owed was in the region of seven shillings, which today is the equivalent of fifty cent. In those days however, the equivalent of fifty cent could land you in long-term debt. My poor mother couldn't walk past the door of the shop while the debt was standing. Instead, she picked up her groceries in a different shop nearby and took the longer way home. She used to walk down Echlin Street with her shopping bag and instead of turning left at the end of the street, she would turn right, cross the road, and go up James Street on the opposite side. Anything but pass the front door of Molloy's. She was so ashamed that she had a bill there and not a foot near the door would she put until the bill was paid.

I wanted to help the situation so one day I asked Joseph if I could work in the shop and, instead of receiving payment, he could deduct the equivalent of my weekly wage from my mother's bill. I started off packing shelves but soon I graduated to serving. Ma had no idea of my plan at this stage; she was paying off the debt by giving a shilling whenever it was spare.

One day, when Joseph and I were in the shop, he saw my mother coming down the street and immediately he went outside to call her over. She nearly died a thousand deaths on the spot. Before Joseph had said a word more to her, she was all apologies to him about the debt. Comforting her as best as he could, Joseph brought her into the shop and reassured her that there was no need to be afraid to walk past the door. He said to her, "Your name is good Mrs Grace." He then went on to tell her that he didn't want to lose her as a customer and that just because she owed him money for back orders of groceries didn't mean she had to travel a longer distance to get a few items.

Joseph had a lovely nature about him. He told my mother that she could pay off her debt in her own time but that I was working in the shop as well and whatever wages I was earning were being knocked off the bill. She was astonished. In fact, the shock of it all seemed to overwhelm her and as such, she became quite upset. Handing her a cup of tea, Joseph sat her down while she had a cigarette to calm her nerves.

Joseph and his own mother were absolute gems. He would regularly encourage me to sing a song for the customers and, of course, I would jump at the chance. We kept in touch long after I moved away from the area. Sadly, Joseph passed away in recent years.

Another business family based on James Street were the Lockharts. They owned the local butchers and their son, James, went on to become a member of the phenomenally successful band Horslips.

Along with Molloy's and Lockhart's, there were two pubs and a little sweet shop called Flanagan's. A lovely lady, Mrs Lamb, used to run the shop for the Flanagans but there were no toilet facilities in the building so she often asked me to mind the shop while she nipped to the loo in one of the nearby pubs. Looking back on it now, I can't but laugh at the idea of her asking a little fat boy to mind a shop full of sweets. I remember one day Mrs Lamb returned much faster than I had anticipated and at the time I was eating a pastry. I tried to swallow it whole. For about thirty seconds, I could only answer with a grunt while I tried to swallow the bloody pastry without choking!

She used to give me the crumbs to eat. That's not as mean as it might sound; in fact it was downright delicious. There was a big board full of cakes and buns that used to arrive into the shop from Boland's bakery every day. After the cakes were sold, the tray would be full with crumbs of icing, coconut, chocolate and whatever else that had been on the cakes and fallen off. I used to call into the shop on my way home from school and Mrs Lamb would give me a large paper bag which I would hold while she lifted up the slab and poured in the crumbs. One day I saw her giving the crumbs to someone else, and honest to God, I got quite upset.

As I said previously, it was an innocent time, but in more ways than one. I know I wasn't the only one who used to believe that if I pulled out my belly button my backside would fall off, and I definitely know that I wasn't the only one who found it absolutely hilarious to call the pedestrian crossings lights "the winking willies".

While we as kids relished the vulgar wit of these nicknames, the older generation used some of the most beautiful sayings and proverbs which unfortunately are rarely repeated today. I remember my father in particular frequently using a variety of adages.

A number of them were country sayings which I myself still use to this day. I think my practice of including those sayings in a few routines was partially responsible for endearing me to rural Ireland as an entertainer. People could identify with the various sayings from having heard their own parents or grandparents use them. It also made people realise that even though I was from Dublin, I was as every bit as much a country boy as I was a Jackeen. One of the sayings my father would use when walking into a pub was "God save all here". It was a way of saying hello. When I was a child, he would introduce me to people as "the son and heir". Now my father didn't have the cross of Christ never mind a wealthy inheritance to leave behind, but it was a country saying that I remember him using frequently.

Not since my father passed away had I heard anyone use them until last year when I was holding one of the first Brendan Grace golf classics. I'm not a golfer, in fact I can't even call myself a fan of the sport, but we decided to hold the event for charity as a number of people from showbusiness enjoy the game as a pastime. As the golf classic in Killaloe received a wonderful response, we decided to follow it up with a second one in Florida. While we were playing the course in Florida, my son-in-law Martin, after taking a belt of the ball, suddenly said, "Ah jaysus, that one was as sweet as a nut." Instantly his words struck me because that was a saying my father always used. In the hour that followed it happened twice more. Two other members of the team, in reference to something they were doing at the time, came out with separate sayings that I had always associated with my father. I hadn't heard these particular aphorisms in over thirty years, and yet here I was after hearing them a few times in the one day.

With this in mind, I was absolutely convinced there was some significance behind it. It continued to niggle at me until I suddenly realised that it was my father's birthday that day. February 22nd. My father didn't really know his date of birth so he always used to say he was born on the twenty-second day of the second month in 1922. All the twos! When the realisation occurred, I felt a shiver go right through me. I wouldn't mind if the three adages in question were common sayings, but they couldn't have been more uncommon. Funnily enough I haven't heard them since that day. Some people might dismiss an incident like that but I always look upon those kind of things as positive little messages from above; a reminder from a loved one that even though they may have passed on, they're still keeping an eye on me ready in their own way to give me a clip around the ear if I need it.

Would you believe, I can recall the exact moment I was told about death. I was six years of age and staying in my grandmother's house at the time. To the back of her house was a Jewish graveyard and on this particular day, a burial was taking place.

The funerals for the Jewish people used to come up Clogher Road to the graveyard while the funerals for the Catholics used to go down the road towards the Mount Jerome cemetery. It wasn't unusual back then for two funerals to meet on the road on their way to their separate graveyards. I remember the hearses that entered the Jewish graveyard had to have curtains on their windows so that you couldn't see the coffin. Part of the Jewish religion also stipulated that a person had to be buried quickly. This may have since changed, but as far as I'm aware, if a person died in the morning, then they had to be buried later that day. Their graveyard also had large tombs as well as graves, but I didn't understand the funeral process so it never really caught my attention until this one particular day. Looking out the back window, I could clearly see everything from the hearse entering the graveyard to the coffin being removed and lowered into the ground.

Curious to know what was in the big wooden box, I put the question to my grandmother. As she sped about the room making the bed, she summarised the entire process – how a person starts off as a baby, grows up, gets old, then a little older, before dying and being placed in a coffin which goes into the ground. If that wasn't bad enough, she then went on to explain how it was something that would happen to all of us in time, including herself, my parents, and eventually me as well. At six years of age, it was a bloody big culture shock to say the least. I was horrified. I got very upset and began to cry.

On that note, I can also remember learning the facts of life. It wasn't my parents who told me but rather my uncle John who was my mother's brother. My parents held very old fashioned views, so issues such as sex education were all seen as tasks better left to someone else. No more than learning about death from my grandmother a few years earlier, I got the whole run down from Uncle John. Diagrams and all.

Funnily enough there are certain songs that I, as a kid, related to death and funerals. As a result, I would burst into tears the moment I heard them. I still can't listen to them today without welling up. These songs first came to my attention through my grandmother's radiogram, which, as those of a certain vintage will recall, was like a piece of furniture in itself. It was a record player as well as a radio and it picked up everything from Raidió Éireann to Radio Luxemburg. Not long after my grandmother filled me in on what eventually lay in store for myself, herself and my parents, I heard a song on the radiogram about a burial. You'd swear I knew the person they were singing about with the crying I did over it. The song itself was a hit record performed by a French group, whose name eludes me, about the three occasions one particular man went to the chapel: his baptism, his marriage and his funeral. Every time I heard it, I related it to the church bell ringing and the coffin going into the ground, and almost immediately the big streaky tears could be seen running down my face.

Another song I never allow my ears to hear is called "My Son". Tony Kenny performs it as does Brendan Shine and Frank Patterson. Frank recorded the song following some encouragement from myself and my good friend Eddie Sweeny. We felt the song was made for Frank to perform as his own son Éanna appeared on all of his shows as a classical violinist. I used to go to Jury's Hotel every year to see Tony Kenny perform and I remember one particular occasion when he began to sing "My Son". I think I was out the door before he had even finished the first line. The lyrics tell the story of a son going off to follow in his father's footsteps. For me, it cuts too close to home because my own son Bradley is also a musician and on the road a lot performing. Honest to God, no amount of willpower can get me to sit through that song.

Crumlin however, despite the funeral memories, was a place I loved every bit as much as Echlin Street. There were so many different individual characters that contributed to the make-up of the street I lived on with my grandmother.

I remember one woman called Mrs Swords whom I think in 1957 won the Glamorous Grandmother competition. Crumlin was also the home to Olive White, a well known model and TV hostess on RTÉ. To me however, she will always be Olive the girl who used to babysit me. I'm told she used to wheel me up and down the street in my pram, more than likely to try and quieten me. I think she was around nine years old at the time but in later years she went on to star in a programme called Jackpot which was presented by Gay Byrne. Needless to say, there was always a bit of rivalry between Olive and her fellow model, my aunt Wyn.

On that same road, there was a mad woman called Nelly who used to constantly stand by the window looking out at people walking by. She used to always shout at Wyn every time she passed. She would say, almost accusingly, "Winnie Myler, goin' off to do your fashion shows!"

Another character from the same area, whom I still see today, is Jimmy Clarke. When my friends and I were kids, he would make us all members of his police force. We didn't do anything, we just had membership of Jimmy Clarke's police force. I met him years later when he was the concierge in Jury's Hotel and we reminisced about those days in Crumlin. I even mentioned him in one of my videos and since then, we always share a private joke about him suing me for royalties.

It was during those memorable childhood days that I developed a love for bikes. Up until the age of twelve I only ever possessed either a second hand bike or a borrowed one. I remember going into Delaney's bicycle shop in Harold's Cross to have my bike fixed and every time, without fail, my eyes would wander over to one bike in particular. It was a three-speed bike unlike any I had ever seen before. I can't remember if it was my eleventh or twelfth birthday but, as a surprise, my grandfather, along with my aunt Wyn and uncle John, decided to treat me to this new animal of a pedal bike!

On the day of the surprise, my uncle John sat me up on the crossbar of his own bike and said we were going for a spin. I didn't suspect a thing until we arrived at Delaney's bicycle shop and was brought inside where I found Mr Delaney standing beside my new three-geared wheels of steel! Coincidentally, the name of the bike was "The Palm Beach". Years later, when we decided to move to Florida, we ended up living in none other than Palm Beach.

As my teenage years progressed so did my longing for a bike that was faster and stronger. I always promised myself that once I got my hands on a Honda, I would set about answering one particularly niggling question. Maybe it was a side effect to living in a big city where a week wouldn't pass without the sound of a siren piercing the air, but any time a fire brigade drove past with its lights flashing and siren ringing, the one thing I always wanted to know was where it was going. At the time however, a pedal bike was my only mode of transport so I promised myself that the moment I bought myself a much longed for Honda motorbike, I would follow the first fire engine I saw. Every young fella at the time had a Honda and it wasn't too long before I was one of them. I was 15 years old, but in those days, authorities weren't as strict with driving licenses, and my forged birth certificate was accepted as valid proof of my age. My insurance set me back about £5 but I had a fairly steady job so the bill didn't leave a lasting dent in my finances.

Despite being something of a novice biker, I was more than able to keep up with the fire brigade I followed. As it turns out, it wasn't anything too dramatic. The crew were responding to a call about small house fire. Naturally it was unfortunate for the house owners but for me, it was nothing like the drama of my previous fire brigade experience when, during one of our Christmas holidays in Dunlavin, the fire truck itself went on fire. I remember there was great pandemonium around the fire station in Dunlavin Square at the time. It transpired that as a cold winter's frost had begun to set in, so did fears of the fire engine freezing over. As a result, some genius decided to place an oil lamp under the engine to prevent it from developing a layer of frost. Something clearly went awry with the plan as it wasn't long before the fire engine was up in flames. Members of the fire brigade from the neighbouring town of Baltinglass were alerted to come and quench the blaze. Fortunately, there was no explosion, but the fire truck itself was completely beyond repair afterwards. The incident featured as a news item on the Frank Hall programme, Hall's Pictorial Weekly. I remember Frank got a great laugh from the incident as did his viewers. Looking back, the idea of a fire brigade going on fire almost sounds like something I would feature in one of my comedy routines.

During my early teenage years, I observed and admired anyone with a striking sense of humour. One such person was a Browne & Nolan's employee called Frankie Kennedy. Frankie was a character renowned for his quick wit. Somebody would make a comment, and he would immediately follow it up with a hilarious reply. Frankie was the kind of man who could be funny without even trying. Everybody loved him. A comical individual, he was a huge influence on me long before I even suspected what my future held. There were certain things he did and sayings he used that I still to this day repeat, not just in my capacity as a comedian, but in terms of general banter. Frankie subsequently went on to join a ballad group but unfortunately we only cross paths once in a blue moon.

Looking back though, I can see he wasn't the only humorist responsible for rousing the performer inside me. I don't know why but I seemed to study actors and performers unbeknownst to myself. It was as if I knew that one day I would be in the same business as them. The comedian Jack Benny, for example, made certain expressions that I observed long before I ever cracked a joke on stage. Every time I watch one of my DVD's, I catch a fleeting glimpse of the different performers inside me. Traits I observed years back in different comedians have since become entwined in my own on-stage personality. On the DVD, I might make a certain facial expression and immediately I can pinpoint it as being that of someone like Jack Benny, Les Dawson, Chris Casey or John Cleese. From a young age my mind seemed trained to hone in on the little idiosyncrasies that can make or break a routine.

I don't think I'm easily spooked, but if there is one thing that is always capable of giving me the goosebumps, it's an old school photograph that hangs on the wall of my pub in Killaloe. In the picture, a large group of school children are standing outside a Catholic church in Limerick for a school tour photo. The picture, which was taken in 1961, was given to me as a gift by one of my closest childhood friends, Frank Savage. As I was examining it one day, something remarkable occurred to me. I was standing smack bang in the centre of the front row line – exactly seven kids in from the left and seven kids in from the right. Anyone familiar with the theatre will know that the lead actor always takes the centre stage; they are positioned right in the centre of the line-up. Considering my friends are standing elsewhere in the crowd, I can't think how I ended up where I did in that photograph. What's more, with the way I'm posing, you'd swear I was part of a school panto rather than a school tour.

Considering what lay ahead of me, that picture truly never ceases to amaze me.

three

*As a student, Brendan was a very intelligent lad. He also had
a quiet friendly manner and was highly thought of by his fellow
classmates. I have known him as a student and a friend and the
one thing I always notice is his wonderful outlook on life. Dublin
in the sixties was a world away from the place it is today but
Brendan was always a person of great hope and he is still that
way today. His heart is definitely in the right place. In fact, his
involvement in charity work has raised phenomenal amounts.*

Brother Con Hurley

The Boss v Bottler

My love of motorbikes led to me breaking my leg three times. In fact,
by the end of it all, I'd say I had run out of bones to break. The
worst crash I was ever involved in occurred in 1969 and it was as a
result of this particular crash that I took an action against Charlie Haughey.

I had just completed the garda exam through a distant learning course with
Kilroy's College, but an injury sustained from a previous motorbike accident
resulted in me failing the medical examination. Following this, I applied for a

job at sea after a cousin of mine, Michael Grace, offered to use his contacts in the Seaman's Union to secure me an interview. As it turned out, my interview with Irish Shipping was successful and I was told where to collect my official papers so that I could go out to sea and effectively become a merchant. Around this time the ambulances and fire brigades were on strike and so the army ambulances were put in place for emergencies. I remember this well because I ended up inside one of them.

As I was on my way to pick up the forms for my new job, an army ambulance shot out of a one-way street and hit me. It turned out the ambulance had just picked up a woman who had suffered a heart attack in Cleary's shop and was rushing her to Jervis Street Hospital when it hit me. Immediately, I – with my broken thigh – was placed into the back of the ambulance alongside the lady with the heart problem. I was conscious for the whole episode and to this day I still have a very clear memory of that painful incident. For a long time afterwards I wondered what had become of the woman in the ambulance that day. About ten years ago I got my answer in front of around one million people. I was telling that very same story on The Late Late Show when a call came through live to the studio. It was from the lady I had shared the ambulance with back in 1969 and here I was now sharing a phone call with her live on The Late Late!

The strange thing about that crash is that it occurred at around 3 o'clock in the day, at which time my mother was in John's Lane Church in Dublin lighting candles to Our Lady in the hope that I would change my mind about going to sea. It worked because, as a result of that accident, I never went to sea. Ma was convinced the crash was Our Lady's way of stopping me from going. I, on the other hand, always felt Our Lady could have chosen a less painful way to stop me.

The action against Charlie Haughey's Department of Finance came about thanks to my father and the influential friends he had made through his job in O'Reilly's Pub. One particular friend was a solicitor called David Bell. When he heard what had happened with the army ambulance, Mr Bell told my father he would take on my case for free. The case was Brendan Grace v Charlie Haughey, the then Minister for Finance. I would give anything to find that court document. David Bell also introduced a barrister to take on the case. They won the lawsuit and a cheque for £1,500 was sent to me from the government. I was 18 years of age when the settlement was made, but at that time you were classed as an "infant" until you turned 21. Imagine, in the eyes of the law I was an 18-year-old infant. The cheque was to be deposited in the bank until I came of age, but David Bell was good friends with the bank manager and so introduced him to my father and me. We decided that instead of leaving the cheque sitting in the account for three years, the bank manager would give me a loan of £1,500 against the cheque. Once I was of age, the bank would reclaim the loan by taking the money in the account.

From the money I got that day from Charlie Haughey's department, I was able to buy my parents their first house. I like to joke that it was Charlie Haughey who bought my parents their first house, because technically speaking, he did. The house, a three bedroom abode in Coolock, was priced at £5,300 and thanks to the money from the claim, I was able to secure a mortgage from the EBS. The repayments came in at £48 pounds a month. To think at the time we probably thought that figure was daylight robbery. Showing my parents the house as it was being built and being able to tell them that it was going to be their new home was without doubt a moment I will never forget. It had always been a dream of mine to buy them a house of their own. While the accident was a bout of misfortune which I cursed at the time, looking back, I credit it with enabling me to fulfil one of my biggest dreams. My mother loved where we lived in Echlin Street. She loved the neighbours, the friendships and everything about the place, but the three flights of stairs were getting to her. Everything we had, coal, spuds, groceries, all had to be carried up those three long flights.

On one occasion we had to haul a fridge up those godforsaken concrete stairs. I had bought my parents a new fridge for £30, which at the time was several weeks' wages. Remember this was back when a new fridge was the height of extravagance. It was a surprise for my mother so I had it delivered while she was out. When she saw her brand new fridge, she nearly put the French population to shame with all the cheek kisses I received from her. Of course, given my own love of chocolate and confectionary, I was every bit as thrilled with having a fridge as Ma was. The claim money also helped me to buy a car as I was beginning to perform regular gigs with my band The Gingermen.

GALWAY COUNTY LIBRARIES

We were on the scene around the same time as the well known group The Emmett Spiceland. To this day, I still think that particular band was lightyears ahead of its time. They were the epitome of showbusiness and of course, we, The Gingermen, modelled ourselves on them. I think for a while we convinced ourselves that we were The Emmett Spiceland. The first place we ever played as The Gingermen was in county Clare. Clare and Limerick were always our favourite places to gig. On the way to gigs in Scariff we travelled through Ballina and Killaloe. I was always in the driving seat back then and I remember being truly captivated by the beautiful scenery of the area each time I drove through it. I didn't know then it would one day be my second home.

When travelling to gigs out in the country, we would use a rented car from Dan Dooley's Car Hire. However, we didn't always follow protocol when renting. we preferred the method of "borrowing" instead. Back then, if someone returned a rented car after hours, they would simply park it ouside the garage and drop the keys into the letterbox. One day I came up with an idea of how to acquire these keys. Using a magnet attached to some string, I slipped it into the letter box to see if the keys would stick. Sure enough when I pulled the magnet out of the letter box, three sets of keys came with it leaving me with the decision of which expensive car I should take for a spin. This became our Friday night routine as the garage was always closed at the weekend. As such, the staff were never aware that their car had been "borrowed". We weren't joyriders by any means, we only used the car to take us to our gigs around the country. Prior to driving off however, we would always disconnect the speedometer so that the person who had previously hired it was not charged for the mileage. Upon returning it the night before the garage opened, I would replace whatever petrol I felt we had used before reconnecting the speedometer. Likewise, if the car got dirty, I cleaned it. This went on for two years and not once were we caught out. In my heart though I really didn't feel I was doing anything wrong. I just thought it was clever. Back then the company was run by Dan Dooley. These days however it is run by his son who is now one of my best friends. In fact after we became friends, I ended up telling him about how fond we were of his vehicles back then!

For some reason, The Gingermen used to perform very regularly in Kilrush and Scariff in Clare. During the weekend we would call to Durty Nellys beside Bunratty Castle where we would spend the day busking. We would busk for drink and Roger, who owned the place back then, used to give us a few pints for providing the music. The American tourists would also pay us tips for singing. If a tourist wanted a particular song and was willing to buy us a drink, then we would sing whatever song they wanted. We earned a fair amount from those tips but it was more of a side earner. We didn't depend on the busking, we just saw it as a nice top up to what we would earn from our mid-week performances. In 1969, we were the warm up act for Sean Dunphy and Anna McGoldrick at a venue in Swords. Neilius O'Connell was their promoter and one night he double booked them at a different venue in Dublin. We went on stage and performed our act as planned but when we finished, there was still no sign of Neilius and the two lads. We carried on singing but despite our best efforts to keep the music going, we eventually ran out of material. There was a big crowd in the venue so management asked us if there was any way we could perform a few more songs until Sean and Anna arrived. We had already performed every song we knew, so returning to the stage wasn't an option. That's when I offered to get up on stage and tell a few jokes. As a result of that spontaneous stint, the jokes started to become part of The Gingermen gigs and that's how my comedy career began.

About two years later, the band parted ways. I have nothing but great memories of the time I spent with The Gingermen. The four of us even had a reunion earlier this year (2009). We think it may have been the band's 40th anniversary but to be honest, it may well have been our 45th. It scares the absolute bejaysus out of us to think back to the exact date we first formed! We never fell out before or after parting; in fact we always remained friends even though we may not have seen a lot of each other in the years that followed. We just arrived at the decision to pursue separate paths. The other three lads already had good permanent jobs outside of the band. I on the other hand always had two jobs. When The Gingermen split up, I was a truck driver by day and a bar tender by night. Not long afterwards, however, my driving job was kicked to the curb as a career in solo entertainment slowly beckoned.

I was performing one night in the old Sheiling Hotel in Dublin when Michael Johnson of the famous 1960's folk group, The Johnsons, approached me. For me, the very notion of even being in the presence of this great musician was thrilling as I had been a long-term follower of his work. With this in mind you can imagine my sheer amazement when he complimented my performance and invited me to Toronto for three weeks to play gigs. At that stage of my life, I had never even crossed the Atlantic to the Aran Islands let alone Canada, so needless to say, his offer wasn't one that required contemplating on my part. I felt excited by the prospect of seeing America for the first time, because back then Canada and America were the one country as far as I was concerned. Sightseeing aside however, this trip became a journey I would never forget because it changed my whole life. In fact, the phenomenal ripple effect from that trip still astounds me.

It started not long after I arrived in Toronto, when I visited a fortune teller in a place called The Daffodil Tearooms. At the time, fortune telling was deemed illegal, but The Daffodil Tearooms had figured a clever way to manipulate the system. In order for them to read your tea leaves without breaking the law, you were charged for a fortune telling session under the guise of paying for tea and a bun. Your bill for the tea would arrive at something like $20, and once you had finished, one of the fortune tellers would approach you to read your tea leaves. The man that approached me was called Zorba. I have no doubt in my mind that Zorba knew absolutely nothing about me, nor did I enlighten him in any way. After looking at the leaves and the tarot cards, the first thing he told me was that a career in entertainment was about to develop for me. He was then able to tell me that I had just arrived in Canada to take up a short engagement entertaining people. He went on to say that the leaves in my tea cup revealed the letter D twice, whom he explained were the initials of a person who greatly influenced me. By this stage, I had surpassed the element of shock and was now completely jolted by sheer astonishment. When he mentioned the initials DD, I freaked because I knew the only person he could be referring to was the singer Danny Doyle. Danny was my absolute favourite musician not to mention a significant role model in my life. What's more, Zorba went on to tell me that shortly after my return home, I would meet two people who would completely change my life. He wasn't wrong either.

When I arrived home from Canada, I decided to trek into Dublin City centre. As I turned the corner from Grafton Street to Dawson Street, I caught sight of two familiar people in conversation with each other. One was the impressionist David Beggs and the other was the RTÉ broadcaster Shay Healy. At the time I was wearing a long suede overcoat and a fedora hat and as soon as he saw me, Shay laughed and said, "Jaysus Brendan you look like you own Dublin."

I can still vividly recall replying with the words, "Well I wish I felt like that!"

Sensing my despondent mood, Shay enquired as to what was wrong. I laughed off my situation with the explanation that I wasn't broke, just badly bent!

As the three of us continued talking, a homeless man approached me and asked for spare change. With my wages from Canada going to my mother and father, all I had to my name was a shilling, so I took it out, handed it to the homeless man and said, "There you go buddy, now you have a shilling more than me."

Around this time, Shay was presenting a programme called Ballad Sheet and was as famous as Gay Byrne. I had never recorded my own music at this stage but, as we were chatting, Shay mentioned that he had a great ballad that might suit me. Called "Cushy Butterfield", it was an incredibly catchy old north of England song, the words of which Shay had adapted to suit Dublin. Before heading away, he promised to send me the lyrics in the post.

It was at this point that David asked me if I wanted to join him at a gig he was to play that night in Athy, county Kildare, in a venue called Pedigree Corner. At the time David was driving a Volkswagen Beetle so I suggested that for the sake of comfort, we travel in my Cortina. Having just given whatever money I had to a homeless man, I realised I couldn't afford the petrol for the trip. I explained my predicament to David and he said he would fill the tank with petrol. On top of that, he gave me the loan of a fiver as well.

We headed off that evening and on our arrival we met David's manager, Sean Clancy. Even though Sean and I had never met before, it turns out I wasn't a total stranger to him as he had heard about my ballad singing. A band had been scheduled to play that night as support to David but a phone call came through to say they wouldn't be able to make it. Just as the panic was beginning to set in, Sean asked me if I could help. As we had travelled in my Cortina, my guitar was in the boot so I offered to perform a few songs. Following the show which, despite the pre-pandemonium, had gone off without a glitch, Sean presented me with £8 for my work. Absolutely thrilled with my night's pay, I repaid David the fiver he had lent me earlier. Prior to leaving, Sean offered to represent me as a manager as he felt he could secure gigs for me. He kept his promise because not long after I was signed up as one of his acts, the bookings began to come in.

Three or four days after the gig with David in Kildare, a package arrived for me in the post. My mother became extremely excited by the sight of the RTÉ logo printed on the front of the large envelope. It was the "Cushy Butterfield" lyrics from Shay, accompanied by a cassette tape of the tune itself. Almost immediately I began including the song in my act. Sean, however, had bigger ideas. Upon hearing it, he told me it was the catchiest song he had heard in a long time and that he felt it had the potential to secure me a recording deal. Following this conversation he introduced me to Mick Clerkin who had just founded the record label, Release Records. Release went on to record most of the showband hits and became the main player within the Irish music industry.

Mick listened to the song and instantly dubbed it a hit. By this point, I was beginning to get extremely excited as the prospect of releasing my own record was no longer a pipe dream but a nearing reality. It was arranged that we would record the song with musical director, and friend, Tommy Ellis. Within five weeks of its release, it hit the number one position in the Irish charts. Immediately, my diary began to fill up and within two weeks, I was listed as the support act to the band, The New Seekers.

Afterwards, a talent scout called Tony Boland approached me and asked if I would be interested in performing on The Late Late Show. The excitement at the idea of appearing on The Late Late Show was without a doubt on a par with having a number one hit. As part of my appearance on the show, I sang "Cushy Butterfield" and introduced a comedy character called "Bottler". Back in those days, The Late Late Show was broadcast on Saturday nights. The Monday morning following my stint on the show, my diary for the following year was completely full.

Looking back, I am shocked by the accuracy of Zorba's prediction. I travelled to Toronto several times in those early days of my career and each time I visited the Daffodil Rooms to see if I could speak with him. Unfortunately he was never there and so I never got the chance to tell him how everything he had predicted for me had come true.

The series of events that led to the number one record and other successes began with that chance encounter with two people, Shay Healy and David Beggs, just like Zorba had predicted. The thing is, if I had met either of them on their own, none of this would have happened for me. Shay gave me the hit song but David introduced me to Sean Clancy who was instrumental in making it a hit. If I had only met David that day, I would probably still have been introduced to Sean but wouldn't have had the hit song from Shay.

My good fortune also brought with it good friends, one of whom was Fr Sean Breen, who went on to become known as the racing priest as a result of the masses he held at the Galway Races. I first met Breener in 1972 in Ballymun where I was the support act for Maxi, Dick and Twink. At the time, he was the parish priest of Ballymun and so approached me, following the gig, to ask if I would get involved in a charity show.

I can't help but smile when I think back to when he mentioned that I wouldn't be paid for my participation in the show. He said I would be doing it "for the benefit of my soul".

On the night of the charity show he never let my glass go empty and afterwards he told me it would have been cheaper to have paid me for the gig. At his funeral mass in March 2009 I described for the congregation how I received my just desserts 25 years after that show when I asked him to preside over the renewal of my wedding vows to Eileen. He said he would be delighted to do so and that all we would have to do is supply the flight ticket to Florida, accommodation and the food. When the bill arrived, I couldn't but laugh when I realised Breener had got his own back after all those years. It would have been cheaper to have just paid him!

As far as I can recall, I wasn't the only performer cajoled into participating in the charity gig in Ballymun. If I'm not mistaken, Red Hurley was also roped into playing "for the benefit of his soul". Red too went on to become a close friend of Fr Breen. He wasn't just a priest; he was a wonderful companion with a remarkable sense of humour.

My friends and neighbours from Florida, some of whom are Jewish, used to insist on going to Fr Breen's mass any time I brought them to Ireland. They always found themselves highly entertained by his wit. They were particularly amused by his way of informing the congregation that he had a hangover and that they weren't to make noise with coins when the collection basket went around. It was Breener's way of saying he wanted notes not coins. Eileen's mother Lillie, who was of the old stock that never witnessed priests take a pint or tell a joke at mass, had a running joke with him about how she didn't think he was a real priest at all, given his carry on. Just like myself, Breener loved the showbands and the glamour that accompanied the entertainment industry.

The Baggot Inn, which became very famous on the cabaret circuit, was where I cut my teeth in the business in the 1970's. We nicknamed it The Maggot Bin. I remember playing there one night and Johnny Logan was my support act. Not long after that he went on to win the first of his Eurovisions and his days of being the support act were well and truly behind him. On one particular night however, a band named U2 was my support act. At the time, Paul McGuinness managed a cabaret act called Spud so I think it was through the ballads and the cabaret that he secured U2 their first airing in the Maggot Bin.

Many will also remember Sunday nights around 1972 when the two big attractions in the venue were myself and the drag act, Mr Pussy, also known as Alan Amsby. Alan became a great friend of myself and Eileen, and I can say with my hand on my heart that he's every bit as funny off the stage as he is on it. Socialising with him and Joe Dolan guaranteed absolutely mad nights out. I will always remember looking out at the long queues outside the venue for our respective shows.

Coincidentally, my future son-in-law Frank Gillespie would later own The Baggot Inn along with Jack Charlton. At the time my manager, Jim Hand, was also manager to Johnny Logan. Jim, at one stage, had the showbusiness equivalent to a full house in poker as his acts had all achieved number one records. Both he and his twin brother Mick had a wonderful sense of humour and made for great company. He possessed the most incredible sarcastic wit and could hold court in any situation.

Johnny's success was phenomenal. He won the Eurovision twice as a singer and once as a songwriter. In my eyes, the odds of winning three Eurovisions are possibly longer than guessing the winning Lotto numbers. When my son Bradley was about five years of age, Johnny Logan was his hero. I even have a lovely photograph of Bradley sitting on Johnny's lap. Brad, who is now a musician himself, had such a smile on his face that day, you'd swear Johnny was Santa!

I have no doubt in my mind that the showbands paved the way for other performers like myself and Johnny, not to mention those on the circuit today. On the rare occasion that I hear their role being undermined, it both hurts and disgusts me. I have great admiration for Bob Geldof and the work he has done but I once heard him making a very unsavoury comment about the showbands and it really pissed me off. The ironic thing is I can see a strong resemblance between Brendan Bowyer's music and Bob Geldof's early material. In the early days, Geldof was like a clone of Bowyer and yet here he was refusing to acknowledge the work invested in the Irish entertainment industry by people like Bowyer.

If you count back to the day I went professional full time, you'll find that I'm 38 years in the business now. Looking back over those years, I think I can safely say that fate has played a huge role overall. The best example that springs to mind is of an incident that occurred one Friday night back in 1972. My grandmother used to go to bingo in Dublin's Liberty Hall every Friday. If I was free, I would bring her to the venue in my Ford Cortina. We had a routine whereby she would go into the shop beside Liberty Hall to buy a bag of sweets while I would run in and buy her bingo cards for her. It was a ritual – she'd get the sweets, I'd get the bingo! One particular Friday night, however, I had been booked to play a short set in a venue the other side of the city, so I figured that if I drove to the gig directly after dropping off my grandmother at the hall, then I would arrive in good time for my slot. While I was on my way to the car, a school friend, Brian Byrne, shouted over at me before coming over for a chat. My car was one of about ten cars there that evening and I leaned against one of them while we chatted. A bus then pulled up and Brian's date that evening stepped off so Brian said his goodbyes. I got into my car and drove towards the venue.

I wasn't in the car two minutes when I began to hear a number of sirens. When I arrived at the other venue, rumours were already circulating that there had been an explosion but I didn't take much notice. After I finished my spot on stage, I travelled over to Eileen's house. By the time I arrived there, the story had broken on the news that a bomb had gone off in a car outside Liberty Hall. Naturally, I was panic stricken as my first concern was for my grandmother. I drove to Liberty Hall to see if I could find her but the whole area had been cordoned off. It was absolute hell waiting. As it turned out, the people inside the hall, while shaken from the force of the explosion, had few injuries. Tragically, a number of people outside the building had been killed.

It turned out to be a paramilitary bomb and in the days that followed the papers carried pictures of where the bomb had been planted. As it transpired, the bomb had been placed in a car outside the building. I got the shock of my life when I realised which car that was. It turns out the car I had parked beside, and had leaned against while talking with Brian, was the very one that contained the bomb. The knowledge of this alone had a terrible effect on me for a long time afterwards. It often occurred to me that if Brian's date had for any reason missed the bus and not shown up at the time she did, there was a very good chance we would have stayed talking and been present when the bomb went off. Even if the bus had been delayed by a traffic light, Brian and I were dead. I still believe to this day that if ever there was one situation in my life that best exemplified the role played by fate, it was that Friday night.

four

In 1973, I went back to sing in Nashville, Tennessee. One day, to my delight, I got a call from Brendan to say that he was in America and would there be a chance of a bed if he dropped into Nashville. I think the best part of Brendan's visit was introducing him to our cat. He and I decided to call the cat Bollix for the craic. We had a bible-thumping neighbour called Faye and it used to be a giggle for us to hear her say: "Bollix ... it's such a purty name for a cat."

Shay Healy

Bren and Eilo

I n the 1300's, a romance between Romeo and Juliet was born. In the 1940's, it was Bogart and Bacall's turn. However, in 1972 St Valentine smiled on Bren and Eilo!

I first clapped eyes on Eileen Doyle when, in the middle of a gig I was playing in Wexford's Talbot Hotel, I heard a woman in the crowd laughing heartily at something I had said. If this were a typical love story, I would be able to tell you about how she had seen my photograph on a gig poster and decided on the spot that I was the man she was going to marry. The reality is somewhat different: she was dragged out to see my gig against her will by her friend Anne Byrne. Anne's brother was a former classmate of mine and it was through him that Anne knew me. In the days prior to that concert, I was involved in two car accidents. I have wondered since then if they were blessings in disguise because I don't think my meeting with Eileen would have come about had those accidents not happened.

I had been scheduled to play two gigs in one night, but while I was on my way back from the first gig, I got sideswiped by another car. As my own car wasn't fit for use following the incident, I called in to a nearby pub, Molly Malone's, where I used to do cabaret. After explaining my situation, the owner gave me the loan of his car so I could travel to the second venue to perform my next show. Travelling home from that gig, a car pulled out from behind a bus and hit me head on.

Before you say it, no I wasn't drinking that night! Anyway, one evening shortly after my eventful night, Anne told Eileen about how a friend of her brother's was on his way to play a couple of gigs when the poor fool ended up in two accidents in two different cars on the one night.

That weekend, Anne and Eileen had planned to travel to Wexford for a break. I was playing there at the time and so there were posters up around the place advertising my show. Noticing the name on the posters, Eileen asked if that was the same fella who had been in the two car accidents. At this point, Anne suggested they go to see me play but Eileen, on the other hand, was adamant that she was going nowhere near any show. After much persuading from Anne, she finally gave in, though from what she tells me, it was entirely against her will. During the show, I obviously said something quite witty because straight away I heard this very unusual laugh coming from the audience. It was such a pronounced laugh that I thought it was a heckler at first. When I looked into the crowd to see where the hearty laugh was coming from, I immediately noticed Anne standing beside the woman responsible. During the interval, I made a beeline for Anne and her laughing hyena of a friend. Straight away I took a fancy to Eileen and afterwards I asked her for a date. Six months later we were engaged.

I was clearly besotted from the word go because my aunt Kay can recall me telling them at breakfast about the beautiful girl I had met at the show the night before.

Prior to meeting me Eileen had been dating a lad who always wore a suit. He was a smart looking guy whereas I was a bit of a clown. I was like a long-haired friend to Jesus, my hair had such length to it and my clothes were downright bizarre to say the least. When Eileen introduced me to her mother Lily, she took one look at me and then looked straight at Eileen and said, "I think he's one of our own!"

I think it was her way of saying, "He's a bleedin' weirdo but one of our own none the less!"

Not long after Eileen and I began dating, I brought her along to a cabaret spot I was playing in the West County Hotel in Ennis. Tommy Drennan and The Monarchs were also playing that night and after I had finished my show, I went back into the ballroom to see Tommy performing with Sean O'Dowd and Dennis Allen. Somehow Tommy managed to find out that it was the eve of my 21st birthday and not only did he make a fuss of me from the stage, he also got the kitchen to present me with a birthday cake. It was an unforgettable night and I don't even have a photograph of it. Tommy was a legendary entertainer back then and I will always remember the pre-21st birthday he gave me.

For some couples, it seems like they were just meant to be together and for Eileen and I this is most definitely the case. We officially met at that concert in Wexford on Whit Saturday 37 years ago this year, however we later found out that our paths had actually crossed a number of times before. In fact, you could almost say I met Eileen before I actually met her.

To give you an example, Eileen's father worked in the Guinness Brewery and every year Guinness held a concert at which some very well known performers would play. In 1967 I played with The Gingermen and, as it turns out, Eileen was in the crowd that night and can distinctly remember the show. A year later I went for an interview for the position of company van driver. At the reception desk, I told the lady what I was there for. I didn't know it then but I was talking to my future wife.

Me dad also knew Eileen very well prior to us going out together. She was on first name terms with my father long before she even knew my name. Eileen worked in St Luke's Hospital while me Da worked as an ambulance assistant with St James's Hospital. It wasn't the emergency ambulance, it was one that they used for transporting patients to and from the hospital. When dropping off patients at St Luke's, me Da and Eileen would regularly chat not knowing that one day they would be related.

Our wedding was such a wonderful day that 25 years later we decided to do it all over again and renew our vows. On both occasions, Fr Breen presided over the ceremony. I remember for our first time up at the altar, Red Hurley was on singing duty. It was a major highlight because Red was already a well-established name in the business. The ceremony itself was held in Our Ladies of the Skies Church near Dublin Airport. We decided to keep the reception very small, to about twenty people or so, as one of Eileen's sisters had wed six months earlier and another was due to get married six months later. With this in mind, we decided to save her father the expense by opting for a small wedding for the very immediate family.

As a wedding gift to ourselves, Eileen and I decided to charter a helicopter to take us from the church to the hotel in Stepaside. Back then, hiring a helicopter was so extravagant, it was practically unheard of. The bill for hiring the helicopter was three pounds more expensive than the wedding reception. The reception was £47 while the helicopter trip was £50! A week or two prior to the wedding however, there was holy commotion over an incident in which three IRA prisoners were plucked from the yard of Mountjoy Prison by helicopter. It seems after the helicopter had been hijacked, the pilot was forced to fly to Mountjoy where he was then made hover over the yard until low enough for the inmates to jump in. Not only was this the same helicopter I had already booked for my wedding, it was also the same bleedin' pilot! Following the incident, I was contacted and informed of what had happened to our pilot. I was told that as a result of the incident, there would be a heavy garda presence accompanying the helicopter to the church in the event of it happening again.

Sure enough, on the morning itself, a huge garda contingent arrived at the church in good time for the helicopter touching down. As if getting married wasn't nervewracking enough, here was a pilot and his aircraft who had been hijacked by the IRA a fortnight earlier. I don't know whose nerves were frayed more that morning, mine or the pilot's.

I always found it strange that I developed such a love affair with helicopters, particularly considering the frightening incident I witnessed back when I was no more than ten years of age. My uncle John had brought my mother, Maggie and me out for a picnic in Lucan one Sunday. Believe it or not, but at that time Lucan was considered the country. He used to take us out for a spin most Sundays in his Ford Anglia. This was the first car I had been in and I remember he had bought it for £25. I can even remember the registration plate – ZH5 740.

As my mother and uncle chatted, I decided to go for a walk down a side road. As I was walking along, I heard a strange spluttering noise coming from a small single-engine plane in the sky. It was so close, I could see it quite clearly. Then everything went quiet and the plane just dropped from the sky. I ran back like the hammers of hell to tell my mother and uncle what I had just witnessed. The picnic was wrapped up and we made our way to the main road. Traffic was held up and I remember noticing the police presence in the area. I never knew what became of the pilot until many years later when I decided to look up the records of the accident. He had died in the crash that day. To this day, I experience recurring nightmares about air crashes. Remarkably, though, it hasn't hampered my love of aviation and I have become a qualified pilot.

On the day of our wedding, Eileen's mother Lillie refused downright to believe us when we said we were hiring a helicopter. Even when, during the church ceremony, the distinctive sound of the helicopter rotors could be heard getting louder as the aircraft approached the church grounds, she still thought we were joking. It was only when we stepped into the helicopter with Fr Breen that Lillie actually began to believe us.

The feeling of being aboard a helicopter for the first time was phenomenal. Having loved helicopters from a young age, the reality that I was finally about to board one was a big dream realised. When we began to ascend, one of the most distinctive features on the skyline was the Sugar Loaf mountain. Pointing to it, the pilot then informed us that was where he was taking us. After soaring over the Sugar Loaf, we made our way to the Pat Quinn Club. The pilot was an absolute gentleman when we asked him about the hijacking. He spoke openly about the day in question and gave us a rundown of what had happened.

Touching down on the hotel grounds, another surprise was in store when we learned that Hal Roach was playing golf on the nearby green. We decided to approach him and ended up having a good chat with him. Lord only knows what he thought when he saw the helicopter arriving to a contingent of army and gardaí. I was beginning to establish a name in the entertainment industry and so the national press picked up on the story of us using the hijacked helicopter. I still have the articles.

For our honeymoon we travelled to London. I was at the stage where I was making enough money to afford my first car and had just bought a lovely Opel Commodore so we decided we would bring it with us. We travelled on the mail boat from Dun Laoghaire. This was before the days of the car ferry so to board the boat, our Opel Commodore had to be lifted on to the deck by a crane. It wasn't a drive on/drive off boat, it was more of a lift-on/lift-off set up. To bring your car to England in those days was unusual.

Our honeymoon was memorable to say the least, simply because we spent it rehearsing my lines for an upcoming theatre show. I had been asked to play the role of the narrator in *Joseph and the Technicolor Dreamcoat*. It was a huge move up for my career but at the time it left me in a dilemma as to whether I should postpone the week in London, which we had already booked for our honeymoon, or take the week and just bring the script with me. In the end, I opted for the latter. I can still remember Eileen reading the opposite parts so that I could practice my lines. By the end of the week I reckon she knew them better than I did.

In hindsight it's a good thing I revised as well as I did as the show is today regularly repeated on RTÉ's Reeling In The Years. The production, which was led by the singer Tony Kenny, involved a lot of well known names in Irish entertainment at the time. It was a cast of brilliant actors all of whom had personalities every bit as remarkable as their acting skills. All, with the exception of one. One particular person, whom I won't name, took a serious dislike to me after an afternoon matinée during which I suffered a bout of the giggles. At some stage during the show, one of the orchestra members, who were positioned in the pit directly in front of the stage, let off an all merciful fart. I remember looking at the conductor Noel Kelehan and even he could not stop laughing. To make matters worse, Tony Kenny, who was playing the role of Joseph, was about to walk on stage to perform a very despondent song called "Close Every Door". This was the point of the show where Joseph was in jail and so the mood for this scene was supposed to be very sombre. Tony is there sitting on the stage floor with these big grey bars around him and I remember the poor man could not keep in the laughter. Seeing me laughing certainly didn't help the situation.

Following the show, a very prominent and well known Shakespearean actor at the time read me the riot act. In a way he was right because allowing yourself to laugh on stage is not the done thing, but on the other hand, if you can't help it, there's nothing you can do. The same actor didn't speak to me for the whole run and I later found out that he had suggested to the director and producer that I be removed from the show.

I was the joker of the pantos, but I always seemed to be able to get away with things like throwing a handful of bangers out on the stage just as another actor was about to walk out and deliver their lines. To most actors, it was hilarious, but the select few always saw it as uncouth and undisciplined. There was no point in trying to change me because it became clear from a young age that the jokery gene was engrained in my genetic make-up. As well as being blessed with a natural wit, my father was also a complete and utter prankster. He was such a lovable character that he would always get away with his pranks, even those he would pull while working as an ambulance assistant with St James's Hospital. Me Da was so well liked that people would phone the hospital to request that they be picked up by Seamus Grace and Bobby Byrne. Bobby, who was the ambulance driver, became very close buddies with me Da not to mention a partner in the now-infamous pranks.

My father had this face mask of a very old and very ugly person that he would sometimes wear in the ambulance while sitting in the passenger seat. It was so frighteningly ugly that I would bet money that a few people nearly crashed their cars when they saw it. Part of me Da and Bobby's job was transporting a corpse from the hospital to the mortuary. On one occasion as they were delivering a corpse to the mortuary there was a member of staff there carrying out a few tasks. When they arrived back outside, me Da decided to put on the mask, climb up onto a barrel and peer in the window of the mortuary. Needless to say, when the poor woman looked around, she caught sight of the mask. Me Da and Bobby presumed she would get a fright and then a good laugh out of it when she saw that it was just a joke. What they didn't bank on was that the poor woman would collapse from the fright. They ended up having to run back into the mortuary and call a doctor to come and revive her. When the woman came around she was hysterical and insisting there was someone at the window. She was convinced it was something supernatural. They tried explaining that it was a mask, but she was so upset by what she had seen that my father thought the best way to calm her down was to actually show her that it was just a mask. So he put on the mask again and after the woman took one look at it, she collapsed a second time. In the weeks following though, she got a good laugh out of it and I have since met the woman in question.

I will never know how me Da wasn't sacked for those kind of things. Bobby once told me about the time a few nurses were wheeling in a corpse. My father hopped up onto another slab and pulled a white sheet over him. He then waited until he could hear the nurses getting closer before sitting up with a jolt. There was pandemonium in the hall that day. He never got into trouble for things like that though because they all loved him for his humour. He could be mightily convincing too.

When my age was still in single figures, I saw a magpie for the first time. I was amazed to see this unusual bird but not half as amazed as I was when my father told me that the bird I was looking at was in fact a jackdaw in his shirt sleeves. I was so young at the time that I would end up wracking my brain for ages afterwards wondering as to why a bird would have a shirt on in the first place.

I loved having him accompany me to gigs in later years. He would never go to see my show though. He would always seek out the dingiest pub in whatever town I was playing in and enjoy a pint there. He loved to meet the locals and various characters of the town. I would drop him off and give him a fiver. In those days five pounds could buy you a good few drinks. On one particular night, as he and I were driving home from a gig, we came upon the scene of an accident at a roundabout near Walkinstown. Before the area was built up there used to be a small humpback bridge where the roundabout is located today.

I remember this because back in 1967 I experienced an unforgettably frightening feeling on that bridge. At the time, I was on my way back home from dropping off a friend in Tallaght and I chose to travel a route through a place called Wellington Lane. The humpback bridge was positioned at the beginning of the road and had a graveyard on one side and a field on the other. Just as I came to the bridge, my Honda motorbike for some reason began to chug before conking out completely on the bridge. It was a good bike, and nothing like that had ever happened before. For some reason, I immediately got a weird feeling. As it conked out, the lights of the bike were shining straight at the graveyard which was located on the bend. I kick-started the bike but as I took off, the bike started performing as though there was another passenger on it. As any motorist knows, you can always tell when there is a lot of weight in the car. It's the same with motorbikes. When you're carrying a passenger on a motorbike, you can always feel the weight of the person on the back. Well on this particular night I could tell by the way the bike was travelling that there was extra weight on the back. At one stage, the feeling of added weight became so evident that I actually put my hand behind me to see was there someone or something there. The hair was standing on the back of my neck at this point because I knew something wasn't right. When I reached Walkinstown, I went into a housing estate. It was about one in the morning, but a car had just pulled in to a driveway and there were two people about to go into their house. I pulled the bike up right outside the house and after expressing my apologies, I explained to the man that I thought there was something wrong with my bike as I could feel the weight of a second person on it. The moment I said that, the Honda fell over. Even though I had placed it securely on the stand after I got off it, the bike just fell flat on the ground. The three of us couldn't make head nor tail of what was going on. I couldn't figure it out, but at the same time, I couldn't get the graveyard out of my head. I wondered was there some connection. I made a few enquiries and found out that a few years earlier a motorcyclist had been killed on that very same humpback bridge. He had driven over at speed and tragically hit the wall. Coincidentally, six years later, the first house Eileen and I bought was located in a housing estate off Wellington Lane.

As I mentioned earlier, a roundabout replaced the humpback bridge once the area began to build up. As me Da and I approached this roundabout that night, we could see some commotion taking place at the other side. It was then I noticed people waving at us to stop. By this stage of my career, I had a white transit van, which had my name lit up on the front as a form of advertising, and the people at the roundabout had mistaken my van with the bonnet lights for an ambulance. When we got out to see if we could help, we saw a motorcyclist lying on the ground after having crashed. I remember thinking he looked like a lad who was only in his early twenties. An ambulance was already on its way but as it happened, there was a doctor living nearby. After being alerted to the accident, he arrived on the scene but sadly, had to pronounce the young man dead. I was up all night thinking about the young man and what had happened. Slowly, I began to think back to the structure of the road prior to the roundabout being installed and I figured the motorcyclist would have been travelling from the same direction as I had been six years earlier when my motorcycle came to a halt. I wondered was it possible that he too might have encountered the same weird feeling I had and that as a result of being quite spooked, had taken off at speed. Maybe it's a coincidence, but I do believe that it's not entirely impossible.

Some incidents are so out of the ordinary that they go beyond coincidence.

Once, when I was performing a gig in Slattery's in Terenure, I spotted Eileen chatting to a woman I knew. I mentioned it to her afterwards and she explained they were friends. That's when I told her that the woman in question had been my first girlfriend back when I was around five. A couple of years later, my good friend Frank Savage presented me with a framed photograph of our confirmation day. After showing it to Eileen, she got the shock of her life when she realised that the boy standing next to me in the picture was her first boyfriend from when she was 13 years of age. It never fails to amaze me how people we associate with our childhood can often resurface in the strangest of places and situations in our adult years.

For example, when I was in my early teens I loved listening to a variety of different radio presenters. Many of these same people reappeared later in my life and I developed strong friendships with many of them. Maureen Potter was one such figure, and another huge favourite of mine was a presenter called Din-Joe. He used to spearhead a very popular programme which consisted of him telling jokes and yarns. My father would be enthralled by this show.

I once wrote to the legendary RTÉ sports presenter Seán Óg Ó Ceallacháin. I have very early memories of my father listening religiously to Seán's radio show every Sunday night. My father was a huge fan of Seán's so I felt compelled to write to him. Even though we have kept in touch through letter since then we have never actually met in person. Another person my father greatly admired was Con Houlihan, whom I have met just twice in my life. As it turns out he knew my father well, but unfortunately I never got an opportunity to talk to him about it. I keep threatening to send him a letter to ask if he remembers Seamus Grace. That was the calibre of people that I looked up to at the time. Cecil Sheridan, Danny Cummins, Chris Casey, all wonderful entertainers in their own right and all main headliners of the Irish entertainment scene. I didn't realise then that I would one day get to work with these people.

Looking back, I can see that I came in just at the right time. When I entered the industry it was becoming more commercial but it wasn't cutthroat by any means. The balance was perfect. The performers I idolised topped the bill at many shows during the 1940's and 1950's. However there were times during my career when my name was top of the bill and they were listed as "other players", and I have to admit it was something I was never comfortable with. I harboured a tremendous amount of respect for these people so it never felt right that I, a relative newcomer, should be top of the bill while these great industry legends were listed as "other players". It never sat well with me. They on the other hand took it with a pinch of salt because they understood that it was a new entertainment era and that new names were drawing the crowds.

Through working in panto, I formed a brilliant friendship with Chris Casey. I had always held him in great admiration as an entertainer and enjoyed being in his company. I learned so much. I absorbed everything, often unbeknownst to myself, just as I had done as a child.

By the time I performed my first panto, I was already on the scene as a balladeer. Most actors remember their first panto for the excitement and sheer jubilation it brought them. When I think back to my first panto, however, the first thing I remember is performing while still in crutches from a motorbike accident. It was 1979 and the great actor Jack Cruise had just passed away. Jack was the icon of the Olympia panto and was greatly loved by the audiences who saw him in action.

Before he passed away he had been involved in the Cinderella panto. As the production was now without its main actor, my manager by some miracle was able to secure me the lead role and I stepped into the shoes of Jack Cruise, albeit in crutches. I was catapulted into centre stage and even though it was a major coup for me, it didn't stop me from feeling uncomfortable. As far as I was concerned, I was still the new kid on the scene and here I was as one of the leads, surrounded by all these stage connoisseurs. Fortunately I got on famously with everyone and spirits were good. One day Danny Cummins called me over and told me the part I was playing wasn't right for me. They had cast me as one of the ugly sisters and Danny was cast as Buttons. Danny said to me he was too old to play Buttons and that I was too young to play an ugly sister, and that as a result, he felt we should swap roles. It made sense, and following on from that I ended up playing the part of Buttons.

I was still on crutches from my accident so they had to be written into the storyline. As part of my first entrance, there was the sound of an off stage crash, which was followed by my arrival on crutches.

While I was exhilarated by the experience of stage, the downside was the feeling of sadness over the passing of Jack Cruise. I once attended a panto and Jack referred to me on stage. It was a little signal to say; "We know you're there in the audience." I once did it to Phil Lynott when he was in the audience with his mother and daughters. Word would come through that a well known person was in the audience and, while I'm not sure if it's still done today, back then, their name would be incorporated somewhere into the script, just as a little nod towards them. As I had already established Bottler, the panto title for 1980 was changed from *Robinson Crusoe* to *Bottler Crusoe*. In the following years, featured pantos included *Bottler and the Beanstalk* and *Bottler in Nipperland*.

To work well in an entertainment production I have always found it essential that the overall atmosphere is a happy one. I want people to enjoy coming to work, not dread it. If someone has an issue or a grievance, my approach is to resolve it and move on. I simply don't like a bad working atmosphere. From what I have heard, this was often the case with pantos. Some actors didn't like the idea of their co-stars having the funny lines and so would demand that the joke be written into their script instead. It's a form of insecurity. What I realised from a young age through my observation of comedians was that you don't always need to be the person telling the joke in order to be the one that gets the laughs. The performer who best exemplifies this is Jack Benny. Benny was without doubt the funniest man alive but he never once told a joke. Someone else would always tell the joke and he would simply react. People would fall about the place laughing at him because his timing was impeccable. Either he was born with a natural comedic timing or it was a skill well honed over years, either way, I have never seen anything like it since. Chris Casey was another example of someone who didn't understand comedy but yet was an incredibly funny person. I discussed it with him a few times and he genuinely couldn't see what people found funny about him.

I performed in pantos from 1979 until 1986 and every year, without fail, Christmas week would bring a nightmare that would leave me in a sweat afterwards. In the dream I walk onto a stage in front of a packed audience when suddenly I forget what panto it is and what I'm supposed to say. Funnily enough, my daughter Melanie, who is also involved in acting, has experienced the exact same nightmare. As a result, I've looked into the meaning of the dream and it's supposed to be a good omen. It brings to mind a saying from years back that went: "If you dream of the bad, you'll hear of the good." In the acting arena, it seems that if you dream you'll have a bad night on stage, it's usually a sign that you will have a good night.

Forgetting words is a strong fear. No matter how many years you're on the scene it still persists. In this respect however, actors have great resilience. Melanie is like me. If she forgot the words to a song she was singing, the chances are the people listening wouldn't detect her mistake because she has this unique skill of being able to invent lyrics and make them work until she gets back on track.

Even though I always found panto quite time consuming, I can still envision myself returning to it at some stage. It's a hankering that for some reason continues to persist. The one person I would loved to have worked with on stage was Jack Cruise. To be honest though, I don't think it would have been a successful partnership as I can't imagine him ever having wanted another comedian in his show.

When I look back over my old panto posters, the one that stands out for me is of *Bottler Crusoe*. Maureen Potter's name was always top of the bill as she was the main act, and this was the very first production where she shared her top of the bill status. As a result the poster read *Bottler Crusoe, starring Maureen Potter and Brendan Grace*. Maureen was the sweetheart of the Gaiety, and every bit as beautiful a person off stage as she was on stage. We always shared great chats following the show when the cast would go for a few drinks. Maureen's favourite tipple was always the unusual collaboration of scotch and milk. Funnily enough, my father used to drink whiskey and hot milk. It's thanks to Maureen that I am now superstitious before a show. It started when we were in a dressing room chatting away prior to a show, and I began whistling a song while she was making last minute preparations. As soon as she heard me whistling, she screamed and told me to leave the room. She then ran me out of her dressing room and, outside the door, she turned around three times and said a prayer. It seems whistling in a dressing room brings bad luck.

When I asked Maureen about it afterwards she was able to recall specific incidents where bad luck had followed. She told me of how someone had whistled in a dressing room only for the entire stage set to fall down not long afterwards. There were even stories of actors who had died on the same night someone had whistled in a dressing room. Maybe it was all coincidence, but whatever the case may be, those in the theatre view it as a way of attracting bad luck.

Another character I once tread the stage boards with was the hypnotist Paul Goldin. Paul, who passed away in 2008, first hit the headlines in the early sixties. Whenever he was performing, he would adopt the most convincing French accent but his act overall was incredibly entertaining to watch. On The Late Late Show one night, Paul performed a hypnotism trick in which he instructed viewers to cross their arms. He then explained that they wouldn't be able to uncross their arms until he clicked his fingers. I tried it at the time and it didn't work, but one lady phoned in to say that her dog had been sitting by the fire when Paul performed his hypnotism trick and now the dog couldn't stand up because he couldn't unfold his paws.

Paul's live shows were every bit as sensational. I attended one such show in the Olympia Theatre. At the time I was still in my teens and, while most young lads would baulk at the notion of getting up on stage and being hypnotised, when Paul called for twelve volunteers, I was first off the seat. I remember he hypnotised me into performing the actions of milking a cow. I can still remember the exhilarating feeling of both being up on a stage and seeing people laugh at my performance.

At the end of the show, Paul told the audience that they would see a leprechaun on their way home. Convinced by his words, I can remember running up the steps of the bus to see if I could find one. As an acknowledgment for taking part, the twelve volunteers were each given tickets for the show taking place the following night. Having enjoyed the spotlight the first night, I presented myself again on the second night when volunteers were called for. As a result, I ended up being on the stage of the Olympia several nights in a row, each night being hypnotised and receiving good laughs in exchange for it. When I got to know Paul as a friend years later, we shared a good laugh one night when I told him about my time as one of his stooges.

Back then, live shows and radio were the main sources of entertainment. I remember when I brought out my record, "Cushy Butterfield", the first people I approached for airtime were the hosts of those much loved sponsored radio programmes in RTÉ. I would stand outside the studios waiting for broadcasting figures such as Gay Byrne to arrive. On their way in, I would stop them and introduce myself.

A radio show called The Farming Independent, which featured three icons of that time, Monica Carr, Jim Norton, and Peter Murphy, was one that rural Ireland lived for and by. Recognising that airtime on their show would be priceless in terms of publicity, I set about making myself known to them by handing them my record when they arrived at the studio in the morning. That's how I made a name for myself with radio listeners – by hanging around and haunting the stars of all the influential radio shows!

Looking back, I think they were bemused by the fact that I, the artist, was out promoting my own record. Normally record companies would send specific people, known as record pluggers, to the radio stations to hawk their latest tracks. I felt it was more personal to do it myself. Irish radio's best known agony aunt, Frankie Byrne, was another broadcaster with whom I formed a wonderful friendship. I remember her coming to my mother's funeral. Her attendance in particular sticks out in my mind because at the time she wasn't in the best of health herself and yet still she had made the effort to come and sympathise.

Despite plaguing them to play my record, the likes of Frankie, Gaybo, Monica, and all those other figures who presented radio programmes, in time began to see me more as a friend than a nuisance. I'm sure I was a headache to them but if I was, it's certainly a testament to their patience that they didn't lose their temper with my persistence. Coincidentally, Monica Carr, whose real name was Mary Norton, and her brother Jim hailed from Dunlavin in Wicklow which, as I mentioned earlier, is my father's home ground. Jim actually went to school with my father and Monica later admitted to me that she once had a crush on Seamus Grace. She often laughed and joked with me that she could have been my mother! Larry Gogan, who is a long-time friend of mine, was always very dedicated to the showbands and upcoming performers. He used to present a number of the sponsored shows back then. Larry's appreciation for music is unique. He has witnessed the change in trends, the fads that came and went, and I don't think there is anyone who will disagree with me when I say he truly is an authority on the Irish music industry.

Another figure of huge influence was Gay Byrne. In my attempts to get The Gingermen an appearance on The Late Late Show, I wrote to Gay Byrne on several occasions. I would usually receive a letter back from the producer informing me that my name was on file and that we would be contacted should a slot arise. Sometimes Gay himself would write the reply, a gesture which I always found incredibly courteous of him. Of course, when I finally ended up appearing on the show in a solo capacity, I sent a letter to Gay Byrne thanking him for giving me a moment in the spotlight on his show. Not long afterwards, I received a letter from the man himself quite literally thanking me for thanking him. I was tempted to write back and thank him for thanking me for thanking him. He too found that, for all the things he would do for people, only a few would reflect their appreciation in a card. In later years he spoke to me about the conspicuous lack of thank you's from people and how I, as a result of my thank you card, stood out in his mind.

It's something I have come to experience myself in my own career. For every ten people I would do something for, maybe one would express their thanks. Personally, I have always made it a point of sending a letter or a thank you card to anyone who did me a favour. I imagine nearly all performers will agree with me when I say people have no problem finding out your address when they have a request, but yet when it comes to sending a thank you note, the address disappears just as fast. Manners were instilled in me as a child. Maybe it was the memory of getting a clip around the ear if I forgot my manners, but either way, good manners were something I carried into adulthood.

Dealing with bad-mannered people however is a skill I've come to acquire over the years. Anyone with a career on stage will at some point have encountered their share of hecklers. I'm lucky I don't get hecklers now, but in my early years there were a few drunken people who would make their presence known. In my experience, a smartass is easy to deal with; a drunken smartass however is slightly more difficult.

When it first began, I would retaliate with a quick answer along the lines of "I wonder if the rest of you is as big as your mouth?" or "When God put teeth in your mouth, he spoiled a lovely ass."

My favourite reply to a heckler though has always been to tell the crowd that he and I used to be a double act. I would then explain that we were called the "sym-bolics", before going on to add that, "I was sym ... he was the other half."

I have found that the best thing to do is let the heckler become a nuisance to the audience and then they will effectively deal with it by telling him or her to either zip it or take a hike.

As a performer, it's tempting to hit back with a sharp reply but in recent years I have become very conscious of the fact that if there is someone heckling, it may be because they have a disability or a condition such as Tourrettes.

Another interesting factor of life in the public eye is being approached and asked for advice on breaking into the comedy business. The reason this fascinates me so much is because I realise I could be influencing, in some way, a future star in the business. One such experience occurred in 1976 when I was playing a show in a cabaret venue called Woody's in Castleisland, county Kerry. By the end of the night, a young American lad and his sister approached me to buy my tape and have a chat. I remember the lad, who at the time was around 17 years of age, was particularly interested in my comedy and I think we chatted for almost an hour while he asked me various questions about being a comedian. I didn't take much notice of it because it's not unusual to be asked such questions, but for some reason I didn't forget him either.

One night in Boston around the year 2000, a girl came up to me and introduced herself a short while before I was to go on stage. She then told me how she and her brother had met me some years earlier in Castleisland. The moment she mentioned it, I could immediately recall the night in question. That's when she told me her brother's name: Dennis Leary. I was so taken aback that I had to ask her if she was talking about "the Dennis Leary". She nodded her head and that's when she told me he was going to be attending my show that night. Dennis was so well known that he was planning to arrive incognito so it was arranged that we would meet up following the gig.

Sure enough, I met him afterwards and we got talking about that night in Kerry. It seems they were in the county that time because his family were

Grandad – me at 18 months.

Grandson – James at 18 months.

Me Da knocking down the Theatre Royal.

Me and my
aunt Wyn.

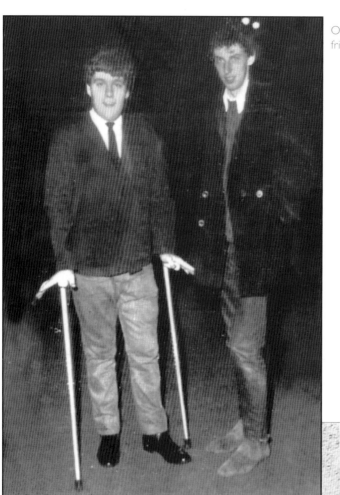

On crutches, with my friend Paul Malone.

Me Da with uncle Pete and me in front of all the bottles – I was destined to be Bottler.

My l'il sis Maria and Pepe.

Me Ma and Da.

With me Da.

My first acting role.

On the ladder to success with The Gingermen.

This photo, given to me by my school pal and lifelong friend Frank Savage, still gives me goosebumps.
I'm only ten years old and already centre stage! Is that destiny or wha'?

Grace in the news.

Me and me Ma.

I learned a lot from my old pal Chris Casey.

Easy rider.

Having a laugh with friends in the Shieling Hotel, Raheny. *From left*; Eileen Reid, Joe Dolan and Tony Kenny.

Big Bottler and little Bottler (my son Bradley).

One of Tralee's greatest treasure's, my good friend Nedeen Kelleher.

Ach, Brendan, ye're an awful man.

Shot with J.R.

Having a chat with
Sir Michael Smurfit
and their Highnesses,
Prince Rainier and
Prince Albert.

from Killarney. He then went on to tell me that he had learned a lot through attending my show that night in 1976 and that it had given him inspiration for his own material. Needless to say, I was fascinated to hear all this because Dennis Leary is a hugely famous actor/comedian in America and Ireland. I can still to this day vividly recall the night he approached me as a teenager with his family because I realised how interested he was in comedy.

Funnily enough, in 1975, the year prior to my meeting with the young Leary lad in Kerry, the Kingdom footballers were playing Dublin in the All-Ireland final in Croke Park. There are many reasons why both counties will remember that day in particular but my reason for remembering it is quite different to most. Tommy Ellis, who was my recording manager at the time, had given me a song written by a friend of his entitled "The Dubs are the Champions". We took a chance on recording it prior to the match but it was made purely on the basis that the Dubs were going to win. Fortunately, the Dubs did win the All-Ireland and we had the record in all the shops the very next day. It soared up the charts so the risk certainly paid off but had the team lost that day, the song would have been shelved which would have been disastrous given the amount of money invested by the record company.

We sang the lyrics to a tune similar to that of "Olé Olé Olé". It was a great catchy song but unfortunately it's nowhere to be found these days. I don't even have a copy of it!

Even though I enjoyed my share of hits, I was without doubt a showband wannabe at heart. I entered showbusiness as a balladeer, but I socialised with the showband stars because I had never developed any great allegiance or camaraderie with the balladeers. I think the glamour possessed by the showband singers won me over. They all had big sound systems, extravagant lighting and personalised vans. It's no big deal now, but back then it was the height of style and luxury.

Once I established a name for myself in the business, I bought a good sound system. This was something that a lot of other acts saw as being a waste of money but I considered it an investment in my career. I saw from the showband performances the big difference it could make to a show. Whenever I played the larger venues, it concerned me that some people might not be able to hear me.

As a result of all the gear, I usually had to transport it in a trailer. One night, when Eileen and I were on our way home from Glencolmcille in Donegal before we were married, I came upon a very sharp bend in the road. I heard a loud thud which must have been a pot hole because next thing all I could see was one of the tyres from the trailer rolling out ahead of me while I was still driving. The tyre then rolled off the side of the road and bounced its way down into a steep valley, leaving me without the option of reattaching the bloody thing. With a trailer full of expensive equipment and now short of a tyre, all we could do was sleep in the car for the night. The next morning, following some roadside assistance, I dropped Eileen off to work before making the dreaded call of shame to her mother Lillie. With my most sincere tone of voice, I explained how the wheel had come loose from the trailer and how Eileen and I ended up booking into a B&B for the night. In separate bedrooms of course.

It was following that incident that I decided it was time to buy a van and employ a roadie. A roadie is essentially a person who travels to gigs with the performer and helps set up the gear. The well known comedian and writer Brendan O'Carroll started off with me as a roadie. At the time Brendan was only thinking of entering the comedy circuit, which naturally was a move I encouraged because I could see he had a great wit about him. We even discussed potential stage names for him and I believe we were going to call him "Benny Loss".

Brendan O'Carroll and I used to do great impressions of Hal Roach, as did Dermot Morgan and my friend Gerry Keogh. Hal was the daddy of the comedians so we decided to perform a skit which we called the Roach Family Five. As part of the routine, myself, Brendan, Dermot and Gerry, along with a cardboard cut out of Hal Roach, would sit around the table, Gerry wearing a child's nappy, Dermot wearing women's clothes, and all of us with our Hal Roach voices. We all spoke to each other as if we were Hal Roach. I later found out that Hal himself had seen the skit and was very amused by the whole thing. That performance was Brendan O'Carroll's first television appearance and, if I'm not mistaken, it was also one of the very first appearances made by Dermot Morgan. It was around the time he developed the character Fr Trendy and the one thing I always remember about him was his constant rehearsing. He was the consummate professional and a wonderful impressionist. The skits he performed of government members were priceless. If Dermot were still alive, there wouldn't be enough hours in the day for him to get through all the material he would derive from everything that's going on at the moment.

Getting back to my roadie situation however, I remember a man working with the Indian Showband suggested a nice lad from Drimnagh called Don Connolly. I went on to employ Don as my roadie. In 1989 I sustained a number of injuries in a motorbike accident. As my injuries presented me from working, we were both effectively out of work so we went our separate ways. Don's brother Tommy later became my roadie for four years, but directly following Don's departure, I employed my cousin Ciarán, who was on a break from his job as a long distance truck driver. He remained on as my roadie for several years. I have many memories from that time but the one memory I know that neither of us will ever forget is of the night we were driving home from a gig in Mayo. As we were driving along, the van began to skid before veering off the road and ending up in a stream, narrowly missing a stone bridge wall by inches. Fortunately, we hadn't suffered any injuries in the crash but when we saw how close we had come to hitting the wall, we might as well have been knocked sideways with the shock we got. The van was a write off and we decided to get a new black wagon, which led to my kids christening us "The A-Team".

When you're on the road so much, boredom can sometimes lead to pranks; pranks that maybe in hindsight weren't such a good idea, or in my case, were hugely irresponsible. One night while Kieran was driving I was in the back of the van having a rest following a gig. I knew I had brought bangers with me so, in the mood for tomfoolery, I decided to light the fuse of the banger and drop it into the doorway beside Kieran. At the time I thought this was going to be hilarious. Normally you hear the banger hissing before it goes off with a bang, but Kieran didn't hear a thing until the explosive noise occurred. The poor lad got such a fright he nearly lost control of the van. He didn't speak to me for about a month afterwards and, to be honest, I didn't blame him either.

Pranks on the road were very much the norm between travelling bands and musicians. The one thing I loved almost as much as listening to the showband performers was meeting them on the road. Between Dublin and Kinnegad you could meet around twenty showband vans either on their way or returning home from a gig. I remember my roadie and I were driving across the Curragh in Kildare when we saw this bandwagon coming towards us. Stories of egg throwing amongst performers when they pass each other on the roads has been well documented and let me assure you my roadie and I certainly played our part in keeping this tradition alive. As the bandwagon approached, I got the eggs ready for take off. Before long I was hopping eggs out the window faster than the other van could drive. Unfortunately, I didn't realise that the driver's window of the other van was open at the time. Johnny McEvoy was sitting inside with a guest from the USA when he was pelted with a stray flying egg. Two eggs broke inside the van and Johnny was absolutely furious with me over it. He has regularly performed on my shows.

The first time I saw Johnny was in London back in 1969. I was with The Gingermen at the time and we were performing a gig in a hospital hall. We were opening for Johnny. I remember there was a huge amount of nurses at the gig all of whom were going crazy for McEvoy. He was famous, rich, and good looking and he certainly attracted the women because they were all flocking around the poor lad. Just witnessing that kind of reaction made me want to be in the business even more.

Mooning was another big thing among bands. As a bandwagon was passing you out on the road, all you would see was a big hairy arse pressed up against the back window. I can't claim a white record however as there was many a time when I stuck my own arse up into the air at a passing wagon. I remember mooning Joe Dolan and his band, but usually when you moon someone, they moon back. The moon was in full bloom back then!

Possibly the funniest mooning incident involved the band, The Branagans; Geraldine, Donal, and Declan. I performed a few shows with The Branagans and I remember on one occasion as we were travelling to a venue, they passed us out on a winding road near Mountrath. Straight away I knew they had passed us so that they could stop and moon us as we drove around one of the bends. As we were driving along, I spotted a squad car behind me, so I asked Brian to pull in and let the garda car pass. The gardaí were now in front of us but of course the Branagan brothers up ahead heard the car coming and naturally assumed it was us. Immediately they dropped their trousers and bared all in the air. My roadie and I were directly behind the squad car and sure enough as we drove around the bend, there were the Branagan lads with every bit of their modesty thrown to the wind. Naturally the garda car pulled in to question the behaviour of the lads, but once the guards realised the lads were in a band, they knew exactly what was going on and let them go. I still maintain it was a testament to Brian's good driving that we didn't crash with all the laughing we did that day.

I call Brian Keane my hand-reared manager as he started off with me as a roadie before progressing through the ranks to manager. Due to the amount of time we spend on the road together, he is also known as my other wife. Funnily enough, it was my wife Eileen who christened him with that moniker. For a Christmas present, Eileen gave him a Zippo lighter with the engraved message, "To my husband's other wife!" Brian first started off with me when he was just 17. My roadie couldn't make the gig at the last minute and as a result I was left shorthanded. I went to a local petrol station to fill up the van. My head was wrecked from trying to find a solution to my roadie problem. I got talking to the kid who was filling the petrol and ended up asking him if he had a driving license and whether he would be interested in a few hours work helping me at a gig. He said he would do it and it was at that moment I hired the lad who would go on to become my full time roadie before progressing on to being my personal manager.

When Brian was still quite young, I advised him to buy a house in Clondalkin. He was only just starting off in the business with me and really couldn't afford it at the time but nevertheless I encouraged him to go for it and fortunately, he heeded my advice. He has since told me about the number of sleepless nights he had back then over whether or not he would be able to make the repayments. Despite his fears, it didn't let him down. I actually encouraged a few people back then to invest in property. The property market was still in its infancy and I could foresee that an investment at that time would later pay dividends. I think, for me, it all stemmed from the advice that was given to me by my record producer Tommy Ellis just as I was starting off. He advised me to buy a house that was slightly more than I could afford; one that I was going to struggle with, and that eventually I would find I could afford it. He was right and his advice was something I passed on to my own kids and people who worked closely with me.

In writing this book I spoke with Brian about the years gone by and, mid-conversation, our memories of the showband years came up. I think many in the industry will wholeheartedly agree that showbusiness was definitely a lot more fun back then. There were so many diverse people involved and a great camaraderie was formed between the different groups. On a trip to Galway from Dublin, you could meet up to ten showband vans on the road, and on some occasions, when we weren't mooning or egging each other, we would actually stop and have a chat and a laugh. There were more people to interact with back then, whereas today it has tightened down so much. It has become a lot more serious. I suppose the difference becomes really apparent when you combine it with the fact that a lot of the people who were in the business back then don't take a drink now. They lived the highlife during the 1970's and 1980's and, as a result, burned themselves out. None of us are getting any younger and the idea of staying up drinking until four every morning is not a luxury our livers will allow us. To be honest, we didn't need to drink to have a laugh. When you're in comedy you can usually create your own amusement, with or without the aid of alcohol.

My past roadies will probably maintain that I'm at my worst when sober. To give you an example, there have been one or two occasions where Brian was driving us back to Dublin following a gig, assuming that I was asleep in the back of the van. I would, in fact, be lighting a piece of paper on fire to leave down beside him, purely to give him a bit of a fright and me a bit of a laugh. Needless to say, Brian would get the shock of his life when he would suddenly see this burning flame going up beside him. Considering, however, what I put Kieran through that night with the bangers, I often remind Brian that he's damn lucky a piece of paper and a lit match was about the worst he got from me!

five

I hired him in the past to perform at number of functions and he always had the crowd in stitches laughing. He performs the role of a drunk very well and of course his Father of the Bride act is just hilarious. Whether he was chatting up the bridesmaid, trying to light a cigarette or giving grief to the mother-in-law, he would have the whole room laughing aloud. His talent is remarkable.

Bill Cullen

Dancing on the Radio

I can remember a time when the rent for our television cost more than the rent for our flat, when Lucan was considered the countryside, and when Tallaght was just a village. I lived in an era where LSD meant pounds, shillings, and pence and where, if you were lucky enough to have toilet facilities, it wasn't unusual for them to be situated somewhere other than in your flat. For the people of the Echlin Street flats, the toilets were located out in the yard. There were eight flats per block and the toilet for each flat was in a little shed-like building below in the yard. The toilets were always locked and each flat owner was given a key which looked more like a small hammer. One particular memory which will remain forever seared in my mind is of when I was about ten years of age and in dire need of a toilet trip. To paint a lovely picture, I was bursting so badly that running up the three flights of stairs to the flat to get the key was not an option. I was a great whistler, so I caught my mother's attention by whistling up at her before following it up with a roar to throw down the key. She wrapped it in some newspaper because the iron key was so heavy that if you got a belt of it, which I did on one occasion, you'd be lucky if you weren't unconscious for two days afterwards. As the key was falling from the third storey however, the newspaper wrapping came undone and it hit the ground with such a thud that it broke. I think I will spare you the description of what happened next, but I can hazard a guess that one word in particular has already sprung to your mind and that it begins with "s" and ends with "e".

The funny thing is when Eileen and I lived in Saggart our house had two bathrooms: one painted in pink, the other in blue. I remember our two young girls would only use the pink bathroom while the two boys would only ever use the blue one. I still have to laugh when I think about that time because I had grown up with a bathroom in the yard and yet here were my young kids refusing to use anything other than colour coded bathrooms.

I am without doubt a highly nostalgic person. I can honestly say I would not like to be arriving into the world today; in fact I'm bleedin' delighted I was born when I was. I experienced two very different Irelands: the old way of life and the new in both the countryside and the city. Someone who saw many different Irelands was the lady I met in 2001 who was born in 1899. At 102 years of age she was as sharp as a tack. She was attending one of my shows so I announced from the show that I had a lady in my audience who had lived through three centuries. Meeting that woman was a particularly interesting moment for me because it would be impossible now to meet someone who has lived in three centuries. The person would have to be over 110 years of age.

Perhaps it's the nostalgic in me but as far as I'm concerned, the old way of life will always offer the best memories. Things were so much more innocent back then and who knows but maybe we were the happier for it? I remember my mother telling me about the time she was in the labour ward awaiting my arrival. She clearly had no idea of what the birthing process entailed because when she saw the woman in a nearby bed being wheeled to the delivery room, straight away Ma called over the nurse and said to her, "That woman in that bed over there came in after me but she's having her baby before me ... will you do me next?"

Of course the nurse tried to explain that she would have to wait for nature to take its course but Ma was adamant that she should be having her baby first since she arrived first. She honestly thought it was that simple.

Another example of innocence from a bygone age was our version of "colour" television. At the time colour television was quite uncommon, not to mention a luxury that was really only afforded by wealthier families. A very enterprising individual would go from door to door selling a blue plastic gel screen which you placed over your television. It gave you "colour" television, even though the colour in question was limited to just blue. People used to buy the screen and then announce they had colour TV when in fact they really only had a black and white television with a blue screen in front of it.

At one stage the Grace family owned a genuine colour television. It came about as a result of my father's love for entering competitions in the *Sunday Press* newspaper. Every week without fail he would complete either the crossword or the spot-the-ball competition. One particular entry led to him winning a colour television. It was absolutely huge compared to the average sized television but the reception on it was rubbish because the aerial was useless. I think we kept it for about two weeks before selling it off.

Films were of great interest to me and my friends. I can remember when Batman was a weekly cinema listing. It would be shown every Saturday and if you had three pence to spare, you had yourself a ticket. If you didn't have the money or wanted to spend the three pence on sweets instead, then you simply bunked in, which was slang for sneaking in for free. Of course, if we were stopped and asked to produce a ticket, we would have our most convincing faces on while we reeled off the age old excuse: "I dropped it." As there were so many kids going to see Batman at the time, we would all have to sit two to a seat. I remember Patch the usher coming down with his flashlight either to tell us to shut up talking or to get us to move up a seat. It was quite difficult for me to share a seat considering I wasn't exactly the skinniest of boys. Whatever film we went to see would often have a lasting effect on my friends and me. If we had just been to see a cowboy film, we would inevitably run out of the cinema afterwards hitting our backsides as though we were on horses. If we had seen a war film, we would walk out like we were soldiers. In our heads we would be on our way to Vietnam rather than James Street. I will never forget a story told to me by my good friend Eddie Sweeney who, when he was around seven years of age, went to see a John Wayne movie with a friend. Eddie had already seen the movie before but opted not to tell the friend, instead preferring to place a bet with him that John Wayne would fall off his horse at a particular point. Needless to say, Eddie won the penny and said to his friend "I told you he'd fall off the horse."

The friend replied that he had actually seen the film before too. Hearing this, Eddie asked him why he had placed the bet if he already knew what was going to happen. In his innocence, the young fella said back to him, "Well I had seen it before but I didn't think John Wayne would be stupid enough to fall off the horse a second time."

As kids it didn't take a lot to keep us amused. We would get great fun out of something as simple as knocking on a door of a flat and running away. Eileen and her friends used to play it as well except they used to call that game "Knocking Dollys".

Another form of entertainment, which I believe a lot of inner city kids still do today, was tying a rope to the top of a lamp post and looping it to make a seat so that we could then swing around it.

When we weren't robbing orchards, which was also known as "Boxing the Fox", we could usually be found playing "beds". "Beds", which today is known as hopscotch, was a game where you would get some chalk and draw eight boxes along the footpath. You would then use an old tin of shoe polish to throw onto one of the boxes before hopping on the remaining boxes on one leg. I was particularly fond of playing with marbles. They were easy to get back then but for some reason are not as commonplace today. For me, marbles always held a wonderful fascination. To receive a bag of marbles would be enough to make my day. However if I got a "gollier" marble, which was a marble that was twice as big, then it was the equivalent to receiving a birthday gift. "Steeliers" were round balls of steel also known as ball bearings. Although if you had those, you were just plain posh.

These days, with regular cheap flights, a day out can consist of travelling to England or Italy. Back when I was a child, we were just as content going to Bray. My mother and grandmother would often bring my sister and I to the beach in Bray. We developed this ritual where we would either get the Number 45 bus out and then the train back home, or vice versa. Dawson's Amusements were in place at the time and for Marie and me, these alone could bring about the same excitement as the arrival of Santa Claus. For a picnic we would walk up to Bray Head which was like a mini Croagh Patrick. My mother would bring the sandwiches and some tea leaves because you could buy a teapot of boiling water from a kiosk on the beachfront. As a result of our trips to Bray, Marie and I developed a taste for banana and sand sandwiches. We had no choice really. The sand would be blowing back up in your face so you would basically end up eating sandwiches consisting of banana and sand.

Bottler came about as a result of a comedy routine I used to perform involving a mother who one day brought her son to Dublin's Sandymount beach. The routine told the story of how a big hullabaloo occurs when the young lad goes missing, until someone spots him in the water. The man runs into the sea, rescues the child and hands him back to the near hysterical mother.

Rather than thanking him however, she takes one look at the child and straight away asks, "Where's his cap?"

As a result of the popularity of that joke, I began to expand the routine by performing skits about my own school days which then led to me wearing a school blazer for the acts in question. With that came the birth of Bottler. You would not believe the amount of times I hear the line, "I was reared on Bottler." People grew up watching him on television and in my shows and even though

Bottler is now 35 years of age, those who were reared on him still see him in the same way they did as children.

What many people don't realise is that Bottler was quite a violent young gurrier when he started off. It surprised me immensely that people liked him as much as they did because in the beginning he wasn't the easiest character to relate to. He had a hatchet, a crowbar, a flick knife and an iron chain. It was so farfetched back then that it was funny but sadly, it wouldn't be remotely funny today as such paraphernalia have since become the norm.

Ironically, Bottler was, and still is, a posh gurrier: his uniform was always made by Louis Copeland!

Even though he is an inner city Dublin character, just knowing that he is as loved by rural people as he is by city people is something I consider an absolute blessing.

Not long after I created Bottler, I was asked to appear in television and newspaper ads for Maxol. The idea was that motorists would receive a token every time they bought petrol and once they had £120 worth of tokens, they would receive a teddy bear called a "Nipper".

For the ad, I was dressed as Bottler and surrounded by Nipper glove puppets. I remember kids used to drive their mothers mental looking for these Nipper toys.

Tom Noonan, who was then managing director of Maxol, brought me into the office and showed me the figures for Maxol's sales following the ad. At the time Maxol was seen as the poor relation to the other fuel companies. They were competing against names like Texaco, Shell and Esso but this ad managed to propel them to the forefront of the petrol game. From the figures produced in front of me that day in Tom Noonan's office, it seems the ad had resulted in Maxol's business in Ireland improving to the tune of 1100 per cent. While I was aware that the Nippers had been hugely popular, when I saw their success reflected in actual figures, I was completely taken aback. The ad was also a major career boost for me and looking back on it today I can see how getting involved in that ad was one of the best career decisions I made.

Television and radio advertisements were a great source of income. The great bonus is the constant television presence it gives you, particularly if your career is that of an entertainer, or like in my aunt Wyn's case, a model.

I remember the sheer pride I felt as a kid every time I saw my aunt Wyn on a television ad. She appeared in ads for Lyons Tea, Irish Coffee and various other products. These ads were not just confined to the television, they were also shown in cinemas. I can remember many an occasion when no sooner would her face have appeared on the cinema screen I would be standing up and shouting: "That's my aunty Winnie!" If Wyn was beside me at the time of my announcement, she would either be vigorously trying to shush me or crouching down mortified by the attention that was being brought upon her by her over zealous nephew. It didn't help matters when I would then point to her and say: "Look this is her here! Look! Look!" I remember some people would become as excited as I was by the presence of a well known face in the audience while others would just shoot me a look of annoyance before roaring at me to shut up and sit down!

While the Maxol ad will always remain in my memory, so too will an ad for skinless sausages, albeit for very different reasons. The filming of this ad took place in Ardmore Studios around 1976 and for the scene I had to be shown eating and enjoying sausages. With several re-takes, which was par for the course when shooting an ad of this nature, by the time the filming was complete I had taken bites out of about 100 sausages. For each re-take I had to have a bucket beside me to get rid of the sausages because with all the takes we did, it was just physically impossible to eat all of them. After going through that, it can be difficult to look like you're genuinely enjoying the food you're supposed to be advertising, so you end up going through the motions of chewing and smiling. For a good while afterwards, I could barely look at a sausage without my stomach turning. These days, whenever I see an ad in which the actor is eating, I always wonder how many takes they had to do to get the shot we see on television. After what I went through with those bleedin' sausages, I can sympathise with them!

On the upside, filming that ad gave me the opportunity to meet one of my acting heroes. Marty Feldman, a very famous actor who had starred in *Young*

Frankenstein, was also in Ardmore Studios filming *The Last Remake of Beau Geste*. Marty was one of those actors whose name would sometimes elude you but whose face you would always immediately recognise as he had these distinctively bulbous eyes. Anyway, on the day of filming, we happened upon each other while we were both out walking the grounds of Ardmore, and given that I was such a big fan of his work, I decided to approach him. I introduced myself and when I said my name, he replied, "Ah yes I've heard of you. Edna O'Brien mentioned your name to me." Edna was the prolific county Clare writer who had authored the hugely controversial book *The Country Girls*. I was immediately stunned by this revelation, primarily because Marty Feldman had recognised my name, but secondly because I had never met Edna! As a result I did often wonder if Marty had mixed me up with someone else that day and unfortunately I have not yet met Edna O'Brien to ask her about it. Regardless, just meeting Marty was an absolute thrill because I was a huge fan of his. I always think of his show, At Last The 1948 Show, as being the Monty Python of its day.

Another ad I made in the 1970's was for the Cross & Blackwell brand, which is now known as Chef. The ad featured me wearing an apron and pointing out the various Cross & Blackwell products available. As part of the ad I had to be filmed washing the dishes and, as the washing up liquid was called Three Hands, they decided to feature me with three hands washing dishes. For this scene they had to source an actor with a long hairy arm that looked somewhat similar to mine.

Around that time, Eileen also starred in an ad for Bisto gravy. Many of you will probably still remember it. For the ad, her script was something along the lines of: "Being married to Brendan Grace isn't easy. He loves his steak and kidney with lashings of Bisto gravy."

One memory of old Ireland that I will always cherish is of the evenings we spent listening to Irish set dancing on the radio. Irish radio was unique like that. I can't help but smile because in all honesty where else in the world would you find people gathering around a radio to listen to dancing? What's more, people would even stand and look at the radio while the dancers were on. The programme in question was called Take the Floor and I remember all you could hear was the distinctive floor-tapping sound of the Rory O'Connor dancers dancing in time with the music of an in-house céilí band. Anyone my age and older will definitely remember this programme.

A radio figure I mentioned in the last chapter was a comedian host called Din-Joe, his real name was Dennis Joseph Fitzgibbon, from Cork. Din-Joe, who has since passed away, was one person I would always have loved to have met simply because he was one of my early comedy heroes long before I really knew what comedy was. As it happens, our style of humour is very similar. I can always picture my father standing by the radio listening to Din-Joe's show and God help anyone who spoke while he was on the air.

When looking back at that time in my life, I can't help but think of the different traits contained within that generation.

Lugs Brannigan, who I also mentioned in an earlier chapter, was one such person who epitomised that particular era. He was a garda of an entirely different age. The thing about Sergeant Brannigan was that he would always travel in a Bedford van that had a sliding door. Whenever he arrived at the scene of a disturbance, he would have the door open and one foot out before the van had even stopped. He would then jump right into the middle of the melée without any pause for thought or hesitation. He was as proactive a guard as you could find. As I lived in the precinct Lugs was in charge of, I personally witnessed the effect he had on gougers. You would see gangs wilt at the sight of him. They would freeze in his presence. He frightened the absolute bejaysus out of them. I remember at the time there was always a rumour going around that he wore an iron knuckle duster underneath his gloves.

Lugs was a gifted boxer and was more than capable of defending himself against thugs. I often wondered was it this element of confidence he exuded that made gangs buckle before him. When I was a kid I once saw him approach six very rowdy drunks one night near the canal at Rialto. He told them all to take off their shoes and socks. He told them to put their socks into the shoes and asked each of them where they lived. Some lived in Crumlin, others in Drimnagh. He then told them all to walk home in their bare feet. He said he would check in at different intervals on their way home and whoever had their shoes back on would be brought off in the van and placed in a cell. While this was going on, I was the other side of the street watching from the window. They did exactly as he said. While they were still being punished for being rowdy, they didn't end up with a blemished record because of their drunken behaviour.

In my opinion he saved the State. Rather than waste everyone's time by throwing someone in a cell, he would instead throw them a punch in the hope that it would cop them on. There were many people previously involved in crime who came up to Lugs years afterwards and thanked him for giving them a belt or two. He taught them a lesson without throwing them in a cell and giving them a tarnished record. He gave them a second chance and for that many were grateful.

In later life, Lugs became a bouncer at the Zhivago club in Dublin and again he was a figure of authority. No one would mess with him. On one particular occasion I approached him outside the Zhivago club, shook his hand and introduced myself. We got chatting about everything from James Street to the years gone by. During our conversation we got talking about his nickname. He told me how much he absolutely loathed it. Lugs was a slang word for ears, and having been a former boxer, he had the look of a broken nose and big ears. He told me that night how much he would have loved to have gotten his hands on the person who christened him Lugs. As his nickname was so well known, people often forgot that he was actually Sergeant Jim Brannigan, they just knew him as Lugs.

I was intrigued by him because I always held a fondness for the gardaí. If I had passed the medical section of the garda exam, I would not only have gone on to graduate as a guard but rise through the ranks. I would even go so far as to say I would have become commissioner. Commissioner Grace if you will. I would definitely have had the ambition to advance through the ranks. My approach towards gougers would also have been hands-on – Lugs Brannigan style.

As it turned out, a very close friend of mine, Eddie Downey, experienced Lugs in the boxing ring. Fortunately for him, Lugs was not his opponent but the referee. A firm ally of Brannigan's, Eddie often regaled me with stories about him and his style. Eddie was himself a champion boxer and in 1952 he held the title of Mr Éire. I first came to know Eddie through attending the health clinic he ran in the Montrose Hotel in Donnybrook.

In the sauna prior to your session, you would meet people from all walks of life such was the large variety of his clientele: judges, solicitors, truck drivers, doctors, postmen, so on and so forth. A famous politician attended his clinic and while he was being tended to by Eddie, his secret service men would stand outside the door.

I always maintained that Eddie had magic hands. Anyone with aches or even stress went to him for help. There were many occasions where I would enter the therapy room and after just one look at me, Eddie would be able to tell that something was wrong. He was well ahead of his time. Tragically, Eddie passed away in the early 1990's. A good friend to many, his loss was felt. He was more than just a masseuse, he was like a therapist and confidante to his clients. He and I had a great rapport and I often confided my most private thoughts to him. A hugely intelligent man, he would give me a lot of insight into psychology and how to read people. I used what he gave me and as a result I find I have become quite an astute reader of people. I can usually tell instantly if someone is of good character or if I want to be friends with them. In the business I'm in, it's necessary to be able to distinguish between the genuine, who want your friendship, and the spoofers, who want something from your friendship.

Over the years I have also developed a great understanding of body language. First impressions say a lot, however for me, it's all in the handshake. When I shake hands with a person, I can immediately detect what kind of an individual they are just by the strength of their handshake and the way they maintain it. For example, I find that a lot of people will shake a person's hand but not maintain eye contact with them for the duration of the shake.

On the other hand, if someone greets you with a hug or by placing their hand on your shoulder, it's usually a positive reflection of their overall nature. I do realise just how fortunate I am to be able to identify the sincere from the duplicitous. After all, the people you allow into your life can have a hugely significant impact. I make a point of surrounding myself with positive and optimistic people. It's the same in work; I thrive in a happy environment. It's important to me that those I am working with are content and in good spirits. Over the years I have seen a number of selfish people who never gave a damn about anyone so long as they themselves were happy. Those are the very same people who are not working today.

I credit many different positive influences with having contributed to my career, but most of all I am forever grateful to the boy Bottler. It's incredibly endearing that people remember him from their childhood as fondly as they do Zig & Zag, Judge and Bosco. Without Bottler and the various influences who helped mould him over the years, I genuinely believe my life would be extremely different to what it is now, and I certainly don't think my career would have brought me in the wonderful direction it has.

six

After coming home from doing the grocery shopping, dad will usually walk into the house and roar "Slaves!" That's how he summons his kids to bring in the groceries.

Youngest son, Brendan Grace Jr

Slaves

There are few kids who would emerge from their childhood without being haunted by memories of buying their dad mascara and foundation whenever he ran out. Although, considering my two girls once walked out of their school only to see me dressed as Bottler and standing beside a Mini Cooper waiting to bring them home, is it any wonder they were hard to shock?

Eileen and I have four kids, Amanda, Melanie, Bradley and Brendan Patrick, and I will always maintain that it's a testament to their mother that all four grew up without being traumatised by the pranks I used to play on them.

On occasion, I would bring them to my gigs. Just before we would leave in the car, I would press my hand against the rear window and leave a handprint. A short while later as we were driving along, sure enough the condensation would fall on the car windows and the handprint would appear. The kids would be chatting away in the back seat when suddenly I would roar, "Oh Jesus kids don't look behind ye." Naturally they would look behind them straight away, see the massive handprint and start screaming!

For a long time I also had them obsessed with the film *Darby O'Gill and the Little People*. There was a stage when we would watch the film on a daily basis. The first time we saw the Rock of Cashel, I told the kids it was Knocknasheega, the castle where Darby O'Gill first met King Brian. I had them convinced of this for the longest time and whenever we went there, they would search frantically for King Brian in amongst the ruins. If we passed the area during the night however, their bravery was somewhat mollified. They wouldn't even want to hear about Knocknasheega because they knew from the film that the banshees appeared there at night. It scared the absolute living bejaysus out of them.

Our eldest girl, Amanda, was named after the song "Amanda" which was a hit around the time of her birth. Performed by the cabaret singer George Hunter, the name seemed to stick with us and so we decided it would be a beautiful name for our first born. The name for our second eldest child Melanie also has musical connections; our baby was named after a singer. During the 1970's, a singer who only went by the name Melanie had a number of popular records, one of which was called "Brand New Pair of Rollerskates". Following that song's release, I created a parody called "Brand New Combine Harvester" which went on to become a number one hit in Ireland. Not long afterwards, Melanie released another song, which by sheer coincidence was called "Look what they've done to my song". The "Combine Harvester" song was a major factor in my career in that I believe it further endeared me to the rural community. A Dublin comedian would have been looked upon as a smartass, but fortunately I managed to break that barrier. Another parody I created around that time was with the Tom Jones hit "Delilah". I decided to record the song using Irish phrases, so instead of singing "my, my, my", I would sing the words "mo, mo, mo". Likewise I replaced the chorus line "why? why? why?" with "cén fáth? cén fáth? cén fáth?".

What's more, all four kids seem to have inherited this creative performance gene. Bradley is a singer and an excellent guitarist, and has toured the world with his rock band, Poison the Well, Amanda is a make-up artist and gifted impressionist, Melanie is a wonderful actress and comedienne, and Brendan Patrick is an unbelievably talented hip hop dancer and rap artist.

The kids are experts at doing impressions of me. They are particularly good at it when I'm not there to verbally cut the heads off them. According to Eileen, they have my every gesture and expression off to a tee. I wasn't present for any of their births although I was there for the conceptions! Each time Eileen gave birth, I was playing a gig and would arrive into the hospital just as the drama had come to an end. The night Amanda was born, I was playing in a hotel in Nenagh. I was still on stage when I received word from my then manager, Val Sheridan, that I was a new dad. Following the show, every speed limit was broken as I sped to the Coombe Hospital in Dublin. In recent times people have come up to me and recalled how they were at the show the night my first baby was born. I arrived in to the hospital at 2.30 in the morning carrying fish and chips for Eileen. Of course, Eileen's stomach nearly turned when she got the smell of them.

After seeing my newborn, I went home to where we were living at the time in Templeogue and nearly broke down the door of the house belonging to our good friends and neighbours, Eddie and Kay. I'm sure they thought someone was breaking in. They opened the top window and shouted out: "Who's that?"

I shouted back: "Daddy Grace!"

I think all the neighbours were woken by the cheers that night. The following day my good friend Frank Savage arrived into the hospital to see us. Frank is the image of Johnny McEvoy and when he called to the ward, the nurses and patients were convinced he was Johnny.

When Eileen went into labour with Bradley, I was due to meet my manager Jim Hand so the nurses gave me a time at which to return so that I wouldn't miss the birth. As it turned out, little Bradley was impatient to see the world and so arrived about twenty minutes after I had left. The birth happened so fast that when I returned, my new son was already in his cot. We decided on the name Bradley as one of our close friends, Burt Rubenstein, had called his son by that name and it was one we had always liked.

When Bradley was a toddler he would often do something or make some expression that would instantly remind me in some way of my father who had passed away two years before Bradley was born. For some reason, of the two boys, it was always Bradley who would remind me of him. He had every antic of my father down to a tee. One particular night I was putting him to bed and, just after I gave him a goodnight kiss, he looked me straight in the eyes and in his toddler voice said, "I used to be your dad.'

I froze. I could feel a cold sweat come over me. For a child of that age to say something like that completely dumbfounded me, especially considering that even though he had never met me dad, he possessed the exact same expressions and gestures that me dad used to have. Even today, I get the goosebumps when I think about what he said that night. When I remember back to how my mother always believed that Marie was a reincarnation of Bríd, then Bradley's words that night really do give me pause for thought. I had noticed several times the different antics in him and how they were so reminiscent of my father but I still couldn't figure out what would prompt a child to say something like that. The uncanny thing is that Bradley doesn't resemble my father in looks. In fact, anyone who has seen a photograph of me when I was in my twenties is convinced it's Bradley. Likewise my 18-month-old grandson James looks identical to me when I was his age. Ironically, there is absolutely no resemblance between myself and my namesake, Brendan Jr.

I think it was easier for the boys more than the girls to deal with what I did for a living. As the boys were schooled in America they didn't have to deal with their classmates knowing that their dad was Bottler. When we were living in Ireland however, our two girls attended Irish -speaking schools and I remember one day showing up on a Honda dressed in pyjamas and a housecoat. I don't think they were ever more disgusted or mortified in all their lives. It worked to my advantage, though, because whenever they wouldn't do what they were told, I would threaten to show up at their school in pyjamas. It would terrify the bejaysus out of them.

As I was always fond of nice cars, it was my ambition to one day own a Rolls Royce. Eventually my dream was realised, but the girls saw it as a nightmare on wheels. I was given strict instructions not to ever turn up at the school in the Rolls Royce otherwise they would pretend not to recognise me. To them it was bad enough having a father who people recognised, never mind him driving a car that would draw attention. To make matters worse, the car had my initials and year of birth on it. You can personalise registration plates in America and England, but you're still not allowed do it in Ireland. Back then I had to use every bit of charm I could muster in order to convince a garage in Tipperary to allow me to book the registration plate BGI 951. I cheated slightly and made it all the one so that the plate would look as though it read BG-1951.

Melanie still reminds me of these things today but I tell her it's payback for the things she did to me when she was a kid. When Melanie was a toddler, she accompanied me to a meeting with my bank manager. Eileen would usually mind the kids if I had a meeting but on this particular day she had to go somewhere, so I said I would bring Melanie with me to the bank. For some reason when I told Mel we were going to see the bank manager, she became ridiculously excited. When I brought her into the bank, she as good as burst through the bleedin' doors of the bank manager's office, before running straight up to him. I will never forget the blood draining from my face when I remember how she looked at him strangely before then trying to look at the back of his head. It was then that little Melanie came out with the question that nearly killed me. "Daddy always said you had two faces, where's your other face?"

Jesus, I was horrified. At the time Batman was hugely popular and one of the characters in the cartoon had two faces which was what Melanie thought she was going to see when she heard that we were going to visit the two faced man. Even though I wasn't present for Melanie's birth, I was in the room, at a distance, when she gave birth to my first grandson, James. There is quite possibly nothing more exhilarating than holding your grandchild just moments after his birth.

My generation will remember a time when attendance in the delivery room wasn't the done thing. It was seen as a private thing which only doctors were witness to and so the fathers always stayed outside. To find out the gender of the baby prior to the birth was also highly uncommon. It was something my mother termed "flying in the face of God". It's a relic of the past that sometimes carries forward but to be honest, I don't see it in my kids or in a lot of other young people. Melanie, for example, could tell us both the first and second names of both her children in the months prior to their births.

My second grandson, who was born in 2008 to Brendan Patrick and his partner Casey, is called Aiden Bradley, and in August of this year (2009), Melanie gave birth to my third grandson, Patrick Francis. For Eileen and me, becoming grandparents was magic. Some people enjoy the grandparenting more than the parenting, but I honestly enjoyed both equally. Even though I was on the road a lot, I always returned home at night rather than staying in a hotel. If, for example, I was playing in Donegal, I would leave at whatever time the gig finished, travel home and then return to Donegal the following evening so that I could avail of a few hours with the kids. It's the reason I never took up playing golf. A number of my friends were hooked on the sport but I was away so much with gigs that if I allowed it to become a passion, it would have eaten into what time I had to spend with my family.

Unfortunately, quality time wasn't always possible as some gigs required overseas travel. At one point I was travelling so much that the kids would often joke that I would have more chance of receiving my birthday and father's day cards on time if they sent them to the Aer Lingus desk at Shannon Airport. Even though this was a commonly told joke, the kids don't really remember the times I wasn't there because our quality time was so good when I was home. I had a van which I converted into a fully equipped camper van. On Saturdays I would bring the kids down to the train tracks in the van. I would take beans and bread and have beans on toast and we would hook up the television and watch either *Darby O'Gill and the Little People*, or *Planes Trains and Automobiles*.

When a train could be heard far off in the distance, we would all run down to the track and place a coin on the rail before running back up to the van. After the train had passed, the coin would more often than not be completely flattened. I would always give them 10p to put on the track. If they asked for 50p coins or a pound coin, I was able to put them off by convincing them that anything bigger than a 10p coin could derail a train.

At the weekend, I would spend time with the kids by bringing them to gigs with me. There was one particular night when I had Amanda, Melanie and their friends Edwin and Jane-Emma in the car and, as we were driving through Kildare, a dog with the most piercing eyes stood out on the road in front of us. We were driving quite fast and I couldn't but have hit it. I stopped to see if I could help it, but the dog had completely vanished. The kids were stunned and from then on nicknamed it the ghost dog.

Every time we were on the road and saw a dog, the kids would scream: "ghost dog!" Today they are convinced I made the whole thing up just to spook the bejaysus out of them. Melanie often jokes that the pranks I played on her as a child have not only left her terrified of dogs but psychologically damaged her as a result.

One incident which definitely had a profound effect on the kids was the day they saw me take food from our household bin and eat it, purely to teach them a lesson about pointless waste. Having grown up in a time where money was scant, I was always eager to instil in my kids an appreciation for simple things such as food and clothes. If that meant disgusting them by retrieving half a loaf from the bin, buttering it and eating it, then so be it. It worked because I only had to do it once to get the message across. Now that they're adults, the kids don't even entertain the idea of food wastage. Any food that isn't used is given to animals. I was always an animal lover. Their childhood was filled with pets, albeit not necessarily their own pets as I would constantly bring home stray dogs. I am fascinated by animals in general and birds in particular.

Melanie once photographed me in St Stephen's Green surrounded by pigeons while I threw bread to them. I can't not feed a bird or a dog. If it means driving a mile to a shop to buy a tin of dog food for a stray, I'll do it. Along with stray animals, I have also brought home a few stray people as well. If I heard that someone hadn't a place to stay for the night, it wasn't unusual for me to give them our spare room. They could be a random stranger, it didn't matter – if they needed a roof over their head, I gave it to them. My kids think it's lovely but slightly strange nonetheless.

Even though I did many stupid things as a young lad, if I saw my kids doing the same, I would lock them up. This was probably why Bradley, at age 17, bought himself a motorbike but hid it from us for three weeks. In the end he decided it wasn't for him. Even though he didn't admit it, I think he probably scared himself while on it. As Bradley is a member of a band, people often ask if I mind him following in my footsteps, but it doesn't bother me in the slightest. It's something he loves and wants to do so I encourage him. I'm very protective of the kids, but I won't hold any of them back.

Just as Brad and Brendan wanted to become involved in music, Melanie was drawn to acting and stage comedy. She is also an incredible singer and can do a wonderful impersonation of Dolores O'Riordan singing "Zombie". In fact it's almost near impossible to tell the difference. She even performed the song for Dolores herself who at the time was taken aback by the similarity of their vocals. Melanie also acted briefly in Ros na Rún as the character Ann Marie. I found it very difficult to watch because it was quite a violent role. In her final scene her character was strangled to death and her body dumped somewhere in Spiddal. From what she tells me though, they have since found her body and have had her funeral.

When I was playing a role in Pat Shortt's massively successful production, Killinascully, Melanie accompanied me to the set in Limerick as my acting coach. You would imagine that acting on stage is no great difference from acting on television but, as I found out, they are positioned at opposite ends of the acting spectrum. You are unrestricted on stage and every move and sound is dramatised to the last, however when you're placed in front of a camera you have to be very subdued and everything has to be toned down.

The one factor that both theatre and television do have in common is that the actors are at a slight disadvantage to everyone else because the public notice their ageing process. Take Anthony Hopkins for example. When we hear their names, we envision them in character. Then, when we see a recent picture or clip of them, we're more often than not a bit shocked by how aged they have become. What we forget is that the character we remember them by was probably from a film made twenty years previously. It's the same with Irish personalities. We remember them in their heyday, so when we see them on a show like The Late Late Show, we find ourselves surprised by how much they have changed. That is the cruelty of showbusiness.

I'm very fortunate I haven't experienced that problem yet. If anything, people say to me at gigs that I look younger now than I did a few years back. It's a lovely compliment to get but it's not down to luck. Theatrical make up in particular has a tendency to leave your skin looking dull and due to the necessity of having to wear such make up for stage, I developed a good skincare routine. I came across a good moisturiser in the States which I use every day. It's a regular moisturiser that you can pick up in a chemist, nothing designer or expensive, but I have never told anyone what it is! I have been using it for around 25 years and I think it's because of that cream that my skin looks even better now than it did years ago.

The first time I wore make-up was for the stage production of *Joseph and the Amazing Technicolour Dreamcoat*. We had a lovely make up artist called Bella so I asked her to show me techniques on how to correctly apply stage make up. My daughter Amanda is now a professional make-up artist so I have the advantage of getting expert tips. There are certain places where you can buy stage make up but on occasion I would run out of an item at the last minute, and so would have to turn to my darling wife and daughters and ask to borrow theirs. I'm sure it can't be easy for a daughter to hear her dad ask to borrow something like her compact powder or blush. When you think about it though, Amanda and Melanie had a father who borrowed their make up and then dressed up as a schoolboy for a crowd of hundreds and sometimes thousands.

When the two girls were younger, they would regularly have a few friends staying over and it often happened that I would suddenly blurt out "Girls can I borrow your eyeliner?" or ask "Did any of ye take my mascara?"

To make things worse, I was clearly being serious so Lord only knows what their poor friends thought. For my birthday one year, Melanie went to Make Up Forever and bought me a ton of stage make up. She knows I love panstick because it suits my skin underneath the strong lights so, after she presented it to me, she offered to apply it to see if it was the right shade. On this particular day, my plan was to remain in the house and finish paperwork so we decided it was the best time to try out the make up. Naturally make up for the stage has to be applied heavily so it looks right under the strong lighting. Off-stage it looks ridiculous because it's applied so thick. Anyway, Melanie layered on the foundation, the powder, the eyeliner, and the blush. I was delighted with the results because I could see it would look great on stage. After Melanie left, Eileen went off to the supermarket. A short while later, I remembered a few things I had to do in the bank and the post office so I also nipped out for a short while. When I walked in the front door over an hour later, I remember Eileen's face just dropped in shock. She just said, "Please don't tell me you got out of the car?" I told her I had been to the bank, the post office and a few other places. That's when she pointed out that I had been wearing a full face of extremely heavy stage make up. To make matters more embarrassing, I went to all the places that I regularly go to where people know me, so I couldn't even rest in the comfort of knowing that it was only strangers who had seen me. I was so made up that the only thing I was missing was a dress and high heels.

I have had plenty of experience in mortifying myself so fortunately I'm not easily embarrassed any more. One example that springs to mind is the comedy act I used to perform where I would go into the audience, usually to an elderly lady, and ask her, "Are you missing anything?" She would say no but then I would pull out from my pocket a pair of ladies panties. They would always be skimpy, very brightly coloured and in total contrast with the woman I had picked. It was always a popular routine with the audience but there were several times when, after the show, I would leave the suit in for dry cleaning without remembering to take the panties out of the pocket. The first time this happened, the person behind the counter panicked when she saw Eileen arrive to collect the suit. The girl had the panties on the hanger with the suit but when she saw my wife turn up, her reaction was to instead give them to me when I arrived. The poor girl didn't know what to think. I didn't even notice that the panties were missing. When it was my turn to collect the dry cleaning, the girl took me aside and showed me the panties they had found in my pocket. Naturally I roared laughing and joked, "Well I wear them the odd time."

There have also been occasions where I have often left a set of horrendous looking false teeth in my pocket following a gig. Luckily the dry cleaning staff know me well by now otherwise they would surely have thought I was some poor unfortunate person who had to wear these dreadful looking dentures.

Another memorably mortifying moment happened to Eileen not long after we first moved to Florida. In America, things are very different. Expressions that an Irish person would use quite freely are often interpreted literally by an American person. One day however, Brendan Patrick did something out of the way to which Eileen said to him, "Brendan I'll bleedin' kill ya!" At the time, one of Brendan's American friends was in the house and heard what Eileen had said. The poor lad got the fright of his life as he was sure that Eileen was being serious. He ended up running home and telling his mother who not long afterwards turned up on our doorstep asking if Eileen had threatened to kill her son. Once we explained the misunderstanding, everything was fine but we teased Eileen relentlessly afterwards!

An incident which I am still reminded of by the kids occurred when I was taking care of Amanda, who was about 18 months old at the time. Eileen was away for the day but prior to leaving she told me where all the baby related products were placed. Unfortunately, I couldn't remember where she said the nappies were kept, so I improvised and wrapped a bed sheet around little Amanda. By the time the sheet was wrapped the whole way around her it was quite bulky, but considering my lack of experience in this domain, I figured I had managed it alright. When Eileen arrived home and looked into the cot, the sight of her baby girl sitting there with a large sheet wrapped several times around her hips didn't go down too well.

For every embarrassing memory however, there is an abundance of cherished ones. For instance, Christmas was and still is a big event in the Grace household. When the kids were younger it was a magical time. Now that we have grandkids, it's like we can relive it again. When I was old enough to write to Santa, the letter was never posted to him but rather pushed up the chimney for him to collect. Kids back then never asked for anything specific. A girl might ask for a doll and a pram while a boy might ask for a cowboy outfit and a gun holster or a toy car. A train set was the ultimate gift and it's a toy I still love today.

When our own kids were small, we would go to great lengths to make Christmas Eve as special as possible. On our way home to Saggart after attending Fr Breen's midnight mass, I would stop the car at the side of the road near our house. At this particular point of the road, you could see right across Dublin. As Dublin Airport was nearby, it was very likely that somewhere in amongst the stars, you would see the little flickering light of a plane. I would have the kids absolutely convinced it was the light from Santa's sleigh. I was so believable, I almost had myself convinced. Once the kids were in bed asleep, Eileen and I would get a little bit of clay and spread it on the floor so that I could make some footprints and have the kids think that the clay had fallen from Santa's boots. We would also make muddy footprints in the hallway and up the stairs. The kids would leave out a bottle of stout for Santa accompanied by some Shredded Wheat and hay for Rudolf. I would scatter some of the hay on the floor to make it look like Rudolf had been in the house with Santa, but to make it even more realistic, I would set up a video camera and tell the kids that we were going to leave it on and catch Santa on tape. Once they were sound asleep, I would dress up in a Santa costume, switch on the video camera and walk over to the Christmas tree with the presents. Keeping my back to the camera so that the kids wouldn't see my face the next day when watching it, I would carefully place the presents by the tree before eating the cake they had left out. Of course in order to make it look as genuine as possible, I would have to drink the bottle of stout as well. When I would play back the tape to the kids the following day, they would be absolutely astonished that we had managed to capture Santa on camera.

There have been many memorable moments in my life but nothing compares to the two occasions I walked my daughters down the aisle.

Our first born was our first wed. Amanda had met Martin Lynch through the pub I own in his home village of Killaloe. For their wedding invitation, we decided to go the less traditional route and send out DVD's on which I, in my drunken role of Father of the Bride, invited people to the wedding. It was highly unusual but very humorous. I'm still working on convincing Amanda to allow me to put it up on Youtube. The wedding day itself, which took place in September 2005, was an absolute fairytale. Whatever about the nerves experienced by the bride on the morning, mine were frayed completely by the time I had the suit on. I think I had a bottle of champagne inside me by the time we had to leave for the church. Amanda and I travelled there in a carriage drawn by horses. Taking my first born to the church was a moving, magical time. There was something about the beautiful horse and carriage that made it even more special. The ceremony, which was presided over by Fr Breen, was held in St Flannan's church in Killaloe. I don't think anyone was short of a few tears when Red Hurley started singing the exact same song he had performed at my and Eileen's wedding 33 years earlier. It was most definitely an emotional day.

Following the ceremony, we went to Dromoland Castle for the reception. We chose Dromoland because it seemed in keeping with the fairytale theme. Just as we did on our own wedding day, Eileen and I travelled to the hotel by helicopter. Prior to the ceremony, the bride and groom hadn't a clue as to how they were going to travel to the hotel as I had arranged it and wanted it to be a surprise. About a year earlier I was playing a gig in Northern Ireland, and while I was on the road I saw a 30ft Hummer limousine. I followed the driver for about three miles before I was able to get him to pull over so I could get his card and book the car for the wedding. That same Hummer was waiting outside the church when the bride and groom emerged from the ceremony as husband and wife. A surprise I arranged for the guests was a fireworks display. Prior to the wedding, I told Amanda and Martin that I had planned to have the fireworks at around 5 or 6 o'clock in the evening when it was bright. When they pointed out that the guests wouldn't be able to see the fireworks properly, I explained that the fireworks had to be held during the day so the lads in charge of setting them off would be able to see where the fuses were. I think Amanda genuinely worried for my sanity at that point.

Prior to the reception, I arranged for actors dressed as figures like James Joyce and Charlie Chaplin to wander amongst the crowd. There is a beautiful entrance to Dromoland and in the weeks leading up to the day I arranged a very elaborate prank to take place there.

I hired two professional acrobats and we planned to dress them in the same wedding attire as Martin and Amanda. The idea was to have them at the top of the long stairs and of course the guests wouldn't know any different because the couple would be at a distance where they would be obscured enough not to have their cover blown. The plan was that they would walk down a few steps before pretending to trip and then tumble the whole way down. It would be choreographed to a tee. At the last minute, I decided to tell Eileen about my prank. The first thing she said was, "It'll kill me mother and probably a few others."

It didn't come to pass. In the end, I decided herself was right.

The weather was so beautiful that day and in complete contrast with that of Melanie and Frank's wedding day in September the following year. If I'm not mistaken, Clare and the surrounding counties endured the worst weather in Ireland that day. It seems we were in the midst of a hurricane, but the location for such weather could not have been more fantastic. The Armada Hotel in Spanish Point, which is situated on the edge of west Clare, offered the most beautiful views of the rugged coastline. Melanie and Frank had opted for a wedding blessing so an altar was set up for the ceremony in the hotel.

Melanie, along with Amanda and Eileen, had been looking at various hotels in which to hold the wedding but no place seemed to be just right. It was getting to the point where all three were beginning to get panicky as hotels are usually booked long in advance. To explain how Melanie decided on the Armada, I need to first tell you about the man who owned it, Johnny Burke.

Johnny and his family have been very close friends of ours for years now. I first met the man himself through playing gigs in an old *sibín* which is now the hotel.

In the early days, Johnny once asked me if I would bring in my guitar and play a few tunes. In return he would keep me in pints. Needless to say, a few tunes turned into an almighty singsong and with the night-long session that ensued, Johnny's till was the lighter for it the following day. Anyone who knows Johnny, knows how much of a devoted follower he was of JFK and the Kennedy family. He even named his son John after the political dynasty's main man. John, who now runs the hotel, was also suitably nicknamed John John.

When I had the helicopter, I would fly to Spanish Point to pick up Johnny whenever I had an afternoon free. We would go for a spin around the county before heading back to the hotel and continuing our long chat. He was a remarkable character and possessed a wit as wonderful as his *seanchaí* ability. The stories he would tell were legendary and the American tourists loved him. Over time Johnny sadly became quite ill. One Saturday evening, he asked his daughter to phone me to see if I could drop by in the helicopter. The following day, my manager Brian, who is also a qualified pilot, flew Eileen, myself, Melanie and Frank to Spanish Point. Sure enough, as the helicopter touched down on the lawn, there was Johnny outside smoking away to his heart's content. He used to absolutely love the thrill of the helicopter landing.

It was a pleasant evening so we all sat outside, had a chat and a good laugh. After a few hours, Brian arrived in the helicopter to take us back to Killaloe. When I said my goodbyes to him, he smiled and said back to me, "You won't see me again." I told him not to be silly as I would be back in Spanish Point within a few weeks. It was then he told me how much he appreciated our wonderful friendship over the years. With that he said something I will never forget: "I'll miss ye."

Just over a day later, word came through that he had passed away.

The last words we shared stayed with me for a long time after that.

Naturally we were going to miss him terribly but yet here he was saying he would miss us. It brought the whole thing very poignantly into reality.

His family asked me to do a homily at his funeral mass in Miltown Malbay, a request which I was more than honoured to oblige. When the priest called me up to say a few words, I simply told stories about Johnny's life, the time I spent with him and the wonderful memories I had of him. During the homily, I think there was more laughter in the church than there would have been at any of my comedy gigs. The stories about Johnny and his life were genuinely funny. It was the way Johnny would have wanted his funeral mass, laughter not tears.

Following the funeral, we all went back to The Armada Hotel. The moment Melanie and Eileen saw the beautifully decorated dining room, not to mention the most magnificent views outside, they knew there and then it was the perfect place to hold the wedding. We all reckon Johnny was present on the day of the wedding itself. In the hotel there is a framed picture of Johnny on the wall. A few weeks later, as we were looking at the photographs we had taken on the wedding day, we noticed that in several of them, the framed photo of Johnny could be seen very clearly on the wall directly behind those in the pictures. If ever there was a sign that he was there on the day, it was that. On the day itself, I think we slagged Johnny in a few of the speeches by joking that he could have pulled a few strings up there and arranged better weather for us!

Fortunately, as both the ceremony and the reception was being held in the hotel, no-one had to set foot outside. Fr Breen presided over the ceremony while Ronan Collins was the MC for the reception. It was only in the weeks following the wedding that we realised seven of the people who had sang at the wedding that day each had a number one song in the Irish charts at some stage: Paddy Reilly, the Chieftans, Seán O'Shea, Dennis Allen, Declan Nerney, Seán Dunphy and myself. Melanie had the Irish top of the pops for her wedding. Also in attendance was Jack Charlton and half of the Irish football team who are good friends with Frank. Ironically, the number one hit song written about Jack Charlton, "Give It A Lash, Jack", had been composed by my former bandmate Liam Littlewood. Liam got the idea from Jim Hand as Jim was always well known for using the phrase "give it a lash".

Frank, who is from Tyrellspass, owned a pub in Boston called The Blackthorn at the time he met Melanie. I had known Frank for a few years prior to them meeting, so when Melanie decided to go to college in Boston, I told her to look up a good friend of mine, Frank Gillespi,e and that he would be able to provide her with a place where she could safely park her car. Somewhere along the line, a romance developed between the two. I think Eileen guessed something was going on, I on the other hand didn't have a clue until Melanie sat me down and told me. The wedding day of a loved one is always going to be special;

Melanie and Frank's day was particularly poignant for Eileen and me. Seven years earlier, they were both involved in a serious car accident near Mullingar.

During the crash, which was the fault of another motorist, they hit an oncoming truck. We found out afterwards that the truck had to be written off. The truck was after dropping off a load. Had he been carrying a full load at the time, he would not have been able to stop when he did and there is no doubt that the outcome would have been much worse. At one point, the front wheel of the car was in on top of Melanie who was sitting in the passenger seat. Just before they were hit, Melanie, for some reason, pulled her legs up underneath her on the seat. Had she been sitting in the usual way with her feet resting on the floor, she would be in a wheelchair today.

She also told me afterwards that a couple of seconds before the crash occurred, she saw her late grandfather Paddy Doyle. To this day she is convinced that he came between her and the truck. No one knows how they both emerged from the wreckage alive. The crash was so bad that Joe Dolan even received word that Mel and Frank had been killed. Earlier that morning, I had left for New York but when I arrived, my connecting flight for Charleston had been delayed. While I was waiting, I decided to make a quick call to my other daughter Amanda who at the time was staying in Florida. The moment I spoke to her, I could tell she was upset by something. She just said, "Dad ring Brian immediately." So I phoned Brian and that's when he broke the news to me about the crash. He explained that Frank was suffering from minor injuries but that Melanie was badly injured and in Mullingar Hospital.

I fell apart. While I was on the phone to Brian, Frank came on and explained that he was going to bring the phone to Melanie. Once I heard her voice, it brought me to life. In the meanwhile however I had to tell Eileen, who was also in America, that Melanie had been involved in an accident. Due to connecting flights, Eileen had to wait about 24 hours before she could see her. It was the worst time of her life. The six hours I had to wait were hell, but Eileen had to wait 24 hours and I honestly don't know how she got through it.

Following the phone call, I went straight to Aer Lingus and explained what had happened. As I travel so much, the airport staff have become good friends of mine and as soon as they heard what had happened, they placed me on the next flight out. I was so distraught at the time that it was only several weeks afterwards when I realised I hadn't actually bought a ticket for the flight back to Dublin that day. They just sat me on the plane so that I could get home as soon as possible. Amelia, who was one of the duty managers at the time and whose son was friends with Amanda, told me to let her know as soon as possible how Melanie and Frank were. A day or two following the accident, I called Aer Lingus to let her know that Melanie was stable. That's when I was told that Amelia's 21-year-old son had just been killed in a car crash. It was like a double devastation for me because I was good friends with Amelia. Afterwards I became more conscious of parents who had lost a child in a road accident. Even though Eileen and I were fortunate that our child had escaped, in a way we could still empathise with other parents who had been through a similar situation.

I subsequently went to see the car wreckage but I'm glad that I had seen Melanie and Frank first. If I had seen the car first, I would never have expected them to be alive after it. It was so badly crushed. I was always grateful to the Mullingar emergency services who were able to act so fast for both Frank and Mel and who were there with them at their very worst. It goes to show, you never know what's waiting for you around the corner.

I was always close to my parents and I found that the older I got, the closer our relationship became. Now that I'm a father and a grandfather myself, I can see how Eileen and I are blessed in that we enjoy not only a close relationship with our kids, but a profound friendship as well. All of a sudden each of them are adults and beginning to start families of their own. You wonder where the time has gone, but then when it comes to your kids and their childhood, doesn't time always pass too quickly? You just think, holy Jesus, here they are having kids. It seems just like yesterday when they were only kids themselves.

seven

The funny thing about Dad and Brendan was that they were two unusual personalities who were worlds apart in the lifestyles they lived. What they had in common was an interest in pure devilment. There was a great wit there between them that crossed all boundaries, but in between it all, they developed a warm friendship and if anyone would approach them when they were together they would be an unstoppable force of humour. When alone or amongst friends however the warmth and kindness between each other would flow. One thing I will always remember is how my father would be on the look out for feedback on Brendan's show any time he was playing in another part of the county, like in Ennis. He knew he would be mentioned, and to be honest, anyone he knew who would be at it would be waiting to hear the joke or comment made about Johnny Burke. I would know by him all day that he was waiting in anticipation to hear something back. When he would hear back what Brendan had said, he'd almost double over laughing.

John Burke, Armada Hotel, Spanish Point, County Clare

Paddy, What's The Time?

I was born on 1 April 1951 but not many people believe me when I tell them my birthday falls on April Fool's Day. Even my daughter Melanie maintains that my mother made it up.

In the week that followed my birth, Leo and Elizabeth King celebrated the arrival of a beautiful baby girl whom they christened Adele and who Ireland would later come to know as Twink.

Maybe the heavens decided for us that we were to become entertainers. On the other hand, maybe it was our gene pool that decided. As I already mentioned earlier in the book, my father possessed the most remarkable sense of humour. I remember him telling me a story about how when he was younger, he had wanted to leave his position in the army. Having no particular reason for wanting to go, he decided to ask a few people how he would obtain a discharge from the force. It was then that someone told him to go to the army doctor and tell him that his sight had deteriorated so much that he was afraid to carry a rifle in case he missed a target. So Dad went to the doctor and told him what the problem was. After examining him, the doctor pointed to a series of lines and asked him to read them, to which my father replied, "What lines?"

The doctor explained the lines were printed on the big card up on the wall. Of course, my father, desperate to obtain a discharge from the army, said back, "What card?"

His ploy worked because the doctor ended up telling him that he was no good to the army with eyesight that bad. That evening, me dad took my mother, who was his girlfriend at the time, to see a film in the Regal Rooms which was part of the Theatre Royal. Before the film started, he was telling her all about how he had fooled the doctor with his eyesight and how, as a result, he was able to leave the army. In those days films had intermissions and on this occasion when the lights came on at half time, my father casually glanced around the theatre only to find the army doctor looking back at him. He had been seated beside him the entire time. My father, upon realising his blind act was up, decided to give it one last go, and so, turned to my mother and loudly asked, "Am I on the right bus for Ballyfermot?" I think the doctor just laughed it off. My father's quick wit never let him down.

The Theatre Royal was a wonderful place. When you think about all the stars that walked its stage, you can really see how it was the ultimate venue in Irish showbusiness. I am incredibly proud to say that I appeared on its stage when I was about eight years of age. My father had brought me to see a panto in which the well known dwarf actor Mick Sereed was starring as one of the three stooges. While the crew were changing a set, the actors used to do different things to entertain the audience. On this occasion, Mick decided to hold a goal scoring competition so he asked for about ten boys to come up on stage. My father coaxed me forward, so I joined the line up. Basically Mick would stand in goal and each boy had to try and kick the ball into the back of the net to win a prize. When it came to my turn, I remember I placed the ball on the stage floor, took a few steps back and kicked it so hard that it knocked poor Mick sideways. Instantly, the whole audience applauded and laughed. Even though I was quite young, I do think something registered in my head that people were actually applauding and laughing at something I had done. Incidents like that seemed to remain somewhere in my psyche and I imagine they all contributed greatly towards inspiring my longing for the limelight.

When I was about twelve years of age, I used to see Mick Sereed around Crumlin. He had relatives living nearby and so was often in the area visiting them. One day, while I was cycling my beloved Palm Beach bike up and down the road, Mick shouted over, "Young fella, give us a cross bar." Naturally I obliged and up hopped Mick Sereed onto the crossbar for a lift to Leonard's Corner which was about four bus stops away. I remember people were waving at him while I cycled along with him propped up in front. He was well known and liked as an actor but he was also one of many who helped mould the industry.

Ireland always boasted a prosperous supply of gifted performers, however it was unique in its style of entertainment. Las Vegas is another place where the entertainment is like no other. I always travelled to Vegas purely for the comedy and the music shows. I never gambled; I didn't even put a dime in a slot machine. Casino games, all of which promised money but instead provided more disappointments than triumphs, never absorbed my interest. One of the first things I learned about Vegas is that there are no clocks or windows in the casinos and as a result patrons don't notice day turning into night. As such they end up staying longer than they had initially planned. All the same, it was a most exhilarating place to perform. Many Irish entertainers have trod its stages, including Paddy Cole, Twink, Brendan Bowyer, Brendan O'Brien and my good friend Joe Mac.

Any time I was in San Francisco or LA, I would always travel to Las Vegas to see Brendan Bowyer and the lads as they were playing out there full time. On a few occasions, Brendan even invited me up on stage to sing with him. Those were the experiences I found particularly exciting not just because it was a Vegas show but because I was on stage singing with Brendan Bowyer. Brendan was an idol of mine when I was a kid. I was still in school when he was number one in the charts. As a young lad, I was delighted that he and I shared the same name. The fact that we would become good friends in later years was something I could never have imagined.

The comedy in Vegas suited me better than the clubs in Chicago, Los Angeles or New York simply because the stage humour in Vegas is clean. Comedians aren't even allowed say the word "shit" on stage which in a way is surprising for a city where one of the biggest casino games is called "craps".

One night in 1977, Brendan Bowyer, Jimmy Conway and DJ Curtain said they were bringing me to see Liberace. They actually had to drag me to the concert because I had no interest whatsoever in seeing a piano player. When the show was over however, I was a changed man and a fan for life. I had never seen anything like that show before or since. I can still vividly remember the moment it exceeded all areas of extravagance when three chauffer driven Rolls Royces arrived on the stage.

Having already been completely blown away by the entire performance, I was even more taken aback when the lads casually asked me if I wanted to meet him. Bowyer knew the crew so he and his band brought me backstage. Unfortunately I had no camera with me at the time, but I did have a small tape recorder to hand. Bowyer knocked on the door and within seconds we were being escorted over to meet Liberace. When we met, the first thing I noticed about him was his incredible graciousness. He spoke to me as if he knew me of old. During our chat, he mentioned about how he had been in Ireland's Theatre Royal and how he had met Mayor Briscoe. I explained that I didn't have a camera with me and asked if he would mind recording a message on the tape recorder for my mother who was a huge fan of his. He was so obliging. The first thing he asked me was how he should address her so I just told him to call her Mother Grace. He then spoke into the tape recorder and said, "Hello mother Grace. This is Liberace speaking to you from the Hilton Hotel in Las Vegas, Nevada. I am here with your son Brendan and he tells me you're the best mother in the world. I hope some day that I get to meet you in person." When I returned home a few days later and played it back to my mother, she cried. She was such a huge fan of his that to hear him addressing her personally was overwhelming to say the least.

I have found over the years that some people in showbusiness have a lovely nature about them in that they speak to you like a friend. There was one occasion in 1977 for instance where I was walking down Oxford Street in London only to realise that Danny La Rue was walking next to me. We didn't know each other personally but I remember, he looked at me and smiled. I shook hands with him and he greeted me warmly. Every famous person I've met, with just one or two exceptions, have impressed me. Although to be honest, I don't like the word "impress" *per se*. People either get my attention or they don't. The words impress and impression are from the same family but can mean two very different things. To me, they are the opposite of each other. I don't set out to impress anyone and I wouldn't expect anyone to do so for me. I'm chuffed when I know the impression I've made on someone has resulted in them enjoying a laugh, but that's simply because I don't strive to impress; I strive to make them laugh. Tom Jones was a quiet person when I first met him. I later found out that he had been experiencing domestic difficulties around that time.

One man who forever had a smile on his face was Bill Fuller, a very successful businessman from Kerry. Like so many others, Bill had fallen in love with Las Vegas and so had decided to make it his home. A man of fantastic wit, he was friends with a lot of the well known stars on the Vegas scene. On one occasion he introduced me to the singer Andy Williams. Back in the 1970's, Bill had tried to convince me to move to Vegas but as the kids were so small at the time, it didn't seem like a good thing to do. I did however visit him whenever I was in the region. In the early 1990's, Bill ended up buying thousands of acres of desert land. Everyone thought he was mad for paying so much for what was effectively a few thousand acres of sand. But Bill was a smart businessman and this was no impulse buy. As it turns out, he had heard there were gold deposits buried in the ground, so he decided to buy the land and establish a gold mine. When Eileen and I were visiting Bill's family on one occasion, Bill offered to drive me to the site and show me the mine. We drove for miles and miles until eventually we arrived at quite a secluded site. Bill had wanted to show me an actual gold nugget they had recently found so he brought me underground into the mine itself. I had never seen anything like it. It was beyond incredible. You see gold nuggets and gold mines in films but you don't ever imagine that one day you would be standing in a gold mine and holding a genuine nugget in your hand.

Unfortunately, the smiles were soon wiped from our faces. Whatever way the door had closed behind us as we entered the mine, it locked shut. As it was a Sunday, there was no one working so we were completely alone on the site. What's more, Bill had left his keys in the jeep outside so we were quite literally stranded underground. Remember, this was pre-mobile phones so we had no way of contacting anyone. Bill tried his best to calm me down but unfortunately it was to no avail and I became quite panicky due to the claustrophobic nature of the mine. After about an hour of banging on the door and trying to get out, a security man came to our aid. He had seen Bill's jeep outside and figured something must be wrong as it had been there so long. It was only afterwards it occurred to me that most people would dream about being locked inside a gold mine and yet here were we not trying to break in, but trying to break out.

Bill, who passed away in early 2009 at the age of 91, was without doubt the hardiest and healthiest man I had ever met. He always made his own brown bread and would even go so far as to carry the ingredients of the bread with him so that he could make it any time he wished. On one occasion, I slept with him. During one of my trips to Vegas, he and I booked into a hotel but there was only one room left. We thought there would be two separate beds but when we arrived into the room there was only one huge double bed. When I suggested going to another hotel, Bill in his distinctive Kerry drawl said back, "Sure this bed is big enough for a family."

Fortunately Eileen is not the jealous type.

When I think of Vegas, one particular incident always springs to mind. It occurred in recent years when I brought the whole family on a trip to Nevada. While we were there, we decided to take a helicopter ride into the Grand Canyon. The helicopter company we chose was one who flew tourists over the canyon before swooping down and landing on the floor where a picnic is then laid out. At the time, another helicopter was in the area carrying an American family. After they too had landed on the canyon floor, we started chatting and that's when they told me their daughter had planned on travelling to Ireland with a friend. They explained that the two girls would be there for the summer to work part time while studying. When I asked where their daughter had found a job, they mentioned that she and her friend were going to look for waitressing jobs but had nothing planned as yet.

At that moment, I took out my mobile. Given that we were on the floor of the Grand Canyon I wasn't expecting there to be any coverage, but being a super optimist, I chanced it anyway. I decided to first call Pat in Dublin's Red Cow Hotel. After trying to convince him that I was genuinely phoning him from the canyon, I enquired if he would have any summer vacancies available. He told me to pass on his number to the family and as it turned out, the two girls ended up working there for the summer. My father often used to say "Always help a lame dog over the stile." As a kid, I had no idea what he was talking about, but as an adult, I completely understood. With that proverb in mind, I was more than delighted to be of help that day even if it was in the middle of the Grand Canyon of all places.

One man who was of considerable help to me was the songwriter Pete Saint John. Back in the late seventies, Pete Saint John had a massive hit record with the song "Dublin in the Rare Old Times" which he had written for Danny Doyle. During a show one night in the Olympia, he told me he wanted to write a song for me. Sure enough he kept his word. We arranged to meet in Marlborough Lane near the Guinness Brewery. When he arrived, he handed me a manilla folder containing the words to a song called "Ringsend Rose" and just said, "That's your's, mate." He was without doubt, one of the most prolific songwriters of his day. Testament to this were the two major hits he experienced in the one year – my own record "Ringsend Rose", and later Paddy Reilly's "The Fields of Athenry".

Shane McGowan was another artist who offered to write a song for me. I'm still waiting for him to sober up however. As we were leaving a London bar, more than likely in search of another one, I noticed that Shane didn't have a coat so I gave him my heavy overcoat to wear on his shoulders. I remember it looked so big on the lad that he probably had room underneath it for four more of the gang. So appreciative was he of the gesture that he offered to write me a song; an offer to which I jokingly replied that I would have to wait for his sobriety to kick in before I'd have any chance of seeing it. Even though Shane was drunk at the time, he didn't miss a beat and with a laugh he shot back, "Sure if I sober up, I won't be able to write it."

There were a number of occasions when I, along with my then manager, the late Jim Hand, enjoyed a boozing session with Shane, although while I "act the drunk", Shane genuinely "does the drunk". Regardless of whether our song ever comes to fruition however, I will always see him as much of a friend as an amazingly gifted icon. His hit "The Irish Rover" which he sang as part of a collaboration with The Dubliners actually came about as a result of a suggestion made by Jim Hand. In an earlier chapter, I spoke about Jim's amazing personality. His work ethic however was even above that again. He was such an astute reader of the industry; an amazing man with an incredible eye for the kind of songs he knew would strike the interest of the public. What's more, he was rarely wrong in his choices. Jim was responsible for proposing the song "Sweet 16" to The Fureys, "The Fields of Athenry" to Paddy Reilly, and to top it all, he was instrumental in getting Johnny Logan into the Eurovision contest. The one thing about Jim was that his acts viewed him more as a friend than a manager.

Paddy Reilly and I were both under Jim's management at the same time. Paddy is by far one of the best singers I know, but his escapades were even better and funnier again. He and I became a double act for years, touring Australia, America and Canada. Paddy was particularly big in Australia and he was always a sure fire bet to bring in a large crowd as his records were constantly being played out there. One particular night however Paddy just couldn't get the notes right on his guitar. He had recently sprained his wrist and playing a guitar for the gig was next to impossible. Fortunately, I knew all his chords so I offered to play the guitar in the wing where I wouldn't be seen while he held his guitar and sang on stage, all the while pretending to strum the chords. To be honest, we needn't have bothered with the scheme because we ended up telling the crowd about it at the end of the show anyway. Paddy had received a standing ovation for his performance, so I walked out and demanded one as well for all my work. And with that our game was up.

One incident which I will never let him live down occurred while we were travelling to Australia. Rather than transporting my merchandise halfway around the world, I instead sought out a company in Australia that would produce it for my gigs there. Paddy however was extremely anti-baggage. Hand luggage for him was a book, and I always reckon if there had been such a thing as an inflatable guitar, Paddy would have been the man who invented it. I would be in the airport with a stack of suitcases, while Paddy would just about bring a duffel bag. The amazing thing was, if we were scheduled to do a press launch in Australia, Paddy would still appear in a fabulous looking suit. I often asked him, "Where in the name of jaysus did you pull that suit out from?" and the answer was usually to the tune of, "Ah it was rolled up in me duffle bag."

Anyway on the occasion we were travelling to Australia, Paddy had just released a new double cassette called "Paddy Reilly sings the 32 counties of Ireland" and I knew it was going to be a huge success. When I saw him checking in his baggage however, I noticed he didn't have his merchandise with him so I questioned him about it. He brushed it off and said, "Ah jaysus Gracer I couldn't be bothered with that kind of thing." Straight away I asked him if he was bloody mad to go on a tour of Australia and not sell any tapes. As it turns out, he happened to have one double cassette in his bag. In the time we were waiting to board the plane, I had ordered the album sleeves to be sent out by FedEx to where we were staying in Australia. When we arrived in Australia, I went to collect my own merchandise so I asked the same company to make about 500 copies of Paddy's cassette. Once all 500 cassettes were sold off, Paddy's wallet was the heavier for it. On our way home from Australia, we had to stop in Singapore to board a transfer flight to Ireland. While we were there, Paddy (with the profits from the cassettes he sold at the gigs in Australia) decided to buy himself a Rolex watch. From those two ordinary cassettes, he was able to buy something that most people could only dream of. Anytime I meet him, the first question he knows I will ask is "Paddy, what's the time?"

One story in particular that I know neither of us will ever forget is the time we visited the Adelaide Irish Centre just shy of completing our Australian tour. When we arrived in, there was a big table laid out for us and on it sat a large variety of Irish food such as soda bread, ham, brown bread and bacon. The woman who had prepared the spread was an Irish woman by the name of Kathleen. In the course of the conversation with the lovely Kathleen, I mentioned that the one thing we missed most from home was the lovely Sunday dinner. That's when she offered to prepare a Sunday dinner in her house just like we would get if we were at home – a nice roast, cabbage, roast potatoes, Yorkshire pudding, the works. The mouths of myself and Paddy were watering by the time she had finished telling us what she would prepare. We were to leave for home that Sunday night so it would be the perfect send off. I think Paddy and I spent the night dreaming of this lunch because we had gone so long without a real Irish meal. The following day, we met at the bar and had a few jars until the taxi arrived to take us to our beautiful Sunday lunch.

When we sat into the taxi, the driver asked us for the address of the house to which I said, "Paddy tell him where we're going."

Paddy replied, "Sure I don't know where we're 'effin going Gracer."

I thought Kathleen had given Paddy the address while Paddy thought she had given it to me. We went back to the hotel and phoned our tour manager in a bid to try and track her down but unfortunately it was to no avail. We then phoned the Adelaide Irish Centre because we knew they would definitely have a contact number for her. Unfortunately the voice at the other end of the phone was a recorded one informing us that the centre was closed on Sundays. There was absolutely nothing we could do. I sat down and I think I cried. I was beyond excited about finally enjoying an Irish dinner, but what upset me more was the thought of the kindly Irish lady who had gone to the trouble of making this dinner and would be left wondering why we hadn't turned up. Paddy and I were so disappointed that we ended up drowning our misfortune in the hotel bar that day. Upon our arrival back home in Ireland, I wrote to the Adelaide Irish Club and addressed the letter to Kathleen. I explained the reason behind our absence and apologised for the mishap. When she later made contact with me she admitted that she cried that day when we failed to turn up but hadn't realised that neither of us had her address. If you're reading this Kathleen, myself and Paddy will still take that roast whenever it's ready.

I have performed with many gifted artists, but I'm especially proud to say I was once a member of The Dubliners. Ironically, it was one of the rare occasions when I didn't have a beard. The band were playing two gigs in Portlaoise and as Luke Kelly was unwell at the time, their manager asked me to stand in for him. Later, in 1983, The Dubliners and I toured Australia. I don't think I will ever forget that trip purely because I had been seated beside Barney McKenna from London to Singapore. Anyone who knows Barney will know that he could talk the hind legs of a horse. Even though we had a tour manager, for some reason I was the one holding all the boarding passes for the group, so with a long flight imminent, I deliberately dropped the boarding passes and mixed them up so that I could be seated elsewhere. Afterwards, Ronnie Drew asked me how on earth I was able to pull a stroke like that. All I could say was: "Ronnie my ears were worn out."

At one stage I also toured with The Chieftans and as we travelled on the Greyhound Bus from New York to Philadelphia, I learned a song from the late Dermot O'Brien called "The Farting Song". The first time he performed it, I found it so funny that the tears were streaming down my face. Now, whenever I have a few drinks on me, those who know me anticipate the performance because it has since become my off-stage party piece. During my tour with The Chieftans I kept a tape diary, excerpts of which I used to send back to Eileen. In a way it was like a log of the tour. Unfortunately, I have since lost the tapes. Thanks to tours like these I was able to see even more of the world, although perhaps sometimes more than I would have liked.

There was one occasion when I was in Sydney and we travelled through King's Cross. It was without doubt one of the most dreadful places I have ever been to. The devastation there at the time simply had to be seen to be believed. Drugs, crime, prostitution and homelessness were all major problems. I didn't realise it at the time, but those problems had given it a worldwide reputation. I'm sorry to say though that I would actually feel safer walking through King's Cross at three o'clock in the morning than I would in Dublin. This is simply because I found King's Cross so heavily policed. The most you would see in terms of a disturbance is perhaps a drunk getting a bit angry and almost immediately the police would be there to quieten him down. When I returned home from that particular trip, I told my kids that I wanted them to some day visit King's Cross. I knew if they experienced it once, it would scare the living daylights out of them as far as drugs were concerned. As it happens, some of them have since seen it and agreed with me afterwards that it was horrifying.

During Christmas 1981, I met the actor David Soul who played Hutch of Starsky & Hutch. At the time, I was busy in the pub kitchen preparing the turkeys that were going to be raffled off as part of a fundraiser, when suddenly my head barman burst in and told me that David Soul was in the front lounge and asking to see me. Even though I was full sure he was winding me up, I went out to see for myself, and sure enough there was bleedin' Hutch standing in front of me.

My first words to him were: "Jesus Christ, what are you doing here?"

I was genuinely starstruck because at the time Starsky and Hutch were big names. You saw them on the television, on Hollywood's red carpet, not sitting on a stool in a Naas bar.

After asking if I was Brendan, he greeted me with a big hug and introduced me to his wife Patti and his driver. David was in Ireland at the time making a miniseries called The Mannion's of America and, as he was staying in the vicinity, his driver had seemingly told him about a fat funny guy whose company he reckoned David would enjoy. He must have told his driver to bring him to see me because all three ended up in the bar talking to me. David subsequently invited myself and a few friends out to visit the set, and when the production had finished, he invited Eileen and me to the wrap party which was to be held that January in Fitzpatrick's Castle Hotel. I knew I would be off work on the night of the party, so I promised I would be there.

The Monday night prior to the event my father suddenly passed away in hospital after suffering from pneumonia. It came as a dreadful shock because he wasn't old by any means. In fact he was just a few days shy of his 58th birthday. I was at his bedside along with Eileen, my mother and my uncle Ned, who was me dad's brother. Both he and me dad were very close and I will always remember Ned leaning over him and repeating the words, "Sacred heart of Jesus I place all my trust in thee." It was as though he knew the end was near. Shortly after that, Dad passed away. On the day of his burial, his friends in the ambulance service gave him a guard of honour while the Garda Siochána escorted the hearse. Even though almost 28 years have since passed, I still find it incredibly moving when I think of that day and the gestures paid to him by his friends. I missed dad hugely following his death as I had always greatly enjoyed his company on our journeys to my gigs. He would almost always accompany me to my shows so needless to say I found it very difficult to get used to not having him there. The night of my father's reposal fell on the same night as the wrap party, but under no circumstances did I want to leave my mother's side. When I told her I was staying put, her exact words to me were, "Your father would have wanted you to be there."

Upon her sheer insistence, I went along and met with David. Quietly, I explained my situation to him. Being a good friend, he was very sincere about the whole thing and told me I didn't have to stay. With my mother's words still in my mind, I decided to fulfil the promise I had previously made and went up and performed a few songs. David also performed a song that night called "The Dutchman". The moment I heard him sing the lyrics, I knew I had to get a copy from him. It was such a beautiful song. As it turns out David was able to give me a recording of it as it was to feature on an upcoming album of his. I subsequently recorded "The Dutchman" and it became a massive hit for me. In fact, it remained in the Irish charts for months. In exchange for the words of the song, I gave David the words to "Dublin in the Rare Old Times". To this day, he sill sings that song as his party piece at various events. He and his then wife Patti had a baby shortly after that, and when they sent me a photograph of the newborn, the note attached read, "We've called him Brendan, after a very sincere wonderful friend we met in Ireland." He must be in his twenties by now, but growing up, he was certainly in good company as David also told me he had named their dog Bottler. David used to live in Hollywood, but he now lives in London and whenever he appeared on The Tubridy Show or The Late Late Show, he often mentioned our friendship.

Even though "The Dutchman" turned out to be my biggest hit, funnily enough, I was singing it for around 15 years before I even realised that it was about Alzheimer's. The lyrics tell the story of a man who was once a sea captain and who now stands on the river bank waving at passing ships, not realising that he was once a part of that world. Maybe it was that particular side of the song that endeared itself to so many. It certainly had an impact on me when I realised the meaning of the lyrics as dementia is something I fear. Losing your life's memories, not recognising loved ones, and not knowing where your life had taken you has to be one of the most difficult things that can happen, not so much to the person, but rather to those closest to them. That to me is the hardest part to swallow.

I remember watching a documentary on Ronald Reagan, who was at one time a leader of phenomenal influence. The documentary revealed how in 1994 he had been diagnosed with Alzheimer's and as the story went along, I began visualising it in my mind. I could see Reagan sitting in a chair somewhere not only unable to recognise his darling wife but with no clue as to the power he once held. It was hard to grasp the fact that here was a man who didn't know that at one stage during his life, he had held the most important job in the world. He didn't realise that he had spoken with world leaders and had been of influence to so many people. I just think it's so cruel that your entire life story could be wiped from your mind and that those you loved most are looked upon in the same light as strangers.

When I look into an audience, I am conscious of the fact that some of those people may have a loved one who is suffering from Alzheimer's or any other disease and that their trip to my show may be the first chance they have had in months to escape their worry and stress. Likewise with the economy. Somewhere in the audience there may be people who have lost their jobs, people battling the stresses of mounting school expenses, mortgage repayments, household bills and so on and so forth. It's not the best time for the economy which is why I'm truly honoured and eternally grateful that people still come out to see me play. Personally, whenever things aren't going right, I always feel that it can't but help to get out for an hour and spend the time laughing. This brings to mind a book I once noticed called *How To Be Happy Without Money*. Ironically it cost £25 which was a fairly substantial sum back then.

Even in 1984 when times weren't economically flush, I remember train loads of people would still arrive in Dublin each week for the live televised show of "Sunday Night at the Olympia" which I hosted.

A very good friend of mine in RTÉ was a senior producer from Kerry called John Williams. It was he who encouraged RTÉ to offer me the show, which subsequently ran for three series. This show alone was so immensely popular that it catapulted my career to a new level. Each week, a train would leave from a different part of the country to transport people up to the Gaiety. It was part of a promotion that when people would buy their ticket for the show, it would also include a train ticket. Whenever the train left from Galway, a local man by the name of Brendan Coffey was always guaranteed to be on board. Brendan, who is well known to most Galway people, has been associated with my career since around 1979. Whenever I played in Galway, Brendan would come along and each time without fail, he would always hold a parking space for me. Even if the gardaí wanted to use the space, Brendan wouldn't be long telling them where to go.

His kindheartedness is probably best epitomised in an incident that occurred on the Isle of Man. At the time, I was playing a show on the island and as Brendan was already there on a holiday he came along to see me perform. The following morning, the crew and I were due to catch the ferry back to Dublin at 9am but we didn't get our alarm call and awoke much later than planned. It was about 9.10am when we arrived at the port and as we had already heard the sound of the ferry horn, we were full sure we had missed our ship. When we arrived at the dock however, there was Brendan Coffey holding up the ship and shouting over at the captain, "He's on the way, he's on the way." I don't know how he did it, but he singlehandedly stopped the car ferry from leaving until we were all on board. In fact, he refused to let the ferry leave the port until we were on. The gas thing is, Brendan wasn't even travelling on the ship. He was still on his holidays and had held up the ship especially for us. Whenever he is in the audience, I always talk to him from the stage and I instantly know from the reaction of the crowd that they all love him. The only other headliners with whom I have to compete for his attention however are the Galway footballers. He is a devoted fan of the team and attends their matches as religiously as he attends my gigs. I don't know if he ever fell asleep in Pierce Stadium while the footballers were on the field, but I have often found him asleep at my shows. Brendan wouldn't just have a quiet snooze however, there would be actual snoring whenever he dozed off.

As well as being a loyal fan, Brendan was an incredible friend. After I was hospitalised following an accident some years back, he took the trouble of travelling all the way to Dublin to see me. When he walked into the hospital room, I could barely see who was there as the hamper of fruit he was carrying was so big. He was and still is an absolute character. Anytime I heard that the train for "Sunday Night at the Gaiety" was to leave from Ceannt Station in

Galway, I knew straight away I could bet good money that Brendan Coffey would be one of those on board.

Those who watched it at home will no doubt remember how at the start of the show each week, Brendan Balfe's voice would boom out over the speakers with the greeting: "Welcome to Sunday night at the Gaiety." He would then list the acts that I would be introducing throughout the show before announcing my arrival onto the stage as host. I would come out, welcome people to the theatre, tell a few gags before proceeding to introduce the first act. It was all very straightforward until one night paramilitary protesters decided they were going to share the stage with me.

This incident, which I don't think will ever leave my memory, occurred during the second show of the first series. At the time I was still very much a novice when it came to hosting a live television programme and while I expected minor hiccups, protestors invading the stage didn't come near the list of things I envisioned going wrong. At first I heard them shouting but I couldn't allow myself to look because you have to remember that this was a live television show and so I had to continue talking straight to the camera as though nothing was wrong. I was in the middle of telling a joke and from the side of my eye I could see a few people from the audience entering the stage, all the while still shouting. In the space of about ten seconds every possible reason for the disturbance went through my head. At first I thought it was a joke of some sort, but immediately I realised it was a protest when I caught sight of them holding up posters above their heads. Instead of carrying placards, they had folded up a number of posters and hidden them underneath their coats before pulling them out as they entered the stage. At one point they were standing behind me with their posters, but something told me that if I continued my comedy routine as normal, the cameraman Ray McHugh would zoom in so close to my face that the viewers at home wouldn't be able to see the protesters. When I looked back at the tape, I could hardly see my ears, Ray had zoomed in so close. It was like we had read each other's minds.

Once the stage manager and a few of the crew were able to usher them from the stage, I proceeded to introduce the first act who was the singer Ralph McTell.

I felt particularly sorry for Ralph because he had been waiting in the wings and hadn't a clue what the shouting and protesting was about.

It later transpired the protesters were members of the Republican army and at the time there was a ban on paramilitaries speaking on television. Section 21 of the Broadcasting Act stipulated that the paramilitaries could appear on television but were not allowed to be heard. They merely identified the show as an opportunity to have their voice heard.

It was a peaceful protest in the sense that there was no violence but it still made headlines in all the papers the following day. I suppose in a way they achieved exactly what they set out to do. It didn't do the show any harm either as the newspaper coverage of the protest gave us maximum publicity. But by the end of the night, my nerves were completely frayed. I wasn't a brandy drinker, but following the show I knocked back half a bottle. In fact Ray and I got very drunk that night to try and subdue the shock somewhat. Ray, who was head camera man at the time, has since become a close personal friend of mine, and has been the director of all my videos since 1990.

In the days following the protest, the director general of RTÉ, Joe Barry, invited Ray and I out for lunch and congratulated us both on successfully holding together the show under such circumstances. It was a lovely acknowledgement to receive.

It's astonishing though to think that there was just a few steps in front of the audience that led to the stage of a live televised show but yet absolutely no security in place to stop someone from walking up. I suppose we lived in an era where we felt we didn't need security. The incident with the protesters however initiated a new approach. From then on there were two security men each side of the stage. I have never since met the protesters nor do I know who they are. There was also never any correspondence from them either to apologise for the interruption or to explain that they just wanted to get their point across to the public. Needless to say, when I saw Paul Stokes emerge from the audience and walk on to the stage of The Late Late Show, it certainly brought back a few memories. If ever there was a baptism of fire, then it's without doubt that I certainly felt the full heat of the flames that night in the Gaiety.

A year later, my nerves were tested again when we experienced a bomb scare. The show was still being broadcast live however it was now called "Sunday Night at the Olympia". Bomb threats weren't all that unusual as it was during the time of the bombings. Bomb scares were in season so to speak. On this particular night, the theatre was packed to capacity. An English comedian, Charlie Daze, was on stage performing his routine when the stage manager, Don Irwin, approached me and told me that the theatre had to be cleared immediately as there was a bomb alert. The gardaí were waiting outside to come in and examine the building and so it was up to me as the host to get Charlie off the stage as soon as possible so that the audience could be asked to make their way outside. I was beginning to fret because how can you interrupt an act being broadcast live on television and then go about clearing such a large theatre without arousing panic?

After I voiced my concerns to the stage manager, Don Irwin devised a plan. I would just walk out on stage clapping my hands and say "Ladies and gentlemen, that was Charlie Daze. We will see you in a few minutes for part two of Sunday night at the Olympia." The production team would immediately bring on screen the ads. A message would then appear on screen stating that due to a break down in transmission, the show would be off air.

I waited until Charlie had finished telling a joke, and when I walked out on stage clapping, the poor lad was astonished to see me as he was still only halfway through his act. When I asked him afterwards what he thought when he first saw me walk out, he said he had figured that the crowd must have hated his jokes and that I was ending it sooner rather than later to relieve him of his misery.

Once I had Charlie off the stage, I faced the task of removing the one thousand strong audience sitting in front of me. So, with a calm smile painted cross my face, I said, "Ladies and gentlemen, due to unforeseen circumstances, we have to vacate the theatre in an orderly manner as soon as possible."

Rather than standing up and heading for the door however, the audience remained seated. In fact, they began to laugh. They thought it was the beginning of a comedy act. Of course, I couldn't mention the word "bomb" or even "bomb scare" but I still had to somehow convey the gravity of the situation, so I repeated the request again, "No seriously, we have to leave the building as soon as possible as there is a slight problem to be sorted."

This time, the audience didn't just laugh but instead stayed laughing for about a minute. Given that bomb scares were already commonplace at the time, I was hoping that by mentioning the word "gardaí", the audience would realise that I was trying to tell them that a bloody bomb was reported to be in the building. At the time, I was in fear for my own life but I couldn't leave until I had seen the last person walk out. The host of a show always assumes the role of captain. Anyone familiar with the rules of the sea will know that in an emergency situation, the captain can't leave until everyone else is safe. Even if it means going down with the ship, the captain cannot leave until his passengers are all safely aboard the lifeboats. It's no different on stage. If you're the host, you're the captain.

So in a calm tone, I explained that the gardaí were in the building and as they needed the theatre to be empty in order to resolve a slight problem, we would have to vacate as soon as possible. I think maybe at that point half of the audience copped that I wasn't joking. Most of them had taken the hint and realised it was a bomb scare.

Once those few got up and began to leave, the rest filed out and followed. I look back on that night and I can't but laugh at how we left the theatre – all the while knowing there was a bomb scare – and then congregated right outside the front door. If there had been a bomb, the building would have collapsed on top of us. Logic would tell you to get the hell away as far as you can from the place but it's something that still happens today.

Once everyone was outside, about twenty detectives with sniffer dogs descended on the theatre and only when it transpired the report had been a hoax, were we allowed back in. I often wondered afterwards why someone would phone the gardaí and report a bomb threat which they knew to be false.

That wasn't my only experience with a bomb scare. There were a number of incidents in which I was hosting a show and had to clear a venue when word of a bomb report filtered through. More often than not, the audience would assume you were telling a joke. Admittedly it's a bit frustrating when people don't take you seriously, but I never let it get to me because I could see precisely why they reacted in that way. When a comedian has to deliver news like that, the immediate reaction of those listening is to assume it's a joke. After all, they're at a comedy show. It brings to mind a very funny scene in Fawlty Towers where Basil Fawlty is performing a routine fire alarm test. He carries out the test and when the guests are outside, Basil arrives out and tells them all to return to their rooms as the test is over. While they were all outside however, the hotel kitchen had gone on fire. Seeing the flames, Basil tries desperately to coax the guests outside again but naturally they don't listen to him because they think it's a test. Any fans of Basil Fawlty will know its one of the funniest scenes in the series but in a way it rings very true for comedians who have delivered news of bomb scares.

People often ask me if I ever drew a blank while on stage, particularly when it was a live show like "Sunday Night at the Olympia". It only happened once, which in forty years, isn't half bad at all.

Every week, we had a special novelty act along the lines of acrobats, jugglers, and tightrope acts. One particular night, we had a novelty act from France scheduled to appear. After the first performer had finished, I went out on stage to introduce the duo, however it was only when I was standing in front of the audience and cameras that I realised I didn't have my cue cards with me which contained the name of the act. I couldn't remember offhand what their name was as it was in French so I kept talking in a bid to stall time while hoping it would come to me. I was so desperate to remember it that I even told a joke just to kill time. It didn't work, and my mind remained blank so I had to bite the bullet and introduce the act by whatever name I could conjure. In a way, you could call it a Basil Fawlty moment. I think I introduced them as "Jondong-bardeau". I also tried to say it in a French accent to make it believable. Novelty acts are normally very smiley and enthusiastic when they go out on stage, but I could immediately detect that these two were furious with me.

The audience loved them and their act went down a storm, but when they had finished they marched straight over to where I was standing. They hadn't a word of English but they still managed to call me every name under the sun. Before I could apologise for misplacing the name, the two of them launched into a tirade of abuse. They were jumping, shouting and screaming to the extent where I was afraid they might be heard by the audience while the other act was on stage. The stage manager attempted to calm them down but eventually I had to be taken away from them because their anger was making me angry. I can understand someone being upset, but these two were blatantly taking the proverbial.

Another memorable night around that time occurred following the show rather than during it. Earlier that evening I had travelled to the Olympia in my own car while Eileen followed me later in her car. After the show, we had a meal and then went for our separate cars. As we were driving out the Naas road, we were in two separate lanes, so I put the foot down on the accelerator to get ahead of her. When I arrived at our house in Saggart, I quickly parked the car, and as a prank, I stripped naked and sat up on the pillar of the front gate. It was about midnight and I could clearly hear Eileen's car getting closer as well as see the headlights in the distance. So I sat there, in the nude, for a laugh.

As it turned out Eileen had travelled a different route home and the car I had seen in the distance was, in actual fact, a garda squad car. Of course they couldn't but see me sitting on top of the pillar stark naked, but luckily they knew I was a prankster. They got out of the car and roared laughing as I, mortified, made my way down from the pillar and over to my clothes. Believe it or not, I was stone cold sober that night so you can imagine the things I did with a few drinks inside me.

One person who won't need to imagine is the TV presenter Bibi Baskin. I think it was around 1985 when I was invited on her New Year's Eve show, the format for which was to be similar to This Is Your Life. A number of my friends were also invited to appear, as were former teachers and people from showbusiness. It was to be a night of reminiscences and humour and the plan was to finish the show by ringing in the new year with the usual countdown.

As I had enjoyed a drop of the champagne that was flowing quite freely that night, I suddenly got it into my head to ring in the new year at 11.30pm instead of 12pm. I knew that the whole nation would be watching so I though a gag like this would be a great laugh. Of course, the moment I started the countdown, the audience immediately joined in. At the time Bibi was incredibly annoyed by what I had done because she felt it was very unprofessional. It was the first time in RTÉ that New Year's arrived twice in the one night.

By 1985, my name in the industry was established. So too, however, was my reputation for regularly changing managers. Seán Clancy, who was my first manager, met me one night while I was out with my latest recruit. He walked up to me, and joked, "Brendan I see you have a new manager! At this rate it'll soon be my turn again."

Seán had a marvellous wit and we always remained friends. He used to work mainly with sound systems and on one occasion he had been booked by a choir to rig up a number of microphones in a cathedral. After Seán had installed all 15 microphones in place on the wall, he realised to his horror that he had forgotten to bring the leads to plug them in. They were all back in Dublin. As the singing wasn't being recorded for television or radio, Seán knew that a choir in a cathedral didn't really need microphones because the acoustics of the cathedral would carry the sound beautifully.

So when the choir master asked him why there were no wires leading down from the microphones, Seán explained that they were in fact a new addition to the sound industry called "radio microphones". He explained that they could pick up sound and didn't need to be plugged in. His spiel worked because following the performance, the choir master told Seán how thrilled they were with the sound and that the radio microphones were the best ever invention.

All that and not one single microphone working.

eight

Are you Perry Como?

Brendan Grace speaking to Frank Sinatra.

Ah Howya, Frank!

In the grand scheme of things, 1989 was a significant year for many reasons. Some people will remember it as the year the Guilford Four were freed following fourteen years of imprisonment. For others, it was the year that Daniel Day Lewis won an Oscar for his performance in *My Left Foot*. For me however, 1989 was the year I found myself standing side by side with Frank Sinatra at the urinals in the Horseshow House in Ballsbridge.

My meeting with Frank Sinatra came about as a result of a chance encounter with the concert promoter Oliver Barry. At the time, Eileen and I were on our way into the Berkeley Court Hotel to meet with friends when Oliver hopped out of a nearby Mercedes and said, "Jaysus you're the right man in the right place." He then asked me if I was gigging anywhere the following night.

As it turned out, I was scheduled to play a venue in Waterford but instinct told me to tell Oliver I was available. My lack of honesty certainly paid off as his next words to me were, "I want to give you the gig of your life. I want you to entertain Sinatra."

Oliver was the man who had secured Sinatra, Liza Minelli and Sammy Davis Jr for an Irish leg of their worldwide tour entitled "The Ultimate Event". The last two shows of the tour were to be held in Dublin and all three were staying in the Berkeley Court Hotel. The funny thing is, on our way to the Berkeley Court Hotel, Eileen and I had actually joked about bumping into Sinatra.

It seems Sinatra's crew were hoping to enjoy a night of Irish entertainment. Oliver commandeered a private bar so that Sinatra and his people could have their corned beef and cabbage party. He told me I would be picked up by limo at Jury's Hotel and brought to the venue where the bash was being held. He didn't dare divulge the name of the venue as he was conscious that the more people who were in the know, the higher the chance the press would hear about it. It turned out to be the Horseshow House in Ballsbridge in Dublin, which was so close that when the limo collected me from Jury's, there was barely time for me to put on my seatbelt. Standing at the door greeting the various dignitaries who had been invited was the comedian Noel V. Ginnity. In the reception area, Ceoltóirí Chuailinn performed alongside the band Stockton's Wing. Immediately, I was escorted into the bar. Through a makeshift curtain, I could see Frank Sinatra, Sammy Davis Jr and Liza Minnelli all sitting together and eating their corn beef and cabbage while laughing and smoking like troopers. Almost as if from nowhere, Sinatra's security men emerged from a cloud of cigarette smoke to grill me over the jokes I planned on using. I ran through the act I had planned and even though I explained my humour was clean, bit by bit they dissected the details before striking it from the list in case it caused offence to Sinatra. When I explained that my Father of the Bride routine was essentially a drunk act but a clean drunk act, I was instructed to abandon it from my line up, again for fear that it would cause offence to the main man.

The staging of the night's entertainment was very informal. No bright flashing lights or grand music, just a very casual and relaxed setting. I, however, was shaking. When it was my turn to perform, I went through the routine that had been approved by security but I could tell that the three stars and their guests were genuinely enjoying the humour. I don't know why, but something in my head encouraged me to go ahead and perform the drunk act that Sinatra's minders had ordered I wipe from the routine. I figured that if I began the act, it was very unlikely I would be physically removed from the bar. I knew that the security team would probably see to it that I was on the receiving end of a few verbal bullets following the show, but at least it would be worth it if the act had made

Sinatra, Davis and Minnelli laugh. So, with my stomach in my mouth, I went on to explain that my next act was an interpretation of an Irish wedding and was aptly titled Father of the Bride. Even though I tried to avoid eye contact with the security team, I could still see them looking at each other as I began the routine and I'm pretty sure they were silently cursing me. Regardless, I tore into the act. I lit up a cigarette, staggered a few steps back and forth, insulted the mother in law, and drunkenly flirted with the invisible bridesmaid. Looking back, I can see why the minders wanted this particular performance scrapped from my comedy set that night. Both Sinatra and Davis were chain smokers not to mention heavy boozers, and I'm sure they felt my drunk act was probably hitting a little too close to home. In that sense, I could see I was running the risk of them thinking I was having a go at them. Either way, caution had long been thrown to the wind and there I was on stage in front of three international stars, performing all the lovely little noises and gestures that accompany extreme drunkeness.

From the moment I began the act, the volume of laughter far exceeded my expectations. It went down so well that I could see Sinatra and Sammy Davis literally wiping the tears away from their eyes they were laughing so much. At one stage, and I still don't know where the inspiration came from, I just looked straight at Sinatra and said to him, in a drunken stupor and almost as though it were an accusation, "You're not Perry Como." I basically gave the impression that I thought I was there to entertain the singer Perry Como. Before I said it, I do remember thinking to myself, "Jaysus you can't say that to Frank Sinatra," but I figured it would either go down a storm or else it would kick up one.

So I moved a bit closer to him again and, in an unsure tone of voice, asked "Are you Perry Como?"

After I said it, there was a slight pregnant pause in the crowd. Next thing I see Sammy Davis falling to his knees with laughter. I always end the Father of the Bride routine by singing the song "I'll take you home again Kathleen". While I was singing it on this occasion, I knelt down beside Sinatra and held the Guinness bottle to his mouth as though it were a microphone. Without hesitation, Sinatra leaned in towards the bottle and began singing along.

All through the act, the photographer Charlie Collins had been taking photographs. He told me afterwards that Sinatra's security ended up seizing the camera and removing the film. I don't know how Charlie managed it, but he snuck a secret roll of film out with him.

When I bowed goodnight at the end of the act, I distinctly remember the first people on their feet were Sinatra, Sammy Davis and Liza Minnelli. The whole room followed suit. It was an incredibly proud moment to receive the applause of three greats; indescribable in fact. When I came off stage, I was actually delighted to find that I was still shaking. It was as if there was no quenching the adrenaline thrill it gave me. Afterwards Sammy Davis Jr went to embrace me in a hug but his arms couldn't reach the whole way around me. He then said to me, "I have never laughed so much. Where have you been? Why haven't we heard of you in America?"

To look at Sammy on the night you wouldn't know that he was ill, but he was dying. It was common knowledge that he was suffering from cancer. Within a month or two of that show, he sadly passed away. We got on so well that night in the Horseshow House, that I would go so far as to say we would have become good friends had he lived.

After a chat with Sammy, I excused myself and went to the gents. Standing outside was Sinatra's bodyguard who told me to wait a moment until Sinatra had finished. At the time, Sinatra's manager, Elliot Wiseman, was passing and told the bodyguard that it was ok to allow me in. When I went inside to the urinal, Sinatra was standing to my left. Honest to jaysus, my nerves were so fraught that I couldn't physically go to the toilet. The best I could do was go through the motions. While we were in the bathroom, Sinatra commended me on my performance and paid me the highest compliment of my career by telling me I had performed the funniest drunk act he had ever seen. He then invited me to join his table. As well as Sinatra, Davis and Minnelli, there were a number of other people seated at the table including Sinatra's wife Barbara, who was the widow of Groucho Marx, one of the legendary comedy figures. When I sat down with them, they immediately began asking me about myself, my comedy and if I would ever consider going to America. We smoked and drank together and for such major stars, there wasn't a trace of egotism or any heightened sense of self worth. All three were far more interested in those around them.

Also in attendance at the party that night was the actor Roger Moore who was a very close friend of Sinatra's. We got chatting and his exact words to me were that I had a comedy gift very few people possessed. Surprisingly, Roger admitted that he wouldn't have been able to do what I had done that night. He went on to explain how in the movies he might have to repeat one scene forty times in order to get it right and that it could take anything up to a week to get it done correctly. Up on stage however, it has to be done right in the space of twenty minutes or whatever length of time you're given. I was thrilled, not just because Roger Moore had paid me a compliment but because I realised I could do something 007 couldn't! I didn't have the James Bond physique but I did have the ability to perform the role of a drunk on stage! On the other hand, is it any wonder I do a good drunk act, sure jaysus I've had plenty of experience being genuinely fluthered. Eileen of course was over the moon to be in the company of this handsome legend. It has to be said he was truly one of the nicest gentlemen you could speak to and meeting him was an unbelievable experience. That night he struck me as the type of person who doesn't take himself too seriously; the sort of celebrity who is aware of his fame but doesn't pay too much heed to it.

In a joke I told prior to the Father of the Bride act, I mentioned Skibbereen. There was no reason for choosing that place; I always used a random place name and that's what came into my head. However, as it turned out, Liza Minelli's agent, Danny O'Donovan, was of Irish extraction and after the show he told me that Skibbereen was where his family came from. He was living in Florida at the time and enthused about how I would have to perform in America. Danny then told me that he wanted me to open for Liza Minnelli's show in Las Vegas. Unfortunately it didn't transpire as he was unable to cancel the contract already agreed with the performer that had been booked some months earlier. Following the show, I learned that Sinatra had also told his own manager that he wanted to book me to play on his next tour. At the time Sinatra was beginning to go downhill in terms of health. An illness, from which he would subsequently die, was beginning to set in.

His management had offered me the opportunity to go to America but I wasn't ready. The children were very young at the time and I just wasn't prepared to move them. I felt they were at an age where it would have been

With fellow comedian, the late David Beggs, and friends.

Grace Shines on Johnny Dawson and Noel Carthy.

Hey there, I know your face!

With my friend, Jack Nicholson.

The Comedians.

Just a minute with
Larry Gogan.

Myself and Tom
McPhail share a joke
with Maureen and
Charles Haughey.

United with Alex.

Rolf Harris and Roger Whittaker in a state of Grace.

Top of the Bill!

Come back Paddy Reilly and tell me the time.

A good man, a cherished friend, the late Detective Jerry McCabe.

My son Brendan Patrick and me with the neighbour Burt Reynolds.

A duet with John Denver.

Delirah to meet you Tom.

His Grace
with the
Maestro.

Michael Douglas
meets me at my
show in Scotland.

On international peace
duty in the Lebanon.

With my friend, Louis Copeland, in full measure.

too much upheaval for them so instead I agreed to perform on the British tour with Sinatra. Even though I rejected the idea of a permanent move to the US at that time, I ended up subsequently becoming his opening act at a number of venues in the States. Sinatra had used a comedian in his show for years, who coincidentally had an Irish connection. He had always held a great respect for comedians and in a way he was a frustrated comedian himself. He liked to hang out in the company of comedians and I think that was part of the reason I was given so much time that night in the Horseshow House.

During the British tour, we socialised together and our dressing rooms were within a few feet of each other. The green room, which is where the artists relax before going on stage, was specifically for Sinatra and his guests. In this room, only the foods and drinks he loved were served. One such food was sourdough bread which Sinatra had specially flown in from a bakery in San Francisco. For the London gig, I had brought along Eileen's parents and a few friends including Fr Breen who I had promised I would introduce to Sinatra at the first opportunity. Upon their arrival, I went to Sinatra's dressing room and explained to him that I had a dear friend with me and that if the opportunity arose would he mind saying hello and maybe posing for a photograph. He said no problem, but when I mentioned that my friend's name was Fr Breen, Sinatra realised my friend was a priest and immediately said, "I'll go to him."

I brought Sinatra into my dressing room and there's Breener sitting back with a glass of Jameson in one hand and a Marks & Spencer's sandwich in the other. Now bear in mind, I had always referred to the man himself as Mr Sinatra, never by his first name, but Breener shakes his hand and the first words out of his mouth are "Howya, Frank!"

You'd swear they were pub buddies for years.

I can still see Sinatra walking up to him and saying "Father I'm very pleased to meet you." The one thing that struck me was that he seemed genuinely appreciative to be in the company of a man of the cloth.

Ironically Breener was usually a man for dressing down. He would almost always wear regular clothes rather than the priest's collar, but prior to the Sinatra meeting I told him I wanted him in the full clerical garb.

After an exchange of small talk, Sinatra said, "Father, will you bless me?"

Breener, without a moment of hesitation, replied, "I certainly will, Frank."

I will never forget the scene for as long as I live. Leaving down his Jameson, Breener went about saying a prayer over him before blessing his throat. After thanking him, Sinatra said, "Father will you pray for me? I need all the prayers I can get." Then he added, almost in a joking tone, "I'm a sinner!"

He then invited us to his green room where he introduced Fr Breen to the various people already there. Of course, as soon as Breener spotted the fancy spread of lobster, prawns and smoked salmon, he made himself at home! Sinatra was bowled over by him. He just loved him.

Eileen and I subsequently had dinner with Sinatra in the Savoy Hotel. At the time, he introduced me to his other guests as "Brendan Grace – my man in Europe." For me, that was quite possibly the highest compliment I could have received.

The publicity that emerged from that one London gig alone was a major factor in my career, and it all started as a result of a chance meeting with Oliver Barry outside the Berkeley Court Hotel. The funny thing is, I don't know if Oliver would have booked me had he not bumped into me that day. It was like he had seen me walking into the hotel and decided on the spur of the moment that he wanted me for the gig. Regardless of the reason, I am indebted to him for the opportunity. To receive a standing ovation from Frank Sinatra, Sammy Davis Jr and Liza Minnelli was a privilege few were lucky to experience. Two or three years later, by which time Sinatra had sadly passed away, Eileen and I had a chat with the family and decided to make the leap across the pond to Florida. When I went over there I met up with Sinatra's management company and as a result I was booked for some very beneficial shows which led to me meeting some very influential people. Thanks to Sinatra, the door to America was already opened for me; it was just awaiting my arrival.

nine

Brendan and I travelled to Baghdad together in 1989. I had arranged for him to perform for the staff of a hospital over there, many of whom were Irish, as it was owned by one of my PR clients. As soon as he arrived, he established a terrific rapport with the medical staff. He was a magnificent guest, not to mention a terrific ambassador for Ireland. It was a wonderful occasion for both the staff and for Brendan as he really enjoyed the experience of the entire trip. As well as entertaining the group with his distinctive humour, he also regaled them with songs and storytelling. His visit was definitely a high point for the staff. They loved him and the feeling was mutual too. In fact, on our way home, Brendan told me how he would love to return to Baghdad to meet the staff again.

Bill O'Herlihy

From Inis Mór to Iraq

It's always nice to be recognised and it's even nicer when the person who recognises you is not mistaking you for someone else.

I experienced this on one occasion, in Lebanon of all places, when I was mistaken for being a member of the Islamic fundamentalist group, Hezbollah.

In October 1989, RTÉ's Bill O'Herlihy, who was responsible for Aer Lingus's public relations at the time, asked me if I would perform two concerts in the Iraqi capital of Baghdad. There was a major hospital there which was owned by one of the Aer Lingus companies and so it was decided that a show should be held for the ex-pats working there. At the time, Iraq was never in the news. In fact I had no idea what to expect when I travelled out there because I had only ever heard about Baghdad in folklore; stories such as *The Thief of Baghdad* and the likes.

Bill and I travelled to Iraq via France and Switzerland and prior to our arrival in Baghdad, we were given a firm warning. You could not be seen to be in possession of money. We were told that American dollars in particular were to be kept out of sight as that was the currency of desire. It seems one US dollar was worth 100 Iraqi dollars.

On the way to the hospital where I was to perform, I noticed massive billboards everywhere displaying different pictures of the one man. In some pictures he was sitting at a desk or posing in a military uniform while in others he was sitting with his family. These were enormous hoardings, well over twice the size of the billboards you would see on the side of an Irish road. As Bill was familiar with the area, I enquired as to the identity of the man peering down from these hoardings. That's when he told me it was the Iraqi leader, Saddam Hussein. Bill explained that every house in Baghdad had to have a photograph of Saddam Hussein. In fact it was compulsory. People were also forbidden to talk about Saddam and if anyone dared speak ill of him they ran the risk of being thrown in jail. I was later told that while the people of Iraq loved the Irish, it was still advisable to be careful of what I said when in public. In fact, the Irish workers in Iraq referred to Saddam only as the *Fear Gorm*.

This was a complete eye-opener for me and naturally I was intrigued because I had never seen or heard of the man prior to the trip.

The hospital in which I was to perform was the very same one Saddam and his family always attended. I was told by the staff that whenever he visited the hospital he was very courteous with no airs or graces about him. It seems he would completely drop his dictator image when in medical care. I often joked that I should have phoned him up and asked him if he was coming along to see my show in the hospital that night, or at the very least have offered to send him one of my videos.

What fascinated me most during my brief time in Baghdad was the culture. You would regularly see men walking around holding hands and naturally, I just assumed these men were in relationships. One of the officials explained that holding hands was just a friendly religious gesture. In fact, if the men didn't hold hands, people would think there was something wrong. Another aspect of the country that astonished me was the absence of local women. Rarely would they be seen out and about as Saddam's regime stipulated that they could only walk the streets at certain times. While it was a ramshackle county in certain parts, in other parts there were huge highways, pristine hospitals and all the signs of a developing country.

Even at that time you could detect its intolerance of other countries and religions. For instance, I noticed that every time I asked for a bottle of Coke, I was given Pepsi. At least I think it was Pepsi, the text on the label was printed entirely in Arabic. It seems Coca Cola was not permitted because of its Western influence. I was told that the people who owned Coca Cola were of Jewish religion and as a result, the product was not allowed to be sold in Iraq.

Iraq also had a custom's search on people leaving the country. You were only allowed to purchase a certain amount in Iraq so there was a general rule that if you were taking too much out of the country, it would be taken from you.

In 1989 Iraq was an entirely different place to the one we see on the news most evenings. It's hard to envisage, but Baghdad was a very quiet city with no trace of conflict. Three months after my trip, the first Gulf War kicked off and that's when the missiles began to fly.

The television footage at the time shocked me as it was difficult to believe that I was looking at the same place. However stunned I was back then was nothing compared to the shock I experienced in later years when I, along with everyone else, watched Saddam's astonishing fall from power as the people he once controlled revolted against him.

As I watched the footage on television of his statue being torn down and dragged along the streets, the one thing that struck me was the sight of people running up to the fallen statue and hitting it with their shoes. When I was in Iraq, I was told that the people showed their disdain for someone by hitting them with their shoes. To see them doing that to the man whose picture was once an obligatory presence in each of their homes was unbelievable to say the least. Even though the city of Baghdad became a very different place over the years, I would still have loved to have returned to the hospital as the staff there were a wonderful audience.

A year later, the Ministry for Defence asked me if I would be interested in travelling to Lebanon for five days to entertain the troops. I was told the trip would also be filmed as part of a documentary. Prior to leaving for Lebanon, I had to hand in my passport to the Irish Army in order for it to be vetted. After taking one look at it, a striking shade of pale came over the face of the army press officer. My passport contained an Iraqi stamp from my trip to Baghdad a year earlier which would have been like a red rag to a bull for the Lebanese authorities. The army immediately issued me with a last minute passport and everything went as planned. Everything except our landing that is.

We were supposed to fly into Beirut but prior to our arrival, a local war had developed and as a result we were prevented from touching down on Lebanese soil. Instead we ended up flying into Tel Aviv and then driving over the border into Lebanon. At the time Hezbollah was at odds with the people in Lebanon but they were remarkably friendly with the UN troops. Despite their penchant for conflict and guerrilla campaigns, they accepted the UN was a peacekeeping force and not out to get them. On a few occasions the troops brought me out in the tanks that the force used and as we were going through various towns and villages, I noticed Hezbollah members pointing at me and waving as though they knew me. There was a bit of a cheer as well and naturally I was beginning to wonder what was going on because it was happening in every town we went through. I found out later that Hezbollah men almost always have beards, and as I was boasting quite a distinctive one at the time, it seems they were saluting me because they thought I was one of them.

During our stay, myself and the film crew were brought to a watch tower which offered the most amazing view of the surrounding area. We had to climb up about 100ft high which was no problem. However, when it came to climbing back down, I froze. I have no difficulty ascending, it's the descending part that I find difficult. At one stage, I was so terrified of climbing down that a UN helicopter was on stand-by to take me from the top of the tower. Fortunately, it didn't come to that.

Towards the end of the trip, the UN troops surprised me and the film crew with a tour of Bethlehem and Jerusalem. One of the first places we were brought to while there was the Hill of Calvary which in itself was a phenomenal experience. Just knowing that I was walking in the same place that Jesus had walked brought about this indescribable feeling of peace and calm. I felt a strange, almost surreal feeling come over me.

The footage shot by the camera crew in Lebanon featured on Kenny Live. I had been asked to appear on the show to talk about my experience out there and throughout the interview, clips of various different scenes, such as the UN helicopters landing, were shown. The helicopter footage was almost like a scene from M.A.S.H. After it was broadcast, I joked to Pat Kenny that Ciarán Haughey had been piloting the chopper. Lebanon was an amazing experience overall and the sense of humour among the troops was wonderful. Bob Hope, who was one of my comedy heroes, also used to regularly entertain troops around the world so I was proud to have been asked by the UN to do the same for the troops in Lebanon.

I'm fortunate that my shows have filled large city theatres, but to be honest, the more remote the venue, the better I enjoy the show.

When I started off as a solo entertainer, I always maintained that no matter where I was booked to play, if I was fortunate enough to be booked in the first place then I would perform regardless of the time or trouble it would take to get to the venue. A year prior to my shows in Iraq and Lebanon, I was asked by the Irish lifeboats organisation, the RNLI, to perform on Inis Mór in the Aran Islands. For the gig I brought along a band and all our equipment was loaded on to the boat in Ross a' Mhíl. Waiting for us when we arrived on the island was a tractor and trailer and after we had piled upon it all our gear, we were brought to the hall where we would be playing to the crowd that night. This was my first introduction to the island and it was every bit as beautiful as what I had pictured in my head. I have played there a number of times since but the funny thing is, the island hasn't changed in any way down through the years.

I have never been to Tory Island but I badly want to play there some time. I love performing in areas that are incredibly secluded; places like Skull in Cork where if you went any further you'd fall off, or Malin Head which is as far north as you can go without being in Scotland.

The one place I absolutely hated playing was the very famous cabaret venue in Wexford called The Unyoke. Situated on the road between Enniscorthy and Wexford, this particular venue was in its prime during the 1970's and 1980's. It was a major venue for cabaret and disco and thousands passed through its doors in the good days. While it sounds like the perfect venue in which to pull the crowds, in my opinion, it was the unluckiest building I ever set foot inside. It got to the point where I would refuse bookings for the place. Something would always go horribly wrong or a tragedy would occur.

I played there for the first time in 1979. A band was on stage before me and during their performance the lead singer was electrocuted by her microphone. When I was booked to play there a few months later, the management contacted me the day before the gig to cancel. The toddler son of the owner had been tragically killed outside the venue. A gig I was booked to play a year later also had to be cancelled when another member of the owner's family was killed driving home from the venue. One particular incident which made the newspapers occurred one night Red Hurley was playing. While he was performing, armed raiders suddenly entered the venue and took whatever money they could find. No one was injured during the gun raid but it must have been incredibly frightening nonetheless.

One incident which I don't think I will ever forget occurred following a show I had performed in The Unyoke. I was driving home in my car while my roadie drove ahead in the van. A short while later, I came upon him on the side of the road as the van lay crashed in a nearby ditch. Afterwards, he told me how he had passed a hitchhiker on the road near the Glen of the Downs in Wicklow and that a mile further on, the same hitchhiker stood out in front of him. He got such a fright that he swerved and hit the ditch. To this day, the guy swears he saw the devil that night. Following several incidents of grave misfortune, I simply stopped playing there. The Unyoke subsequently closed down and not long afterwards, it burned to the ground. If I'm not mistaken, the burned out shell of the building is still there. I have since met Eddie the owner and he too always felt the venue was cursed. My heart went out to him because he experienced so much tragedy in his life. Prior to the club's life as The Unyoke, it was a tiny roadside pub. Eddie had built it up into a successful venue and for a time, before the bad luck kicked in, it was a supreme place to perform.

While The Unyoke was without doubt the unluckiest place, it wasn't the only venue where I witnessed misfortune. On one occasion when I was due to perform a gig in a beautiful three-tiered theatre in Glasgow, a member of the audience tripped and fell over the balcony. Fortunately he didn't die from the fall but he was quite badly injured.

I myself ended up in an ambulance during a show in 1977 in Ballina, county Tipperary. There were no steps up to the stage so instead I used a chair. As I stood on it however, my foot went through the seat and I ended up causing severe damage to my groin.

Then of course there is the misfortune of a non-injury kind. The type where a power cut occurs right before you are to go on stage. Funnily enough this has happened to me on a few occasions. In 1985 for instance, I was about to perform in a hall on Achill Island when the electricity went out and the entire island was suddenly left in darkness, except for one house located about 100 yards from the venue. The owner of the house generated his own electricity so after asking if we could share his supply, we went in search of cables. Eventually we had enough cables to come in the door of the venue which was located at the back of the hall. The downside to this however was that the stage was situated at the other end. To overcome the obstacle we decided to bring the equipment to the other side of the hall. We then asked the audience to turn their chairs around and instead they watched us perform the show at the back of the room.

In forty years of performing however, I have experienced more good fortune than bad when it came to gigs. In a way I made my own luck. In the early days, I always invested back in my business and purchased equipment which other entertainers felt was a waste of money. One of the first things I bought was a Binson Echo. It was savagely expensive and normally associated with showbands but I found it was wonderful for spreading my voice right through a venue. I also acquired a follow spotlight. Some performers ridiculed my investment in such equipment, but I felt that if people in the larger venues couldn't see my facial expressions or hear what I was saying then I was at great risk of losing potential laughs. Such additions to a show can make a huge difference to the end result. Considering I have been using a strong spotlight for all these years now, I am fortunate that I haven't suffered any eyesight damage or headaches as a result. The spotlight that hits me when I walk out on to the stage is two kilowatts. It remains on me for the entire show and while it may sound like no big deal, it is actually the equivalent of standing in front of car headlights for an hour.

Another feature that I introduced to my stage show was that of backing tracks. I think I was the first person in Ireland to do so. By the time I began this practice, I had already enjoyed a number one hit with "Cushy Butterfield". I felt it would be much more convenient to be able to perform the song to the music rather than having musicians with me every time, so from my record producer Tommy Ellis I obtained a copy of the music to sing against. By the late 1970's, I had carried out quite a lot of audio recordings, but as we approached the 1980's, the record label I was signed with, Solo which was part of Release Records, was about to be sold. Solo owned all my recordings, so upon hearing the news of their disbanding, I enquired with Mick Clerkin about the possibility of buying the rights to all my own recordings. We agreed a deal and the figure we reached could have easily bought me a four bedroom semi-detached house in Terenure at the time. Fortunately however, I was able to foresee the value of the recordings and while buying my back-catalogue of recordings was a decision that dug deep into my wallet at the time, it was never one I regretted. Some performers might find it hugely annoying to have to buy the material they created, but it didn't bother me because the Solo label had been hugely responsible for promoting my act in showbusiness.

I always loved singing but I can't pinpoint which side of the family I inherited it from as both my parents possessed quite a gifted singing ability. My mother's party piece was always the song "Oh my heart is broken, Cherie". Dad would always try to make her laugh mid-song and it was rare that he wouldn't succeed in doing so. Dad himself loved to sing the song "The Dying Rebel". Any song that had Wicklow in it was always his song.

We enjoyed a wonderful chat on the flight that day and I do think we became genuinely good friends as a result.

Not long after "Lady in Red" hit the big time, I was inspired to write a witty parody of the song which was to be sung in a drunken manner. Fortunately, it wasn't long before the opportunity to air it came my way. Chris's record company were giving him an award in Fitzpatrick's Castle and Chris had invited Eileen and I to attend the function. It was only after I arrived that I figured Chris would get a good laugh from the drunken parody of his hit, so I decided I would get up and perform it. The crowd were laughing so hard, there may well have been a few wet seats by the time the song was over. Chris, who hadn't heard it before, ended up with a pain in his face from laughing. Following that night, a friend of mine George Hunter told me that I had been standing beside a young man at some stage during Chris's party who I appeared not to know. He then told me that he thought the man in question was trying to get my attention but that I hadn't seen him. I couldn't place who George was talking about so he pointed out the man in a photo. I said, "Jaysus his face is a bit familiar alright."

George replied, "That's because he's Bono."

I nearly passed out. I had met Bono unbeknownst to myself. One U2 member who did manage to catch my attention however was Larry Mullins. Larry approached me many years ago in Clontarf Castle as he had wanted to attend my show but couldn't get tickets. Needless to say, I was awestruck at meeting him and told him that if getting him a seat at the show meant bringing in a carpenter to make one, then so be it!

In the bigger venues, such as theatres, I always keep a box or two free just for those kind of last minute requests. One night around 1989, Chris De Burgh contacted me about acquiring last minute tickets. He had tried to secure tickets for my show in the Gaiety but they were all sold out. I told him to come along and that a theatre box would be ready for himself and Diane. I had a backing track to Lady in Red with me so I asked him if he had any objection to me performing on stage the parody I had sung at his award reception. As it turns out, Chris actually wanted to hear it again. The theatre box I had reserved for him was only a few feet away from the stage and on realising the close proximity of the two, another idea was inspired. I figured it would be a great surprise for the audience if, after I performed the parody, Chris would suddenly stand up and sing the actual version. When I ran it by him, he was equally as enthusiastic about the idea. The show began and no one in the audience knew what lay ahead. They didn't even know Chris was in the venue.

Following my parody, which was sung in the voice of a drunk, I then said to the crowd, "Well that's how I sing the song, but I think this is how it's supposed to be sung." With that, the spotlight shone on Chris who immediately burst into the lyrics of "Lady in Red". The crowd went crazy and after he had finished they gave him a standing ovation. I jokingly started to slag him from the stage for taking the spotlight away from me. I think my words to him were along the lines, "I'm here working my ass off all night and all you do is get up and sing one lousy song and you get a bleedin' standing ovation!"

Regrettably, I don't have a photograph or a video of that night.

My good friend Roland Soper, who wrote the first Eurovision hit for Ireland, was in the audience for this particular gig. Afterwards he came back stage along with his wife Phyllis and said, "Grace I don't know how you pulled that one off but ten out of ten!"

A few years later, I met The Edge, Bono and Larry one night in Boston when we were staying in the same hotel. My son-in-law Frank Gillespie and I had just been to the U2 concert and when we returned to our hotel, U2's manager Paul McGuinness spotted us in the lobby. He came over and asked us if we fancied joining himself and the lads for a bit of a party in their suite upstairs. We walked into the room with Paul and sure enough there was Bono, The Edge and Larry. For some reason Adam Clayton wasn't there though. The Edge came over to me to say hello and I couldn't believe that he was actually delighted to meet me given that he was this legend of a musician who had just played to 50,000 fans. His exact words to me were: "We were all brought up on Bottler!"

Bono also came over and started talking about Bottler and how he grew up listening to my comedy. I couldn't get my head around the fact that here were these three worldwide legends and yet they were spending time talking to me. It seemed surreal. I told Bono that night about the time we met at Chris de Burgh's party and how I hadn't realised it was him. It was truly a night where the term "phenomenal" doesn't do it a fraction of justice.

There have been a few downright bizarre incidents in my life like that. I remember watching a movie one night and realising that I had not only met three of the stars that were acting in it, I had also made them laugh. The three stars in question were Frank Sinatra, Sammy Davis Jr, and Charles Durning. I first met Charles Durning when I was involved in the celebration marking the reopening of the Gaiety Theatre. The event was called "The Night of a Thousand Stars" and it was the first time I performed the Father of the Bride on stage. Famous faces were everywhere that night and I remember even the president at the time, Paddy Hillery, was in attendance. Charles Durning was staying in the Westbury at the time and had been invited into the concert. I was fortunate to meet him afterwards and to this day we still keep in touch.

There was one incident with him, though, that I will never forget. Nor will he for that matter. We had met up in New York and as we were walking towards Rosie O'Grady's for lunch, people would literally stop and look at him. The man was iconic and I was fascinated by the reaction to him. All of a sudden, these two Irish lads walk straight up and say, "Ah Jaysus, howya Bottler?" It was very funny at the time because Durning was known worldwide and yet they hadn't paid him an ounce of attention. Afterwards, as he and I were walking along, he started laughing and said jokingly, "All right, how much did you pay those two guys to upstage me on the street?"

Charles Durning introduced me to Dom DeLuise who had starred in all the Burt Reynolds movies. I later met Burt himself through my son Brendan Patrick as he attended his acting class in Florida. A very charismatic man, he couldn't have been more down to earth. It's always lovely to meet someone famous and find that they are incredibly unpretentious and not in the least bit affected by their fame. They treat you more like a friend than a fan.

Phil Lynott had that quality in abundance. When I was in his company in London, you could see that people were almost transfixed by the lofty superstar in their presence. Even though he was so famous, you couldn't detect a trace of ego in Phil if you tried. He had a great sense of humour and always had a smile on his face. In fact, he used to love it when I would tease him that he wasn't black, just slightly tanned. Regrettably, I never had a photograph taken of the two of us, so when his statue on Grafton street was unveiled, I had a friend photograph me standing beside it. Funnily enough, I found out in 2009 from my aunt Kay that Phil and I were actually distant relatives. It seems he and I shared the same great-great-grandfather. I don't know how the link works out but it seems our family tree shows that Phil and I are third cousins. According to Kay, my grandmother Maggie was attending a relative's funeral where she bumped into a cousin she hadn't seen in some time. In the course of the conversation, this particular cousin told my grandmother that she had a famous grandson. When my grandmother asked who he was, she replied: "Phil Lynott." That's when my grandmother laughed and said, "Well I actually have a famous grandson as well, Brendan Grace."

I, needless to say, was absolutely gobsmacked to hear this revelation. In school, I learned that my family are descendants of Strongbow. The only regret I have about that relative is that he's French. I'm not too fond of them, particularly after the incident in the Olympia where I was read the riot act by the French duo. Strongbow's name was Le Grote, which as far as I know, means "fat" when directly translated into English. My classmates teased me mercilessly about that in school, saying, "Ah sure no wonder your name is Grace!"

I later learned that Strongbow is a descendant of Brian Boru so it's not a half-bad bloodline to descend from. I remember hearing a story as a child about how several of my ancestors were killed in the Battle of Clontarf. To be honest, I don't think Boru was involved in the battle at all. I'd say he lived next door to Clontarf and just went in to complain about the noise.

On my father's side of the family, my great-grandfather hailed from an era where they were highly educated. He was the schoolmaster and as a result was known around Dunlavin as Master Grace. His father before him was known as a hedge schoolmaster in the area. Oliver Cromwell's reign in power had brought about a ban on children being educated. As a result, many defied the ban and instead gathered by a hedge in a field where they would conduct their lessons in secret. When I was younger I sadly didn't take enough interest in the matter to ask my grandfather about it, so I never knew much about what his father and grandfather had seen or what they had gone through. I don't know if they were ever caught teaching or whether they escaped detection. In fact, it's only in recent times that I realised just how steeped in history the Grace family are. Even though my mother was reared a Dubliner, her side of the family had roots in Wexford. Their surname was Meyler and they were a business family from Wexford town. The uncle I favoured, Jimmy, ran the fish market which today is run by his son. Whenever I would go to Wexford on my holidays Jamsie would take me with him in the fish truck on his deliveries to a variety of different houses. A very charitable man, he would often bring a bag of groceries or some fish to people who couldn't afford them, and he always had a bag of sweets for the kids. That was commonplace back then; people looked out for each other. Everyone loved Jamsie as he was so good natured with never a bad word to say about anyone. Even as a kid I was always fascinated by his kindness. He would take me everywhere in the truck and as a result of being in the company of boxes filled with mackerel and trout, I would arrive home smelling to high heavens of fish. You would imagine it would be difficult to stomach, particularly for a city kid, but it never bothered me. Slurry on the other hand got the better of me once or twice. Of course my country cousins would take one look at my face going green and joke, "Ah you're a Dublin Jackeen alright."

Even though I was born and bred in the city centre, I have a hands-on understanding of rural Ireland. I had the advantage over other kids in that I had places like Dunlavin and Wexford where I could do stupid things like get stuck on a shed roof or fall flat on my face in a pile of muck. I can see how that freedom benefited me and I would even go so far as to say it is a crucial component of any childhood. If my relationship with the country hadn't developed, I firmly believe my comedy would be very different and not in a good way. I was always drawn to the countryside which probably explains why I gradually moved from living in the city centre to living outside the city in Saggart before then settling in both Florida and the real Irish countryside of Killaloe, county Clare.

Having grown up in the city however, I developed a love of buses and trains. It's a love I carried with me into adulthood and for my fortieth birthday, Eileen bought me a vintage double decker bus. I should clarify first however that the bus was a present for my actual fortieth birthday as opposed to the fortieth birthday celebration she threw for me when I was turning 39.

That's right, Eileen threw me my fortieth birthday party when I was 39. She felt it wouldn't have been as big a surprise if she had waited until I was actually forty because she knew I would be expecting a party. With that in mind, she decided to bring things forward by a year.

Her plan worked because I didn't suspect a thing. She had gathered together a large group of family and friends in Scruffy Murphy's on Dublin's Lower Mount Street, and staged a "This Is Your Life" celebration. It was the easiest venue to trick me into going to without arousing any suspicion. On the big evening in question though, she couldn't get me to leave the house. My manager Jim Hand, who was in on the surprise, had asked me to meet him for a few drinks in Scruffy's. As I was quite tired and not in the form for going out, I decided at the last minute to postpone the meeting with Jim until later that week. Of course this made an almighty mess of Eileen's plans so she had Jim phone and coax me into meeting him. He said he had something special to tell me so, against my will, I went to meet him in Scruffy's. When I walked in, everyone I knew was standing in front of me singing happy birthday. I remember thinking, "Jaysus, am I 40?" For my actual fortieth a year later, Eileen bought me the double decker bus.

She had heard through David Keane, the brother of my tour manager Brian that there was a CIÉ bus for sale. At the time, I was in another part of the country playing gigs and when I turned into the driveway of our house in Saggart, the first thing I saw was this massive double decker bus. I was astounded.

At one stage I would have given anything to have been a bus conductor so in a way owning my own bus was a dream realised. My close friend Frank Savage is a retired bus driver and conductor and any time I would meet him in the city while he was working, I would always beg him to give me a go behind the wheel.

The remarkable thing is that the bus Eileen bought me would have served the area where I lived as a child. Not only is it very likely that I was on this bus countless times as a young lad, but Frank would also have driven it at some stage as it was in operation up until the 1980's. It's the old fashioned Dublin bus, the kind that didn't have a door at the back. The practice in place was the hop-on, hop-off system. It's now approaching its fiftieth birthday and, without a doubt, it will always be my prized possession. At the moment it is being remodelled and should be ready next year.

There is a slightly eerie side to it however. In fact, it's almost impossible not to experience quite a strange feeling when standing inside it. For me, one incident in particular made me wonder if there was a reason other than its age that gave it that distinctive air of eeriness. As I was turning in the driveway late one night, the inside lights on the top deck of the bus suddenly came on. Not knowing what to make of it, I went to investigate. There was definitely no one around and when I went inside the bus, there was no explanation as to what had caused the lights to come on. I felt a shiver travel down the back of my neck while I was there and to this day, I still don't know what happened that night. The kids always reckoned it was something supernatural because there were a few occasions when they too witnessed the lights suddenly coming on.

Whatever the reason, it definitely evokes those memories of a different time. This is why, when I first got the bus, I set about organising several trips for senior citizens because I knew they would remember that same style of bus from years ago. I even had Frank, an ex-CIÉ driver at the wheel. People would stand and wave when it passed because it's so unusual to see a bus like it these days. I know my mother would definitely have loved it. Ma had sadly passed away four years earlier. When you're close to your parents, I don't think you ever get used to the idea of not having them there. I still talk to both my parents and I do believe they're up there looking out for my sister and me.

In recent years, when I step down from the stage and talk to a member of the audience, I usually hone in on a lady who reminds me of my mother or perhaps my aunt or grandmother. Then I talk to them, sing them a song and give them a DVD as a gift. It has happened on more than a few occasions that the woman would laugh and say to me, "You picked me the last time I was at your show." It has occurred several times but it's just pure coincidence.

Very shortly before Ma died, she spent the night at our house in Saggart. I had a meeting to attend in town that evening for which I was wearing a brown pinstripe suit with a tie. The moment she saw me she remarked on how well I looked and warned me that I was to wear that same suit to her funeral. I told her I would and when that sad day arrived, I did exactly as she asked.

Fr Breen hosted the funeral ceremony before being joined by Fr Brian Darcy. At the time, the dentist John O'Grady had been kidnapped by the Border Fox Dessie O'Hare and Father Darcy had been chosen by Mr O'Grady's in-laws, the Darragh family, to deliver the £1.5 million ransom. From what I can recall, O'Hare was caught by the gardaí before Fr Darcy gave him the ransom. Yet, despite being involved in such a long and harrowing experience, Fr Darcy still travelled straight to the church afterwards to be at my mother's funeral.

During the ceremony, Red Hurley sang "Ave Maria" and if that wasn't enough to start the tears, John Sheehan of The Dubliners walked up to the altar and began playing "The Marino Waltz". There wasn't one person in the church who could stop from welling up when that music was played. John's performance was completely out of the blue. I had introduced my mother to him a few years earlier as he was the man who had written and performed her favourite piece of music, "The Marino Waltz". It seems I had also mentioned it at one stage to The Dubliners how my mother absolutely loved that tune, and John, obviously remembering this, decided to play it as a fitting tribute to her during her funeral mass. It was an incredibly moving gesture and I often wondered if I thanked him enough for what he did that day. Eileen was my rock during that time as I was completely devastated by the loss. The night after my mother died, I had been scheduled to perform a show. I was planning to cancel but Eileen and a few friends advised me to do exactly the same thing I had done the night of my father's passing because it was what my mother would have wanted. On the occasions of both their deaths, I had to perform shows. It was difficult but I seemed to get strength from above. I was deeply upset over her passing, just as I was when my father died, but in some way I drew comfort from knowing they were together again.

ten

For our tenth wedding anniversary, we decided to go to Miami.
One day during our trip we went to the supermarket, and of course
Brendan was in his absolute element going through the different
aisles. He loves nothing more than browsing the shelves for various
groceries. By the time he was finished looking at everything, he had
a full trolley but he didn't bring it to the checkout. He just enjoyed
going around and picking out the various items that caught his eye.
We could have gone out for a meal and enjoyed a bottle of wine but
no, it was straight to the supermarket to go looking at groceries.

Eileen Grace

Dinner With The Graces

I was always a big lover of sweets. In fact, the one thing that equals my love of confectionery is discussing with people the sweets that were in shops years ago. I could happily talk about that for hours on end. As well as being able to recollect the perils of sucking a sweet that had a three-pence coin hidden inside it, I can also vividly remember the first time I tasted ice cream, not to mention that glorious day when the shops of Ireland introduced the phenomenon that is Tayto crisps. Unfortunately, my love of crisps almost had me arrested.

A friend of mine, Mick Kinnelly, worked for King crisps and, as I loved their flavour, I would regularly buy bags of crisp seasoning from him. The seasoning was a white powder but it tasted delicious, especially on homemade crisps. When I first moved to America I decided to bring the crisp seasoning with me in a few ziplock bags. Of course, as I was going through customs, the official's eyes lit up when he saw these plastic bags of white powder. He was sure he had caught me carrying cocaine. I could tell what he was thinking and all I could say to him was, "You probably won't believe me but it's crisp seasoning." To my great relief, he let me through with it.

My diabetes limits my intake of these salty goods. The condition, which is a little known fact about me, has been my companion since 1994. I have type two diabetes which I discovered could be treated by making improved changes to the diet. Sadly, the diet amendments didn't help my condition so I now take medication for it instead.

Prior to being diagnosed, I possessed all the symptoms of diabetes. On one particular night while I was out enjoying a few drinks with the entertainer Padraig Browne, he mentioned to me that I might be diabetic. Padraig was himself a diabetic and so was *au fait* with the various symptoms of the condition, one of which is frequent trips to the toilet. He had noticed that throughout the course of the night I had been to the toilet several times so he advised that I get checked for diabetes. Not long afterwards, I went to see a doctor I knew on Baggot Street. He took a few samples and his opinion there and then was that I was a diabetic. Once it was actually confirmed, I went into complete denial; I just couldn't accept that my lifestyle had to change. Eileen once told me that she wished she had been diagnosed with it instead of me because her lifestyle would have coped with it far better than mine. A diabetic has to have a routine which is impossible for someone whose career hours are the complete opposite to routine. My hours are so unpredictable that it plays havoc with my condition. To make matters worse, every single bleedin' thing I love is completely out of bounds for a diabetic.

I don't want the condition but I have it regardless so I feel I might as well make the best of a bad situation and encourage some awareness among people. Given my love of sweets I'm probably not the best role model for diabetics but

I still want to help highlight organisations such as The Diabetes Federation of Ireland, if they'll have me of course. I would also like to raise awareness of diabetes in children. It's harder for a child to understand why they can't eat certain foods like other kids their age and, when you think about it, wasn't poisoning yourself with an overdose of sweets all part of the fun of being a child?

I am fortunate that none of my kids inherited the condition. Of the four, Melanie has the biggest sweet tooth while Brendan Patrick is a vegetable junkie and very into his healthy eating.

Just like Padraig Browne diagnosed me prior to the doctor's official confirmation, I too have gone on to spot the symptoms in other people, some of whom are colleagues of mine in showbusiness. When they went to a doctor about it, they found I was right. To be honest I reckon that as many people have diabetes and don't know it as those who do have it and are aware of it. I am convinced my father was a diabetic but didn't know it.

My mother-in-law, Lillie, found out by accident that she had diabetes. She didn't possess any of the symptoms so it goes to show that you can live with it without knowing you have it. The condition however is more common than people realise. For instance, Eileen and I were at a function and there were ten people at the table. Of the ten diners, seven were diabetics.

In a way, it's not at all surprising that I found myself with this condition as I was always very fond of chocolate and sweets. The confectionery I enjoyed during my childhood probably set me on my way to becoming a chocoholic.

When I was a child, we used to have a sweet called a Lucky Lump. It was a sugary sweet moulded into the shape of a pillow. The reason it was called a Lucky Lump was because there was a three-pence coin, also known as a thru'penny bit, hidden inside the centre of the sweet. There's not a hope in hell any confectionery company would get away with producing a sweet like that for today's market. Not alone was there the risk of the chewer choking on the coin, there was also the matter of hygiene as the coin wasn't even wrapped in foil. You would literally suck the sweet until you saw the coin protruding through the sugary coating and, of all the sweets, it was definitely my favourite.

Fizz Bags were another love of mine. These were little bags of sherbet into which you would dip a lollypop. Trigger Bars, Flash Bars and Macaroon Bars were all about a penny in price and if, as a kid, you went into a shop with just six pence to your name, you could truly poison yourself with all the sweets you could buy.

Brendan Fassnidge, a very well known entrepreneur whom I dubbed Mister Mercedes as he owned a high-profile Mercedes dealership in Dublin, was once a classmate of mine and would always arrive into school with the best sweets as his family owned a sweet shop in Palmerstown. At the time, there was a chunky chewing gum called Long John Silver and it contained the most fabulous orange flavour. On occasion, Brendan would bring in a few of these chewing gums to share amongst the class. But before passing them around, he would chew them for an hour to extract the flavour. You would really only "loan" the chewing gum on to the next person. This was regular practice and I hate to admit it but I can still remember being one of the borrowers.

In that same school, there was a teacher called Brother Linnane who was known for having a notorious sweet tooth. His sense of smell was equally as strong as his penchant for all things sugar and if one of his students had sweets such as toffees, Brother Linnane would immediately pick up on the scent and demand they be handed over. Of course, he would see to it that the sweets wouldn't go to waste.

As far as I can remember, when Tayto was first launched they were called Star crisps. Not long afterwards, Perri crisps arrived into the shops. Perri, at three pence a bag, were seen as the "poor man's Tayto". I can still vividly remember the first time I tasted a crisp and there was absolutely nothing you could compare it to; it was a new phenomenon. Before they arrived, the only snacks available were of a chocolate or a toffee nature. My kids never believe me when I tell them that to buy a pound's worth of Tayto back then, (which were four pence in price and there were forty sixpences in a pound), you would very definitely have needed a wheelbarrow to carry them home. I love that I lived through that time and that I can identify with those early days. If ever the government began giving out fun ministries, I would like to be the official Minister for Sweets and

Chocolate. If we can have a minister for every other bleedin' thing, then I don't see why something as everyday as confectionery should go unministered.

I love remembering many of the fads that came and went and those that stayed and became almost part of our daily diets. When King crisps first came out, I was 15 years of age and, thanks to my forged birth certificate, I had secured a job driving for a Dublin company. While I was on my way to make a delivery one day, I spotted a King crisp van and immediately abandoned all work related plans. Instead, I followed the van from Dublin city centre out to Sutton so that I could trade with the driver something in my lorry for a few bags of his crisps.

On another occasion during my time working for that same company, I was driving a lorry filled with potatoes. Being 15 years of age, safety was the least of my concerns and as I drove around a corner in Churchtown, the back of the lorry swung to one side and the entire load of potatoes fell off. An old man who was walking along at the time was, within a matter of seconds, completely surrounded by about two tonnes of potatoes. I panicked because I knew I would be fired once the boss discovered what I had done. At that moment, I spotted a nearby wall that another vehicle had previously hit so I went over and took a large chunk from it. I then threw it up against the cab of my lorry so that I could tell my boss the lorry had simply hit some stone debris that was already on the road from a previous collision with the nearby wall. I have since met the boss in recent years and fortunately he accepted my belated revelation in good spirits. In fact, we shared a good laugh over the incident.

Since those adolescent years, I have witnessed changes in various confectionery products that have actually upset me. For example, when the box of Dairy chocolates was taken over from Rowntree Macintosh by Nestlé, several of the chocolates were changed. Personally, I think they changed it for the worse because the originals were lovely. Admittedly, there are far more serious things going on in the world but I did warn you at the start, I could talk about chocolate for hours!

Black Magic is another collection that was changed. Not one of the sweets that were in the original Black Magic box remain in today's selection. With Roses, the coffee sweet is now redundant. With Double Centres, it's half the box. Milk Tray is the most unchanged, although they did take out one particular sweet and it's removal devastated me at the time. I still haven't quite overcome the disappointment. It was a chocolate fudge sweet with a slice of almond on the top. I can still remember when Milk Tray was sold loose in tins. When I was a child, biscuits were almost always sold loose. You would pick however many you wanted and your selection would then be placed in a bag and weighed. My favourites have always been the old faithfuls, Mikado, Coconut Creams, and Chocolate Goldgrain, however Raspberry Custard Creams have my eternal love.

When it came to loose sweets, Bullseyes were practically part of our daily diet as kids. Aniseed balls, which we nicknamed Nancy Balls, were hard sweets that would take an hour to suck down. They were a form of gobstopper except they had a seed in the centre. Gobstoppers were also available when I was a kid except back then they were known as hard boilers.

There used to be two sweet factories in the heart of Dublin, one of which was called Lemons and created very affordable types of sweets, while the other was called Urneys, whose sweet collection I loved. I can still remember the names of the various bars Urneys created. Their big sellers were the Royal Cream, Two & Two and the Regal Milk.

The Royal Cream was a bar I knew intimately. It consisted of nine squares with three delicious fondant fillings: strawberry, orange and mint. The Two & Two chocolate bar consisted of two fillings – fudge in one half, vanilla in the other, while the Regal Milk was the token bar of plain milk chocolate, yet every bit as delicious as its two shelf mates. Another big seller for Urneys were chocolate éclairs. At the time Urney's sponsored a Raidió Éireann show which was presented by Gay Byrne. This was during Gay's very early days of broadcasting and the radio spot in question was called Urneys Mystery Parcel. Basically, listeners would send in an unusual item and if it was the most unusual that week, the person who sent it would receive a hamper from Urneys consisting of all their chocolates. I was working as a messenger boy in Brown & Nolans at the time so I wrapped a parcel in the dispatch area and plastered upon it every postal sticker I could find. "Urgent", "Fragile", "This Way Up", "Printed Matter", every label I got my hands on found its way on to the parcel.

There was nothing inside the box; it was solely about the brightly coloured parcelling. A few days later, the effort paid off! I can still remember the moment Gay Byrne said, "Brendan Grace from 2E Echlin Street, Dublin 8, you have won this week's parcel and what a parcel it is!"

He wasn't wrong either. The hamper was absolutely huge. Containing a selection of every product Urneys made, it was without doubt a chocoholic's fix. During the Urney-sponsored radio programme, there was a serialised segment called "Dantro, The Planet Man" and the funny thing is, anyone I've mentioned it to, including Gay Byrne, cannot recall it.

Along with possessing a love for childhood chocolate memories, I also hugely enjoyed the television advertisements that were broadcast years ago.

Ricey Scully, a great friend of mine and a radio presenter with Midlands 103, once presented me with a format for a television series. Ricey was always an ideas man and on this occasion, the idea was "Brendan Grace's Ireland". The show was to consist of me visiting the different aspects of Irish life. One topic that I personally would love to see become part of a show like that is life of yesteryear. I am an avid nostalgic and love reminiscing about the various programmes that were broadcast years ago. I particularly love discussing the various ads that appeared on television back when Radió Teilifís Éireann was still in its infancy and known as "Teilifís Éireann – Bealacht a Seacht" which meant Irish television channel seven.

I think I can actually remember the first two advertisements that were aired when RTÉ opened – Lyons Tea and Mobil Oil. I would genuinely love to host a programme where a panel of people talk about the old ads they remember from years back. Another trivial thing I would love to do is see if people can remember the animals that were on the old coins. From what I can recall the farthing had a snipe bird, the ha'penny displayed the image of a pig, the penny had a hen, the threepence had a rabbit, the sixpence had a greyhound, the shilling had a bull, and the two shilling had a salmon. The funny thing is I couldn't tell you what's on the back of a twenty euro note! Irish people love looking at the way things used to be and I think that's why the likes of Reeling in the Years are so popular.

When it comes to radio however, there is no beating Brendan Balfe. Brendan is the daddy of radio nostalgia in Ireland. I personally have always associated the past with happiness more so than sadness and as such I do not identify with the stories that painted those times in a miserable light. Admittedly, it was an innocent era, but we were always genuinely happy. These days I read about kids as young as six being prescribed anti-depressants, and it makes you wonder if perhaps we really were happier as a society when we had damn all. For instance, when I was a kid we were delighted to get twopence pocket money. To acquire our little fortune, we would bring a glass bottle to a shop in return for which we would get twopence. Naturally the availability of discarded glass bottles was greater in places where large crowds would gather, so for kids, these places were like goldmines. It was the equivalent of finding a euro left in a trolley except back then it was like finding a euro in about ten trolleys. It was common practice but we were actually recycling without realising it. If you were going to the shop to buy a drink, you would have to bring an empty bottle with you for the drink otherwise you were charged a twopence deposit for the shop bottle until you brought it back. **GALWAY COUNTY LIBRARIES**

A familiar line in several of my jokes as Bottler is: "We were so poor we never had any food." The reality however is that while, yes, we were indeed very poor, Marie and I never went without in terms of food.

My mother and father were both great providers. Ma used to make delicious burgers called rissoles. These burgers contained onion, breadcrumbs, thyme, beaten egg and mince. By the time they were ready, they would be massive. As it was quite a big meal in itself, the dish was particularly good for families who were watching their cash. My mother, who had acquired the recipe from her own mother, passed it on to me when my own love of cooking began to develop. Last Christmas, I gave the recipe to a beautiful charity cookbook which consisted of well known personalities sharing their favourite dishes. In fact, following the publication of the book, people wrote to me about "Rissoles *á la* Grace".

I have always loved cooking. It was a skill I had to acquire because of the hours I keep. Due to nerves, I can't eat prior to a gig so it's usually in the early hours of the morning, following a show, when I sit down for a meal. It wouldn't be unusual for me to arrive home at three in the morning and cook myself a full dinner.

I think I was seven years of age when I created my first meal. I knew my father loved mushrooms and my mother loved toast so one morning, not long after we moved to Echlin Street, I made them both breakfast. The toast was perfect but the mushrooms were raw because I didn't realise they had to be cooked. My poor father didn't want to upset me so he ate every single one of the raw mushrooms I had left in front of him.

Up until the age of twelve, I wasn't aware of other vegetables apart from potato, cabbage, and turnip. Carrots were not seen as proper vegetables because they were only served as part of a stew. You would never see carrots on a plate unless there was a stew attached.

For as long as I can remember I have always loved things like the skin of the chicken, the crackling crust on the pork or the fat on a slice of beef. Unfortunately, these are the parts that most chefs tend to discard, as I found out much to my grief on one particular occasion in Las Vegas. I was attending a major helicopter convention along with Ciarán Haughey, Barry Mooney, John Barnacle and a few others from the helicopter business. When we queued up at the carvery for lunch, there was about five people ahead of me. I noticed that a new side of beef had just been introduced and I figured that by the time it was my turn, I would be able to get some of the lovely fat on the beef. My mouth was watering at the sight of the beef fat, but just as it was coming to my turn, the chef grabbed the knife, ran it along the crispy fat and threw it in the bin before I had the chance to stop him. I was so disappointed that when it came to my turn, I told him I was going to cry myself to sleep that night.

India is one place I would love to visit purely out of an interest in experiencing the way in which they cook their dishes. I am very partial to high velocity Indian food and can whip up a number of traditional dishes. I am also very proud to say that I can cook a curry so hot it would open your toes. I will make anything from crisps to dip to stuffed oysters and every time I make a dish I always try to add a different ingredient to see if I can improve it in any way. This is probably why I love browsing through supermarkets. If I'm on tour in a different country and have a few free hours in the day then I will usually pass the time by going to a supermarket. I will shop for food to bring with us on the road but I equally enjoy browsing through the different foods even if not with the intention of buying. I'm spoilt for choice with the American supermarkets because they are so huge. When we moved there first, I would accompany Eileen to the supermarket and wander off with the trolley, filling it up with a variety of ingredients for meals I had in mind. For some reason I just get a great kick out of browsing through the aisles.

While Floridian supermarkets have every kind of product imaginable, the one thing they don't have are Easter eggs. As such, this necessitates two egg runs from Ireland. I begin stocking up the moment they appear in the shops in February. Needless to say, I always end up with Easter eggs left over. Come July in the Grace household, there will still be a few sitting in the fridge. When I'm home in Ireland I usually pack between two and three huge suitcases with nothing but Easter eggs. I pack them in such a way that not one egg will be cracked when the suitcases are opened in Florida. With all my years travelling back and forth I have picked up a few tips and tricks when it comes to packing. On one occasion for instance, I had a hankering for a rhubarb tart, and so Laura, the owner of a coffee shop in Killaloe, generously made one and presented it to me on the morning I was to leave for Florida. I carefully secured it inside a postal box and addressed it to my house in West Palm Beach. When it arrived, not one crumb had fallen off. The kids were so fascinated by this that they took a photograph of it and had it printed on an apron for me.

When I moved to Florida the absence of chippers really disappointed me; they just don't exist in America. This was a massive let down to me considering I know most chippers in Ireland. Whenever I gave directions to someone, I would almost always direct them by chippers rather than road or street names. The Morrelli family who own a string of fast food restaurants around the country are close childhood friends of mine.

I also miss the Irish confectionery when I'm in Florida, but my dislike of the American sweet selection is largely a good thing because it means I have a healthier diet while I'm there. I'm less likely to snack on junk food. In America, my daily diet consists mostly of fish and salads. Foods such as seafood and pasta are also a love of mine but my main weakness will always be bacon and cabbage. It's easier than you think to find cabbage in Florida, but one thing you won't ever find is a parsnip. For some reason they can't be found for love nor money across the pond. Turnips on the other hand can be found everywhere but go by the name rutabaga. I love the whole cooking process. There is something about it that I find hugely invigorating. It has become a running joke amongst the kids that every time they visit, there's always either a saucepan on the boil or a pan on the hob.

My favourite cook is without doubt Paula Deen. She is hugely famous in America because of her cookery show and I for one am a full-on follower of the cookery gospel according to Paula. She creates the heartiest dishes and doesn't tolerate minimalism or skimping on ingredients in any way. Italy is a particularly wonderful place for this style of cookery. The Morelli family, who I referred to earlier, hailed from a farming area in Italy and are fabulous cooks. I have been great friends with them for about 45 years now and can still remember the first time they opened a chip shop in Ireland. Over the years they set up each of their children with a shop and now the whole family is involved in the business. When I was a teenager there was a chipper on James Street but the Morellis also sold homemade ice cream in their chip shop so it was worth walking the extra distance to Thomas Street for it.

Everyone can remember where they were the moment JFK's assassination was announced. Well I remember exactly where I was – standing at the counter in Morelli's. My father was always a particularly big admirer of JFK, but became an even bigger fan after he visited Dublin and travelled up Echlin Street. It goes without saying, my father was incredibly proud for a long time afterwards that Kennedy had actually set foot on our street. Unfortunately I was so young that I didn't appreciate the significance of it at the time. What's more, I had a direct view of the man himself as I was propped up on me dad's shoulders. Another president to pass through the street was Bill Clinton. He was approaching the end of his presidential tenure at the time and was visiting the Guinness Brewery as part of his trip to Ireland. Coincidentally, Joe Duffy was performing the live commentary from the landing of the flat that I used to live in. Several times throughout the show he even mentioned that he was broadcasting from "Brendan Grace's old home".

While I am getting used to not having a chipper near where I live in Florida, I don't think I will ever grow accustomed to the confectionery on offer in the States. The American chocolate and biscuits are appalling and when it comes to Taytos and Perri crisps, I always stock up on my supply when I'm home.

The one thing I cannot fault America on in terms of food is the price. Eating out in Florida is a fraction of the price of eating out in Ireland.

The family and I always make a point of meeting for a meal every Thursday night in a hugely popular restaurant called The Dune Dog. Thursday night in this restaurant is known as lobster night and for our meals we would all have lobsters, crab legs, chicken, corn on the cob, potato salad and a variety of other side orders. With the meals, we might have beers or wines. By the end of the night, our bill for the entire family would come to the equivalent of just €70. In Ireland, the same meal combined with drinks would probably arrive at a total of a couple of hundred euro.

In America, value for money is simply the done thing. In a way it reminds me of an Ireland where five pounds was almost impossible to spend in one go with the amount you could buy for it. For instance, I once came across an old crumpled up five pound note in my granny's table drawer. Every house had a table drawer in which could be found everything from sewing needles to a pack of cards. It was obvious the money had been sitting there for quite some time and had been forgotten about so with pound signs in my eleven year old eyes, I took it. It was the equivalent to a week's wages back then and as I couldn't spend it all on my own, I decided to enlist the help of my friends. For a while we lived the life of Reilly. I bought them fish and chips, bus runs, funfair tickets, sweets and so on and yet after all of that I still hadn't spent so much as ten shillings of the five pounds. Now I was left with the responsibility of loose change. I couldn't bring it into the house or my mother would be asking questions so eventually I had to own up. With my most honest face, I told my mother I had found the five pound note scrunched up on a wet road. When I gave it to her she immediately wanted to bring it to the local shopkeeper in case someone had lost it and would return looking for it. I managed to convince her, against her better judgement, to keep it but by jaysus it took some persuading.

Getting back to America however, you will rarely find a restaurant that is less than top class because Americans don't tolerate anything less than 100 per cent. Since we moved there, I have found that if an American person isn't happy with something, they will say so straight out. The Irish on the other hand seem to have a habit of putting up with poor service and not wanting to rock the boat. When I'm home in Ireland, I'm always annoyed about things like sandwiches with their see-through ham and apple pies with damn all apple. It's a bone of contention with me because here you pay so much for so little, whereas in America, a restaurant sandwich has thick bread and is bulging with filling. It also automatically includes side orders so when you order a sandwich, you quite literally receive a meal. I have in the past bought an apple pie in an Irish supermarket just to cut the top off and see how much apple has been placed inside. Honest to God, there have been a few occasions where there wouldn't even be a teaspoon of apple in the filling but loads of dough and pastry. Fortunately, I do see a change beginning to take place in the culture of "give the consumer as little as possible" and it's not before time either.

The funny thing is, people seem to think that Ireland became an expensive place to live as a result of the Celtic Tiger era, but I noticed the huge difference between American and Irish prices from the moment I visited the US in the 1970's. From day one, I noticed the phenomenal difference in even the basic grocery shopping. Despite these few misgivings however, I can't imagine not returning home on a regular basis.

I have to get my fix of home. And Perri crisps.

eleven

Brendan and Eileen were a big part of our family and were always great fun to be around. Very rarely would you see my father doubled over laughing, but Brendan had the capacity to do that. He had so much time for Brendan. It could be hard times or good times, but Brendan was always a welcome guest in our house. Brendan and Eileen were very much part of family occasions and we shared with them many wonderful times over the years, from birthdays to the Dingle Regatta and so on. They are such beautiful kindhearted people.

Eimear Mulhern on behalf of the Haughey family

See Ya, Boss

Fr Brian Darcy, the official pastor to the entertainment industry, once introduced the tradition of holding a confessional mass every year for people in showbands and showbusiness.

It was like a general absolution ceremony and lord knows, some needed it more than most. Even though I was and still am very good friends with Brian, I never went to this annual mass. I never felt the need to go to confession; I prefer to talk direct. You can get confession over the internet these days and even the pope himself has an email address. I'm surprised he's not on Facebook at this stage.

While I don't entertain the idea of confession, that is not to suggest that I am not a believer. I regularly attend mass in my parish of Jupiter in Florida and, as I mentioned earlier, I do genuinely believe my parents are looking over me. Kathleen Keane, mother of my manager Brian, is a deeply religious person and regularly talks to my mother. Even though my mother died twenty years ago, Kathleen has often come up to me and casually said, "Brendan I was talking to your mother last week."

When I enquired with Kathleen as to the nature of their last conversation, she explained that Ma wanted me to know that she was very proud of me and that I was to keep an eye on my health. Kathleen's not psychic, she just has a direct line.

While I consider myself a believer, I will admit there were moments where my faith was rocked. For instance, earlier this year two priests formed the subject of a TV3 documentary entitled Ripping off the Rich: The Playboy Priests. The programme featured the story surrounding Fr John Skehan from Kilkenny and Fr Francis Guinan from Offaly, and their involvement in one of the biggest scandals in US history to hit the Catholic Church. The two priests had been charged with stealing from their parish of St Vincent Ferrer's in Delray Beach, Florida and were suspected of having embezzled millions of dollars of Church funds throughout a forty year period. Needless to say I was shocked by the details, not just by the enormity of their crimes but because I had personally known these two priests. What's more, I had helped them fundraise. Naturally, I was completely oblivious to what was really going on behind the scenes.

I knew Fr Guinan personally, however Fr Skehan I met only briefly. Eileen and I very often met them both out at dinner as they would have frequented the very same restaurants as us.

Even though I was not a part of Fr Guinan's parish as he was based in a different part of West Palm Beach, I willingly carried out a number of fundraising shows for him. It was very common for Irish entertainers in Florida to perform charity concerts for Irish priests so I was more than happy to play my part. In fact, shortly after we moved to Florida's West Palm Beach in 1993, one of the first shows I did was for Fr Guinan. It was incredible just how much was raised on the night of the gig. Prior to going on stage, Fr Guinan took me aside and asked if I would give special mention to a local couple who had donated $50,000. When I went out on stage, I said my few words and then went on to acknowledge the couple who had made the generous donation. This was followed by a huge round of applause when suddenly, a man stood up and announced that he would match that amount. I was barely into my second joke of the night and already we had raised over $100,000. The generosity of the people was just incredible however it makes what the priests did all the more tragically sad. When the news about their crimes first broke, everyone, including myself, was absolutely shocked. No one had suspected any wrongdoing.

Shortly after we moved to Florida, Eileen and I attended mass in our parish church. In the middle of the ceremony, when it came to the part where you shake hands with the people around you, a man sitting in the pew in front of me turned around and reached out his hand to me. I nearly bleedin' collapsed when I realised the man was none other than Perry Como. Perry, a native of Florida, was a very religious man and had donated quite a substantial amount of his money to the church. He was such a true gentleman. In fact I spoke with him following the mass and we shared a good chat about his time in Ireland and how he had recorded one of his specials there. While he was reminiscing, he mentioned Twink who had been on the show with him. In fact his exact words were 'that broad saved my ass'. I think he had forgotten a line on the show and Twink had rescued him before anyone noticed he was in trouble. He also spoke about a barber shop he went to for a shave during his trip to Ireland. The shop in question was based on Dublin's Thomas Street and was called Como's. The irony of it is that Perry Como had actually started his working life off as a barber.

Our own parish priest is a Sligo man called Fr Aidan Hynes. Like myself Fr Aidan likes to get his fix of home so he regularly travels back to Sligo to visit his lovely mother and family. We always miss him terribly when he's away because we absolutely love attending his mass. He always makes a point of singing and every Easter Sunday he sings the Easter bonnet, which isn't even a hymn. Regardless, he still sings it and his parishioners can never get enough of it.

Moving to Florida was exciting more so than nerve wracking. We decided we would try it for two years and if we didn't like it, we would move back to our house in Saggart. The kids had absolutely no objection to moving; in fact we were all willing to give it our best shot. We always knew we would leave, it was just a matter of when. As my own sister Marie was already living in Florida, the only draw back to moving was leaving Eileen's parents Lily and Patrick. As it transpired, we saw each other every three months or so as either we would fly home or they would travel to see us.

Approximately a year after we moved to West Palm Beach, Eileen and I were looking through the real estate on offer in the area when we noticed that the address of one particular house read Galway Court. Other addresses for that same area included Limerick Court and Kerry Court. We were highly amused by this and so went along to check it out. We immediately fell in love with one of the properties and today part of our address is Galway Court. In actual fact there are two ironies to our address. I mentioned earlier about how I once owned a bike called the West Palm only to move to West Palm Beach years later. Another story behind our address involves the name of the complex in which we live: Rolling Hills.

Twenty years ago, I was interviewed by broadcaster and radio presenter Robert Walsh for Cork local television. We had separate dressing rooms where we prepared for the show but when we arrived down to the studio set, we realised we were wearing the exact same suits, right down to the ties and shirts. We were so identical that when we saw each other we couldn't but laugh out loud. What's more, we were both similar in weight so we were almost like twins when we stood next to each other.

We joked about which one of us was going to be returning to the dressing room when Robert suddenly suggested that we both remain in the same suits and make reference to it during the interview. The interview itself was such a laugh that I told him to let me know when the show was going to be aired. With that, we swapped business cards and I remember his address in Cork was Rolling Hills. It caught my eye at the time because it was quite an unusual name. When Eileen told me she had found us a house in Rolling Hills, for a moment I thought we were Cork bound. Unfortunately, I haven't met Robert in the years since to tell him of the irony. Even though we said we would remain in Florida for just two years, over four years had passed when we remembered our initial plan. Sixteen years down the line, we have absolutely no intention of ever leaving.

We were fortunate that it worked out so well for us. It's a completely different lifestyle and would probably have been quite the culture shock had we not travelled to the country on holidays in the years prior to the move. In a way, we were pre-prepared for what to expect. Some things, however, you are never prepared for as I found out much to my mortification. In my defence though, we had only just moved there. It happened one day as I was trying to phone directory enquiries, the number of which is 411. By mistake I dialled 911, which is the phone number for the emergency services. When I realised what I had done, I immediately put the phone down. A couple of seconds later, a call came through from the local police station asking if they were through to the Grace residence and if everything was ok. Once I explained my accident, I enjoyed a good chat with the policeman on the other end of the line. No sooner had I hung up when the door bell rang. The station had sent a local cop around to double check if everything was ok. On another occasion, I was cooking turkey when the smoke that arose from the oven set off the kitchen fire alarm. Almost immediately the phone rang. It was the local county fire department. I explained what had happened but while I was still on the phone, I could hear sirens outside. Two bleedin' fire brigades had turned up outside my house, hoses at the ready. Between the cops calling one day and the two fire brigades on another, the neighbours must surely have thought they were living next door to the Osbournes.

Florida is a strange place in that those who were born there usually move to live elsewhere. There are very few real Floridians in the place; it's full of blow-ins like myself. One such blow-in is the Australian golfer, Greg Norman, whose daughter is a friend of my son Bradley.

The complete opposite to the blow-in community is the actor Burt Reynolds. Burt is known as Mr Jupiter as he was born and raised in the area and still continues to live there. A gentleman through and through, he has donated quite a substantial amount of land to the state so that it can be used for public parks and children's playgrounds. As I mentioned earlier, I was introduced to him through my son Brendan Patrick who was involved in his acting class.

The one thing I love most about dividing my time between America and Ireland is the balance. In Ireland I am recognised, but in Florida I'm anonymous. Most of my neighbours have no idea what I do for a living, so in that sense I get to enjoy the best of both worlds.

I once went into our local supermarket in West Palm Beach to pick up a carton of milk and a few other general items. As I walked by a mirrored area, I caught sight of my reflection. I remember the first thought that went through my head was: "Oh sweet Jesus." I realised I was wearing a long shirt, boxers and sandals, but had completely forgotten to put on my trousers before I left the house. Not one person even noticed. The lifestyle is so laid back. On the other hand, if I had walked around a supermarket in my boxers in somewhere like Manhattan, Boston or even Dublin, chances are I would have been arrested. Fortunately the dress code for where we live in Florida is "as lightly as you can".

As with every American state, Florida too has its own Irish community. Not long after we moved there, Eileen and I chose to visit a local restaurant called McCarthy's. Ironically, my son-in-law Frank and I now own that very restaurant. After we got chatting with the then owner, John McCarthy, he introduced us to a number of Irish people living in Jupiter who are still close friends of ours today. One of these people is Tom McPhail from Enniskillen. I call him The Duke because I'm convinced he's the reincarnation of John Wayne. His party piece is "The Isle of Innisfree" from the film *The Quiet Man*. I subsequently had the opportunity to introduce Tom to Maureen O'Hara and during that meeting, he serenaded her with a rendition of that song.

Another fellow country man with whom we became acquainted was the chef, Ken Wade, and his wife, Jenny. Ken was formerly the executive chef in Mayo's Ashford Castle and currently owns his own restaurant in Florida called Paddy Macs. When we first met him, he was the manager of a well known restaurant called Harpoon Louis. The situation from which our friendship sprung was unusual to say the least. Myself, Eileen and the kids had a meal there one evening with my sister Marie. When I went to pay for the meal, the *maitre d'* very discreetly returned and explained that my credit card had been declined. I tried a new credit card but that too was declined. I then discovered that the reason the cards had been rejected by the machine was due to the time difference. It transpired that the first card I handed the *maitre d'* expired on October 31st. Even though we were in the restaurant at 8pm on the 30th, in Ireland it was 1am which made the date the 31st. My card was on Irish time and so was declined because it had technically expired. The second card I had given the *maitre d'* was the new card I had been carrying with me, but it too was declined because it wasn't yet November 1 which was the date the card was to be activated. Basically my old card was out of date while my new one wasn't yet in date. Fortunately I had the cash on me and as I went to pay the bill, Ken approached me. The moment he spoke his first word, I could hear the Dublin accent, "Ah jaysus, Brendan Grace!"

After I explained the problem with my credit card, Ken refused to take the cash from me. He just smiled and said, "It's on me."

Since that night, we became great friends. I'm sure our paths would have crossed at some stage anyway as it's very rare that there would be two Dubs living in an area like Jupiter and not meet at some stage, but that particular incident sped up the process somewhat.

When I bring friends over from America, they are amazed that everyone recognises me. I always joke that I'm world famous ... in Ireland!

Americans by their nature get starstruck easily. They are in awe of anyone on TV. I was queuing with my family for the Empire State Building when an Irish family further up in the queue approached me and asked if I would give them an autograph and stand for a photograph. Naturally I was happy to oblige. The funny thing is that even though the other 99 per cent of people in the queue hadn't a clue who I was, over a dozen more of them still came up and asked for my autograph. When I asked them who they thought I was, their actual reply was that they didn't know but figured I must be famous if the other family had wanted my autograph and photograph. That's exactly the way most Americans react simply because they are so media driven.

Having lived there for 16 years now I am even more convinced that Americans don't speak English. They speak American. Believe me there is a huge difference between the two. So many words and descriptions are different in America that when I began performing gigs there, it was incredibly difficult at first to know which words I had to change. It was something I had to take very seriously as there was a risk that when I arrived at the punchline of a joke, no one would understand what I was talking about. Even something as simple as referring to the boot of the car has to be changed because Americans haven't a clue what a car boot means, they only know of it as the trunk. The word fortnight is another one they can't comprehend. In that regard, you have to ensure that your act is thoroughly translated to suit the American audience.

If I were to tell a joke to an American audience in the exact same way that I would tell it to an Irish audience, the two reactions would be very different. From the Irish audience I would get a good laugh. To the American audience though, I might as well be talking in Russian. The funny thing is, however, if I were to tell the Irish audience a joke in the same way I would tell it to an American audience, the Irish listeners would still find it funny because we understand American terms and phrases. We're far more cosmopolitan than Americans, probably because we grew up watching American programmes and cartoons.

When it comes to crime, Florida reminds me of the Ireland in which I was reared. In the area of West Palm Beach for instance, you could take off for the day without locking your house doors. I think the reason the area has such low crime statistics is simply because there are cop cars everywhere. Their presence is known and as such it is the people who feel safe and the criminals who feel threatened.

In Ireland, unfortunately, the gardaí are handcuffed, but through no fault of their own. They just haven't been provided with the resources.

It also doesn't help that the law appears to be on the side of the criminal. It really pisses me off no end to see a situation like with the Mayo farmers who were protesting peacefully and yet were jailed, whereas someone who has committed a really heinous crime is given a suspended sentence. It just makes no sense. When I'm in America, I listen to Irish radio all the time so that I am *au fait* with the news.

In Ireland during the sixties and seventies, the worst crime you could commit was robbing the gas meter. The meter was a system whereby in place of receiving a bill for your gas supply, you would instead insert a shilling into the meter box which would in turn allow you a certain amount of gas for your house. A man would then come around to collect the money. We often inserted holy medals and foreign coins to make the meter work but of course when the gas man came around he would separate the Irish coins from the other "currency". I remember on one occasion when he handed back the foreign tender to my mother. I, being quite young at the time, pointed at the handful of Irish coins and said, "Eh mister, would you not give her some of those coins instead?"

During my earlier trips to America, the one thing that always fascinated me was the variety of items available there that couldn't be bought in Ireland. When I first began travelling to the States, I used to bring home cases of Budweiser. My friends would be astounded by this American beer because at the time we only had Harp, Carlsberg and a few others.

Once, my aunt Wyn and her husband Bud bought me a television watch. There was a wire attached which went up along your arm and into your pocket to the receiver. It worked very well and picked up plenty of programmes, but only in America. The second I arrived home, the television went blank. It picked up every American channel imaginable, but no way could it pick up RTÉ.

While I loved the gizmos, I was equally as fond of the old fashioned devices. When I was living in Echlin Street I had a lovely neighbour called Mrs Mackey. I remember she owned the most beautiful gramophone which I absolutely loved. She even gave it to me as a gift and I still have it today. No doubt it contributed in some way to my love of music. To be honest, I have always believed it is in the make up of a comedian to want to do something serious, artistically speaking. You often hear of comedians being manic depressives. Personally I think it's because they can make everyone laugh except themselves but I don't think it's necessarily the trait of a comedian. I know of several people in comedy who suffer from depression and are manic depressive but I think it has more to do with the genetic make-up of a person. I suppose if you look at a clown, the smile is literally painted onto his face. It's his job to make others laugh and as such you never see the true expression underneath all the face paint. Even though he is making everyone laugh, behind it all, his personal situation could be very different.

Take rodeo or bull fighting in America. If the matador is injured or comes close to being gored by the bull, rodeo clowns are immediately sent in to distract the animal. They could be bricking it with fear of being gored by the bull themselves, but they will never show it. In a circus ring, if something goes wrong or someone falls, the clowns are sent out to entertain the crowd while the matter is being rectified. That's where the saying "send in the clowns" originated.

I have met people who are in the comedy business and are so involved that they can't get a laugh from someone else's jokes. I'm very fortunate that is not the case with me. I love laughter, whether it be from the joke of a professional comedian or just a funny person. In saying that, there is never a night when I'm not grateful that people have taken the time and trouble to come out, sit in a seat for two hours and laugh at my performance. Of course, if you dwell for too long on the fact that there are a few hundred people watching every move you make, it can be quite off-putting, particularly for a solo performer. I try not to think about that because even after all these years, it can still make me nervous.

To understand where I am coming from, picture in your head your workplace. Now imagine that you are working but that there are a few hundred people sitting there watching your every move, ready and waiting to say "Ah you put that screw in wrong," or "You didn't do your calculations right." I think it would more than likely drive you mad. Jim Carrey once made a movie called *The Truman Show* about everyone constantly watching him and that is exactly what the life of an entertainer is like.

When you're on stage, you can't see the crowd because the spotlight is focused on you. As it leaves the rest of the theatre shrouded in darkness, it reminds you just how lonely an experience being a performer can be if you let it. Even when you're off stage, there is an ever-present expectation from people to be made laugh. People often approach comedians and say, "Tell me a joke!"

I've often joked about it in my act down through the years that if you go to a friend's house and if they or their spouse is a plumber or a carpenter, then chances are you're going to have a leaky tap that needs fixing or a chair that needs mending and you're going to end up mentioning it to them. We don't separate the individual from their job title.

It's something I myself am guilty of. When I think of John Cleese, I immediately think of the devilment he got up to as Basil Fawlty. However, what we often fail to recognise is that when this comedy genius is not performing, he appears to be quite a serious individual. I once read that the legendary comedy duo Abbott and Costelloe didn't speak to each other when off stage. It was the same on occasion with Laurel and Hardy. Off stage, they wouldn't talk because they simply didn't like each other. Of course people don't detect the hostile atmosphere in a performance because it's the job of the comedians to make the audience laugh and therefore, the audience really shouldn't see if something is wrong.

Maybe the key to remaining in love with the business is not to bring your work home with you. I stand by that rule. When I rehearse, I do it somewhere away from the house or on the way to a gig. If there is something specific I have to say, I note it in my cue cards to prompt me, but otherwise the flow of the show comes naturally.

Maureen Potter is the one person I know who never needed cue cards. Before a panto started, people would often send in requests if it were a child's birthday and Maureen would always recall these requests from memory. She could reel off ten minutes of names without needing notes. What's more, she could do it every night; she was known in the business for it. For a child to hear their name being called out on the panto stage was and still is a big thing. It's up there with Santa reading out the letters on Radio One from the North Pole.

Maybe it's in a bid to tap into their serious creative side, but you often hear of entertainers taking up songwriting and often with great success. A number of well-known comedy entertainers down through the years have composed songs that went on to become hits that are still played today. In 1969, when I was in Dr Stephens Hospital in Dublin, I wrote a song called "Industrial Fair". It was actually a song about a chimney, one of those really tall ones that you never see nowadays. From the hospital window I could see the top of this chimney right over the rooftops and for some reason felt inspired to put pen to paper. It sounds weird to say a chimney inspired a song, but I chose interesting words for the lyrics and when it was put to a tune, it actually became quite a catchy song. I decided to include it in the track listing for my first LP "Grace Before and After". To this day, people remark on that song and still ask me to perform it, which is something I find very surreal as I wrote the song at a time when I didn't even know I was going to be a performer.

During the early days of my comedy career, people often asked if I felt I would have made it as a singer. Due to people enquiring about the singing side of my persona, I decided to record an album called "Don't Laugh at Me Because I'm a Fool".

The idea for the name came from Norman Wisdom's song of the same title for the movie *Trouble in Store*. On the album I led off with Ken Dodd's hit "Tears For Souvenirs" followed by "Smile" written by the daddy of comedy, Charlie Chaplin. I think I chose the works of these artists simple because I was as influenced by their singing ability as I was by their comedic timing. It was a dual admiration so to speak.

I have written many songs over the years but one that I am quite proud of is one you will never hear me perform. In 1985, I wrote the lyrics to a song about the moving statues in Ballinspittle. A number of people were being very cynical about this bizarre occurrence at the time, but I simply saw an opportunity to inject some humour into the situation. From this I created a very tongue in cheek song about people travelling to Ballinspittle in their thousands, some to witness the phenomenon, others to set up chip vans, and even more to sell Our Lady key rings, ashtrays and mugs. Everyone was on the bandwagon. If the Mother of God had realised just how much of a windfall she was after creating for Ballinspittle at the time, she would have surely returned and demanded a slice. I thought the whole thing was very funny so I put together a song about statues that were moving around the place and playing hide and seek. We had to record it about twenty times because the musicians would invariably find themselves overcome by a dose of the giggles. It was one of those songs that would most definitely have been a hit, however it never came to pass because I dumped it. I played it to my mother one night and while she laughed at the humour of it, she pointed out that it might offend more people than it would please. As so many had placed their faith in this phenomenon, it was easy to see how it could cause mass offence. Regardless of how much laughter the song was capable of inducing, if a project didn't garner my mother's blessing, I didn't press ahead with it. I knew I simply wouldn't enjoy performing the song unless I had first acquired her full approval, and so with that "The Statues of Ballinspittle" met its demise.

I must admit I once had my very own experience of moving statues.

One night, as I was driving home from a gig, I decided I needed some fresh air so I parked the car near the chapel in Birdhill, county Tipperary. As I was standing outside, there was a car coming towards me and whatever way the lights of the oncoming car reflected on the statues outside the chapel, all I could see were these statues coming at me. I nearly destroyed my trousers with the bloody fright I got. I was physically shaking after it. It was an illusion of some sort created by the lights of the car but it seemed so real.

Regardless of whether my performance on stage was that of a singing or a comedy nature, I always made a point of using a sauna or a steam room during the day to relieve my voice. I found this particularly beneficial, especially when smoking was permitted in bars. While I usually frequented the sauna of Eddie Downey's clinic in the Montrose Hotel, I subsequently decided to acquire my own. To endure the heat, I always found I had to have a portable TV or a radio in the sauna as a distraction. All was going well until one day I stepped in to the sauna and noticed the TV wasn't sitting properly. That's when I realised it had melted from the heat. While some people treat the sauna as a form of quietness and relaxation, I on the other hand would almost always be on the phone while in there. This brings to mind an incident which occurred about twenty years ago while we were still living in Saggart. I was sitting in the sauna when the phone rang and a man with a soft Northern Ireland twang asked if I was Brendan. He then went on to tell me that he was Daniel O'Donnell. Naturally I thought someone was winding me up so I replied, "Ah come on, who's acting the bollix?"

I was so sure it was one of my friends pulling my leg and despite the caller's best efforts, there was no convincing me otherwise. The poor guy kept insisting he was Daniel and eventually I got so frustrated with him that I just told him to forget about it and hung up. I figured it had to be a joke because Daniel O'Donnell would have had no reason for calling me. Five minutes later the phone rang again. It was Seán Reilly, a good friend of mine and currently Daniel's personal manager. When he explained his reason for calling, I was red with embarrassment. He told me that Daniel had been trying to get through to me because he wanted to ask me a few questions about Saggart as he was thinking of purchasing a property there, but that I had hung up on him twice. Immediately I phoned Daniel and apologised profusely for my blunder. He was so polite about the whole matter and we ended up chatting about Saggart and the property he was thinking about buying. He pressed ahead with the sale and, along with being my neighbour, he became a good friend. I also developed a lovely friendship with his mother Julia and often met her when she was visiting Daniel. As well as having an incredible personality, Julia is a marvellous cook and makes pancakes to die for. On one occasion, when I was performing a gig in Dunloe, she wasn't feeling well so couldn't attend. She did however send a few neighbours down to the venue carrying a plate of pancakes for me. That night I brought the plate on stage with me and told people that they had been sent by Julia O'Donnell to fatten me up.

One year when a number of my American friends were over on holiday, I brought them to my house in Saggart. Just as Daniel gives his visitors tea, I ply mine with a few drinks. During the course of conversation I told them there was a very famous Irish singer living nearby. As there was quite a large group, they were making their way around by bus, so we had the driver bring us up to Daniel's house.

Even though Daniel wasn't famous in America at the time, once I pointed out the house of this famous Irish singer, the Americans immediately had their cameras out snapping away. I for some reason thought Daniel was away at the time so I went out and rang the bell on the electric gates outside his house. For a laugh I then got down on my knees, like you would at an altar. To my horror, the gates suddenly began to open. Daniel walks out, sees me on my knees like an eejit and shouts out "Ach you're an awful man. I have no peace with you coming up and kneeling down outside my house all the time."

Daniel has a great sense of humour and takes no offence when I mimic him because he knows there is no malice intended by it.

Both he and his lovely wife Majella get a great kick out of my Daniel impersonation act. His fans on the other hand have reacted to the gag with hate mail. It's actually a testament to their loyalty to Daniel that they feel so offended on his behalf. For instance, there was a sketch I created called "Daniel's Kilt" which I performed on one of my DVD's. This one in particular ignited several hate letters lambasting me for mimicking him. Clearly they thought I was having a go at him and so hated me for it. The funny thing is those gags always met with Daniel's approval. He simply loved the humour of them and so had no objection to me mimicking him.

Charlie Haughey was the exact same. Whenever I was in his company or if I were performing for a function at which he was in attendance, I would tease him relentlessly with the mimicking routine, but it was all done in good spirits and good taste. Like Daniel, he too was comfortable with me performing a gag at his expense. I was always a firm Haughey supporter and have been good friends with the Haughey family for many years now. I first met Charlie through my manager Jim Hand at a Fianna Fáil function in the Grand Hotel in Malahide back in 1978. It was the first of many party events at which we would meet and over time we became good friends. In turn, Eileen became close to Charlie's daughter Eimear while I developed a friendship with his wife Maureen who was, and still is, the very epitome of a lady. His son Ciarán and I also became very good friends through our mutual love of helicopters.

On a number of occasions, I accompanied Charlie on the campaign trail all while in the character of Bottler. Charlie possessed a wonderful sense of humour and over the years he shared with me many an entertaining yarn. I remember when he visited West Palm Beach, we decided to go out for a drink. Of all the places we decided to go to, we chose a local restaurant where, in order to afford a burger, you would very nearly need a mortgage. I decided it was my treat so I handed Charlie the wine list from which he chose one of the top bottles of champagne. After we had polished off two bottles of it, I think my heart nearly stopped when I saw the three figure sum on the bill. The following night, when it was Charlie's turn to take me out, he didn't falter. He chose a beautiful restaurant and when we arrived he told the waitress to bring out the most expensive red wine they had. He then turned to my son-in-law Frank Gillespie and said, "Life is too short for drinking cheap wine."

That was classic Charlie. He was incredibly full of banter and fun, not to mention a wonderful storyteller to boot. Some people, due to being of quite a tall stature, are able to command a room from the moment they walk in. Charlie, however, possessed the same commanding force and more, even though he was quite small in height. That same night in the restaurant, he and Frank were engaged in conversation about Gaelic football and at one stage, Charlie asked, "Did you hear what I said about Páidí Ó Sé? I phoned the Late Late Show and told them he wasn't actually born in Kerry."

I have zero interest in sport, but even I was intrigued by this little revelation. Charlie went on, "Páidí wasn't born in Kerry at all. I told them he had been carved out of the rock of Mount Brandon."

When Charlie left that night in a limousine, I'd say he thought he was back in power again with all the waving he was doing from the back window. Another occasion which springs to mind whenever I think of Charlie is the evening his son Ciarán and I were returning from Inishvickillane some years back. Ciarán, who owns Celtic Helicopters, was piloting the chopper that evening and landed it outside Abbeyville to pick up Charlie who was Taoiseach at the time. We then made our way to Dublin airport. As we approached the runway, air traffic control held us back until the runway was completely free of traffic. This meant Ciarán had to hover the helicopter until we were given the all clear to use the runway. Once or twice Ciarán asked for permission to cross the active runway but was each time was refused. Suddenly Charlie said to Ciarán, "Tell them who's on board."

With this, Ciarán gets back on to base and explains he has the Taoiseach in the helicopter with him. Straight away the response comes back, "Oh, please come on in."

When Celtic Helicopters was first launched in Abbeyville some years ago, a blessing was performed on each of the aircraft by Charlie's brother, Fr Eoghan Haughey. Blessings such as these were the done thing back then and I'm sure the practice still goes on today but probably to a much lesser extent. I remember there used to be one day each year when people would bring their motorbikes to churches around Dublin to have them blessed. I suppose in a way it was a request for divine intervention to keep the driver and passenger safe. Perhaps I should have had the priest wash my bike in holy water considering the number of times I crashed while on the bleedin' thing.

A substantial number of people still have their houses blessed and I would usually avail of a two-for-one opportunity and have Breener bless the bandwagons as well. On the day of the Celtic Helicopters launch however, the aircrafts were lined up on the lawn outside the house so I, noticing the opportunity for a gag, went to an upstairs room in Abbeyville where there was access to a balcony. With a plate of sandwiches in my hand, I began my drunk act and started firing sandwiches towards the helicopters as if they were birds. In keeping with the character, I adopted a drunken stupor and shouted down, "I'm jusht feedin' the hel-copters."

On one occasion, Charlie invited me on a yachting trip with him. At the time, he owned a yacht called The Celtic Mist which he and his family were planning on sailing from Malahide around the coast to Inishvickillane. One day Charlie phoned me up and invited me on board for the journey from Kinsale to Inishvickillane. I was absolutely delighted by the invite because I knew it would be great craic. The weather however suddenly turned appallingly bad and they had to port until the skies calmed. As a result, the departure of the yacht from Kinsale had to be postponed for a few days. Charlie contacted me about the delay, however their rescheduled departure time coincided with gigs I had on so I explained my situation and bid them well. The day I was to join the Haugheys on The Celtic Mist was the same day it went up on the rocks and sank near the

Mizen lighthouse. They subsequently had to be rescued by one of the life boats and fortunately no one was injured. At the time it was a huge news story.

Looking back, however, I can see it was just one of a number of incidents in which I was prevented from venturing near the sea. Apart from the Haugheys' yacht sinking and the occasion when I was knocked down by the ambulance while on my way to collect my forms for my job at sea, there was another incident which occurred around 1974. Not long after Eileen and I got married, our good friend Red Hurley gave us a very unusual dog, an Afghan Hound. Red had given us the dog on a Friday and as such we decided to name the dog Friday. Not long afterwards, I bought a fabulous dinghy, the type to which you could attach an engine, and I was really looking forward to using it. I left it in the back garden and when I looked out one morning, the dinghy was in absolute shreds, courtesy of Friday.

The nature of this breed of dog is mischievous, but I still to this day can't figure out how he managed to shred it to the extent he did. It wasn't remotely possible to repair it. I was furious at the beginning but my mother's words, "It broke a bigger cross," entered my mind and instead I wondered if something tragic would have happened had I ever brought the dinghy out on the water. Maybe it's coincidence but even Eileen has noticed how fate always seems to intervene in some way to stop me from going near water.

There was another side to Charlie that few were aware of. When it came to his constituents his kindness towards them was extremely profound. Several people have told me how Charlie used to call to their houses with a hamper or give them a few quid if they were short. The thing is Charlie would never tell you about this himself. There were quite a number of generous gestures like those but while most politicians would use them as an opportunity to brag about the good work they were doing, Charlie would always keep it to himself.

Likewise when Melanie was in hospital following her accident, Charlie arrived in late one night to see how she was. When her husband Frank arrived in a short while later, he found the former Taoiseach sitting there having a long chat and a laugh with Melanie. He was a true gentleman like that.

I don't think I will ever forget the last time I spoke with Charlie. It was just a few days before he passed away. His wife Maureen was there, as were his sons Ciarán and Connor. We had a great conversation about old times and a good laugh about various things which had happened throughout the years. When it was time to leave, Charlie insisted on walking Eileen and I out to our car. There were a few steps outside his Abbeyville house and, as he was too feeble to walk them, he remained at the front door. He then stood to attention and saluted me with the words, "I'll see ya, Bottler."

In return, I saluted him back and said "See ya, Boss."

Eileen and I were acutely aware of how ill Charlie was at the time and we suspected that our meeting that evening would be the last we would enjoy with him. To be honest, I still can't look back on that evening without being moved by the way he bid me farewell.

Charlie's name came up recently during a chat I enjoyed with another Fianna Fáil politician. I had been scheduled to do an interview on Midlands Radio with my good friend Ricey Scully. As I was sitting in the studio enjoying tea and cake, in walks a very familiar looking person and starts eating the cake along with me. It was none other than midlands' local, An Taoiseach, Brian Cowen.

We ended up chatting on Ricey's show together and from what I was told afterwards the station's switchboard was jammed with well-wishers. During the show, Brian Cowen started reading out the dates of my gigs which, for me, was a surreal experience because here was the Taoiseach, leader of our country, promoting my show. Following the interview, we went over to the Bridgehouse Hotel for lunch where I regaled him with stories about Charlie Haughey which absolutely fascinated him. I have no interest in politics these days but I would definitely consider Brian to be a close acquaintance and my heart goes out to him at the moment given the crisis he has to deal with, not to mention the large level of public unrest being directed towards him.

Another person for whom I have great admiration is the Limerick businessman JP McManus. I first got to know JP through performing at functions he hosted. Despite his phenomenal success, he remains the most down to earth gentleman you will ever meet. I don't think the man has ever once in his life developed airs, graces or ego.

Around ten years ago, when the horse Istabraq was in his prime, JP approached me and asked if I would write a song for him. After we had a nice chat about the history of the horse and how it came to be such a racing phenomenon, he explained that he wanted the song to honour the man who had first discovered Istabraq's potential.

It seems the trainer John Durkin had seen the horse compete in a race and instinctively knew he was witnessing a prospective champion in action. With this in mind, John immediately brought Istabraq to the attention of JP McManus. Sadly however, at the age of just 31 John contracted an illness and passed away in 1998. Essentially the song was going to be an accolade to the horse because at the time it was winning absolutely every race in which it competed. But over all, it was to be a fitting tribute to John.

I wrote out the story JP had shared with me and developed it into song lyrics. I then created the air that would accompany the song and to this day, I consider it to be one of the best tracks I ever created. I have never actually performed the song on stage as it was a private piece of work that was to accompany a series of photographs. I do think I may re-release the song someday but accompanied by different lyrics. It had the kind of tune that could easily feature as the score of a movie so it's not beyond the bounds of possibility that it may resurface once again.

Not many people know that I was once involved in the horse racing industry, albeit briefly. It began in 1982 when Tony Durkin, a man well known in the construction industry, convinced me to buy a horse. I thought he was bleedin' mad. I was bad enough on motorbikes never mind a racehorse. Anyway, I decided I would buy the horse and give it to Eileen as a birthday gift. Instead of presenting her with the horse however, I felt it would be more fun to give her a card with a treasure map and cryptic clues.

We all headed off in the car with Eileen in the driving seat, baffled as to what the end result would be. Every time she found a clue it would lead her to another part of the country. She was wracking her brains trying to figure out what we had in store for her and as soon as she had settled on one notion, the next clue would completely scupper it.

At one stage she thought it was a piece of jewellery then one of the clues involved a key so this led her to the idea that it was a house or a car. Eventually the clues led her to the stables in county Carlow and it was there she met her hairy gift, who she later christened His Grace!

We entered him in several races and in every race he would win the first half. His Grace would begin by leading but his luck never lasted and he always fell back.

Fr Breen was as delighted with the horse as Eileen was and he regularly joined us at various meetings in which His Grace was running.

I remember talking to Breener about the horse one evening and after describing the horse's tendency to veer to the left all the time I asked him if he knew how I would go about curing it. The answer I got was to put a bit of lead in His Grace's right ear.

Intrigued, I asked how I would do that, to which came the reply: "With a gun!"

As it turns out, that's exactly what happened as the horse became quite ill.

In later years, not long after I composed the song for JP McManus, Eileen and I were invited over to Cheltenham for one of the Istabraq celebrations. While over there we met a man called John Coyle and his wife Fiona. As well as being a pro golfer, John is also famous for being able to sing "Danny Boy" in Chinese. Having heard him sing it myself I can say with full assurance that you really have not lived until you have heard "Danny Boy" in Chinese.

That night John and I paired up and began singing, and even though myself, Eileen and the kids were living in America at the time, John somehow managed to talk me into making county Clare's Killaloe my second home. Little did I know that a pub located on Killaloe's main street would also later come into my possession through very bizarre means. Tom Elliffe and his partner Lorraine, in the company of the resident bulldog, Jessie, had owned the pub "Richardsons" for several years and from the moment I stepped inside the front door of the bar, Tom and I became good friends.

One particular Tuesday night in 2002, I was burning the midnight oil and when I woke up the following morning, I not only had a bad hangover but a pub in my name as well. I distinctly remember waking up to Eileen's word's, "Did you buy Richardson's pub last night?"

With absolutely no memory of the previous night's events, I naturally laughed it off. However, when my lovely wife told me she had received a number of phone calls about it, the memory wasn't long returning. I remember saying, "Mother of jaysus, I was there with Coyle and a few of the lads all right, but I don't remember buying the bleedin' pub."

As far as I could recall, the worst I had done to my wallet that night was buy a few too many rounds, but slowly flashbacks began visiting and I realised I had bought the bar itself.

Tom was very honourable about the deal that day. The euro had just been introduced to the country but I, going by what few recurring memories I had of the night, somehow assumed the deal had been done in the old currency, the Irish punt.

When I went to see him about the purchase, I was prepared to pay in punts, but Tom, being an absolute honest gentleman by nature, informed me that our deal had actually been agreed in euros. Even though the euro was worth a lot less and Tom had the opportunity to gain quite a bit extra financially by going along with my assumption that we had done the deal in the old currency, he remained upfront and sincere about it.

We were good friends before that, but I always believed it was that particular incident that made us even greater friends.

twelve

When I was young I was a big Grease fan and totally in love with John Travolta. On one occasion, Dad arrived home from a trip to America with a Grease album, autographed to me by John Travolta. I was so chuffed! It wasn't until I was old enough that I recognised the writing as being my dad's, and not John Travolta's. There was another memorable occasion where early one Christmas morning, I awoke to see Santa placing toys into the stocking at the end of my bed. I said nothing as I was terrified I would scare him away. This particular Santa Claus would always phone us each Christmas. Needless to say, this was all before I was old enough to realise who I was talking to on the phone!

Amanda Grace

A Bar and a Farting Bulldog

When I bought the pub, with it I inherited the dog Jessie, who was as well known around Killaoe as Tom or myself. In fact such was Jessie's regime around the pub that I often used to joke it was he who ran the bar and that we were just his tenants. Jessie also used to fart to his heart's content. To make a bad situation worse, he would usually break wind by the fire. I swear to god, he could clear the bar with the smell. You really haven't lived until a bulldog has farted in a warm bar. Customers used to buy him Tayto crisps all the time. He absolutely loved the bloody things, which needless to say, probably didn't help his flatulence.

After I took over the pub, we renovated it and named it Brendan Grace's Bar. A pub with photographs always held a fascination for me and it was something I wanted to replicate in my own establishment. There is always a great novelty value attached to the photographs we display in the pub simply because many of the people in the pictures are well known. I also have a picture of Fr Breen in the bar and when a number of my American friends first saw it they were convinced it was the pope. Those with particularly bad eyesight would ask, "Brendan did you and Eileen meet the Pope?" Of course they were usually corrected with the reply, "No we didn't meet the pope, the pope met us."

Another picture which has a great story attached to it is of the actor Jack Nicholson and myself. Dr Michael Smurfit regularly booked me to provide the entertainment for his corporate events and on one occasion in 1999 he had asked me to perform a show at a function in the K Club. He told me Jack Nicholson would be in attendance however, as the event was being held in a golf club, I thought Michael had said Jack Nicklaus, the golfer. I remember telling Eileen at the time that Jack Nicklaus was going to be there. When I later walked out to do my piece for the crowd, who do I see sitting up in front but Jack Nicholson, the movie star, wearing white runners under his suit no less. He loved the show that night and afterwards he and I ended up drinking pints of Guinness together well into the small hours. We were actually the last two to leave the bar. Eileen wasn't in attendance at the show so I decided to phone her while I had the man himself beside me. Both of us were well on the sauce at this stage and we decided it would be a great laugh to put him on the phone to her. So I said, "Howya love, I want you to say hello to Jack."

Yes, even after all these years I still call her "love", particularly when I'm drunk and can't remember her name.

So himself goes on the phone to Eileen and says "Hiya hunny, this is Jack." To which he gets the reply, "Jack who?"

He told her his name but she thought he had said Jack Nicklaus as she had heard me mention that he was going to be a guest. He carried on chatting away to her but the poor thing didn't know it was in fact the Hollywood movie star she had been conversing with until I told her the morning after. The kids were fascinated by the idea of their dad getting drunk with undoubtedly the coolest star in Hollywood, but they were far more impressed by the photograph of me with Bon Jovi's drummer Tico Torres. This meeting came about after JP McManus booked me to entertain the guests at a golf tournament in Scotland. It was during that event that another popular wall photo was captured – me with Michael Douglas.

A particularly eye-catching photograph that features in the pub is of Pavarotti and me. Pavorotti apparently never stood for photographs with fans as he was particularly mindful of germs and the effect that something as simple as a cold could have on his voice. When I spotted him in the Westbury Hotel in Dublin one day, I decided to approach him but his minders immediately stopped me. For some reason, Pavorotti made the exception and beckoned me forward so I could have a photograph taken with him. Personally I think I got through the barrier because fat men harbour a type of allegiance to other fat men.

It was the same with the comedian Les Dawson. The moment we met, we became instant friends. Les was my mother's favourite comedian. When she was alive I tried my best to arrange a meeting between the two of them. Unfortunately it never came to fruition. She had only passed away about two months when I received a phone call from the singer Sonny Knowles telling me that Les Dawson was coming to Dublin the following day. Sonny was booked to play the same event so he filled me in on the details about how they were going to meet in the Gresham Hotel for lunch at noon. We arranged that I would drop by the hotel at that time and that Sonny would introduce me to him. The second I stood in front of Les, he hugged me. It was incredible to meet him in person because he was as much my favourite comedian as he was my mother's. Eileen and I, along with Sonny and a few others, went out for drinks with Les and his fiancé Treacy that evening and by the end of the night, Les had extended a wedding invite to myself and Eileen. We actually became lifelong friends and we still remain in contact to this day. I told him about my mother and how she was such a fan of his routines and I am still convinced that she pulled a few strings with the big man upstairs to make that meeting happen for me! The reason I am so adamant that she was instrumental in our meeting is because on the night we went out for drinks, Sonny got up and told the very same joke that my mother used to tell at the ladies' club. It was a joke I had given her and it was her absolute favourite, and when Sonny told it, Eileen and I just looked at each other stunned. Sonny had just picked a random joke to tell; there was no way he could have known it was the one gag my mother loved to tell. To me that alone was a little signal from her.

Another idol of mine who I had the privilege of meeting was the late John Denver. I own every record he ever released and I used to sing all his songs in my early days of performing. When he came to Cork in 1992, he was singing to a huge crowd when he began to trip up on the words of "The Banks of My Own Lovely Lee". He had insisted on singing it it was clear that the words were beginning to elude him. As I was standing at the side of the stage after having introduced him to the crowd, I could see he was struggling so I went out and helped him sing it. To meet my idol was one thing, to perform with him however was above and beyond anything I could ever have dreamed of. Off stage he was so thankful for my help. Sometimes meeting your heroes can leave you disappointed, but if anything my meeting with John Denver left me with an even greater admiration for him. To this day the photograph of he and I singing on stage still garners plenty of attention from visitors to the bar.

On another occasion, I introduced the singer Kris Kristofferson to the stage at Siamsa in Cork City. This was another opportunity I got thanks to the promoter Oliver Barry.

While my excitement at meeting John Denver was almost off the radar, it was nothing compared to Tom's Eliffe's reaction the night he met Clare hurling manager Ger Loughnane.

For the length of time I had known Tom, he was a steadfast supporter of Loughnane. Some people have JFK's photo up on the wall in line with that of the pope, but in Tom's eyes, what Loughnane had done for Clare hurling in 1995 and 1997 made his photo as deserving of a place on the wall with the best of them. One night Loughnane happened to call in for a drink so naturally we lined him up for a photograph. Tom was so excited you'd swear Clare had won the All-Ireland all over again. You can tell just by looking at his expression in the photograph how proud he was to meet his hero.

Sadly, in 2006 Tom developed an illness which seemed to catch up with him very fast. The whole town was absolutely devastated when the news emerged that he had passed away. I myself was grief stricken. The loss of such a close friend hit me hard. Tom is buried in the local graveyard in Killaloe, but to be honest, we always feel he is here in the pub with us. Given that Tom always sat by the pub's open fire, we decided it fitting to dedicate the wall around the fireplace especially to him. Countless photographs of him smiling with various friends now don the stone walls and for me, that one small area of the pub is a place that evokes many a memory of a wonderful friend. Maybe it's the presence of a fireplace, but it's a part of the pub that seems to draw people. When I first became acquainted with the pub, I was fascinated to learn that customers used to cook sausages in the fireplace as well as make toast.

Over the years I have made some wonderful friends in the pub. From Tom Eliffe's partner, Lorraine, who keeps me in coffee, Charlie O'Connor who bakes me cakes, and Coleman O'Flaherty who sings for us at the drop of a hat, there are countless locals who have helped make Killaloe as much of a home for me as Florida or even Dublin. Naturally, there are far too many people to mention, but I'm grateful to every one of them for their friendship and witty banter.

While the interior of the pub catches the interest of many, the exterior seems to equal it in terms of appeal. When the smoking ban came in, I immediately had an outdoor smoking room constructed. It's sheltered and heated but best of all, it has a lovely atmosphere and as a result I've often found more non smokers out there than smokers. I go out there to smoke now and then, but of course I only smoke to check that the smoke alarms are working.

This is actually not my first time running a pub. I once owned a pub called Brendan Grace's Place in Black Church near Rathcoole but I sold it in 1979 after an incident in which three raiders broke into the bar late one night. At the time of the break in, my mother and father along with my sister were finishing up for the night. After the raiders had gained entry into the premises, they locked them in the bathroom and told them they weren't going to hurt them but that they just wanted cash. They then asked my parents and sister if they wanted anything to drink. My father requested a bottle of whiskey and minerals for the girls. Once they were out of the vicinity, one of the raiders contacted the local garda station and informed them that three people were locked in the bathroom of Graces pub. The pub never felt the same following that night, so I put it on the market and sold it off.

From the moment I bought the bar in Killaloe, the first photograph I knew I wanted on the wall was that of my father and me enjoying a pint of Guinness. It's also surrounded by treasured pictures of my mother, sister and family. The photographs on the walls of both the bar and lounge documents both my public and private life and each time I look at them, I always spot one I forgot was there. Friends of mine from America particularly love picking out the various well known faces in many of the pictures. Every year, usually around September, I bring a group of my American neighbours and friends to Ireland. After stopping off at my pub for a few warm up drinks, we then head off around the country in a large coach. Some of them love it so much that they have ended up buying property here. We travel all over to places such as Kerry, Galway, Donegal, Wexford, Cork, and absolutely everywhere in between. My American friends are aware I am involved in showbusiness but they never realise just how well known I am until they come on our coach tour. One particularly memorable day, which occurred not long after we moved here but long before that Tuesday night when I bought the pub, we brought our American friends to East Clare so they could see our adopted home village. When we came over the bridge in Killaloe and were heading out the Scariff road, there was a Clare County Council lorry in front of us and a number of council workers filling in parts of the road. As a result we were held up in traffic. While we were waiting,

I got it into my head to get out of the coach and go up to the council lads and pretend to give out yards about the hold up. I went up waving fists, guns blazing but the lads recognised me so they knew I was only pulling the proverbial out of the ones on the bus. Of course the Americans were all taking photographs of the incident and it was only when we looked back at the pictures years later that we realised that one of the council men in the picture was in fact the father of a man called Martin, who me daughter Amanda would subsequently marry. The gas thing is, she hadn't even met Martin at this stage. It was just a complete coincidence. The coach tour is our annual tradition at this stage. In fact it's known as no-rules tour! The bus driver is bribed from the word go and he is also very much of the understanding that whatever schedule he is given at the beginning will more than likely be changed at a moment's notice usually to accommodate pub stops.

We regularly went to the restaurant Moran's of the Wier in Kilcolgan. I absolutely love shellfish so it was a place I always favoured visiting whenever I was in that neck of the woods. In fact around the time of the Galway Races, I would always call to Moran's and perform an impromptu show. Unfortunately however it got to the point where after about three years, I had to stop doing it because the whole place would be blocked up due to so many people arriving for it. I remember a number of people would even arrive by helicopter. It just got to the point where it was no longer impromptu. People who were later involved in tribunals were all there. Figures such as the Bailey brothers, Patrick Gallagher and a number of other big developers were all in attendance and each and every one of them had the living bejaysus slagged out of them.

Anyone who has been to my shows will know I always involve the audience in my routine. I might just talk or sing to someone but if I spot a person who bears an uncanny resemblance to a celebrity, I will usually point it out. For instance, I was performing a Christmas show in 2006 in the Bridge House in Tullamore when during my act I noticed a table to my right where one of the men sitting at it was wearing a white suit. I had limited vision of the crowd due to the strong spotlights, but when I looked at him a second time, I remember thinking he must be a tourist. Before I finished the gig, I began performing a medley of songs. During the routine, I saw a guy with a beard in front of me so I stepped off the stage with the microphone and said, "Ah howya Rolf?" Obviously it was a joking reference to Rolf Harris. At this point, I looked over to the man in the white suit and I said, "Howya Roger?" because the man in question looked similar to Roger Whittaker. I like to interact with the guests as much as possible at functions such as these so I walked over to his table. The song I was singing at the time was very well known so I put the microphone to the man in the white suit as if to ask him to sing. Again, it was all in keeping with the joke that he was Roger Whittaker. When I gestured the microphone towards him, without hesitation he picked up where I had left off, and that's when it dawned on me, "Jesus, Mary and Joseph, he actually is Roger Whittaker."

Following the gig, I went out to the lobby where I approached him. I said to him "I think I'm about to be very embarrassed when I hear your answer, but have I Roger Whittaker in front of me?"

Accompanying his reply with a smile, he said, "You have!"

I couldn't but apologise profusely. On one hand I was over the moon to meet this legendary singer, but at the same time, I was immensely embarrassed that I hadn't realised who he was sooner. I explained to him that I had assumed he was a tourist who just happened to bear a slight resemblance to Roger Whittaker, but fortunately he had found the whole episode quite funny so didn't mind in the slightest. We stood talking for a while and he said to me at one point that it was the funniest act he had seen in all his travels. As it turns out, he and his beautiful wife Natalie live in Offaly and after hearing so much about my show from people in the town, he made a point of attending. We exchanged phone numbers and not long after that gig, he phoned to invite Eileen and me to a celebration in Offaly marking their 40th wedding anniversary. Considering that on the night of the show I had referred to another man as Rolf, I thought it was particularly funny if not a little ironic that when we arrived at the anniversary party on the beautiful grounds of their Offaly home, standing beside Roger was none other than Rolf himself!

On the night, Rolf performed a party piece for the audience which was absolutely hilarious. Overall he's a wonderful entertainer but I later discovered that he is also a talented accordion player to boot. I went up afterwards and performed my own routine in which I welcomed the guests to Roger and Natalie's celebration. It was like Father of the Bride except tweaked to suit the occasion. It was completely ad lib; I just made the whole thing up as I went along, but I could see Rolf laughing so much that at one stage, I genuinely feared we would be phoning for an ambulance for him. Following the performance, Rolf came up to me and said the same words the actor Peter O'Toole had said to me some years earlier, "That's the funniest drunk I have ever seen."

When Peter O'Toole saw the Father of the Bride act at the reopening of the Gaiety Theatre he had said, "That's the best drunk act I have ever seen. Take it from me, I know what I'm talking about."

I often find that some people think I am genuinely drunk when I perform this act. For instance when I recently attended Larry Cunningham's book launch in Cavan, I performed a drunk act on the stage. Afterwards, a number of people approached me and were actually astonished to find that I was sober. It seems my drunk character is so convincing that many thought I was genuinely plastered. Eileen and I had a similar reaction to a drunk act performed by Dean Martin at one of his performances. In fact, to this day we still don't know whether he was really drunk or just acting.

A look through the photographs on the walls inside the pub will tell you many different stories about my life and the people I have met. Unfortunately however there is one entertaining story which you won't find on the wall. It occurred in New York in 1991 when I spotted the actor Gabriel Byrne sitting at the other side of a bar I was in. I had never had a proper chat with him before but was a fan of his work so I walked up to him to say hello. After greeting me, he embraced me in a big hug and said, "Ah sure jaysus, wasn't I reared on Bottler!"

He asked me why I was in New York and when I explained I was performing a show that night, he said he would come along. Sure enough, come nine o'clock he turned up at the venue. During the course of the evening, I announced to the audience that he was there which in hindsight probably wasn't the smartest thing for an entertainer to do, because naturally the crowd's attention leaves the stage and focuses on the star. Following the show however, we were enjoying a few pints when we suddenly decided to go to Eamon Doran's pub. Close by, there was a horse and trap which carried tourists around Central Park so we decided to avail of that particular mode of transport rather than trying to hail a cab. The person controlling the horse was a girl with a shaven head and looked absolutely identical to the singer Sinead O'Connor. They were so alike that I actually had to ask Gabriel if Sinead O'Connor had taken on a second job. As it happens he too had seen her before and reckoned she was a double for Sinead. Naturally, she immediately recognised Gabriel and was delighted to have him as her passenger.

As we were trotting along Park Avenue on our way to Doran's pub, Gabriel suddenly spotted a deli. Without hesitation, he asked the Sinead look-a-like to pull the horse over to one side for a moment while he ran over and bought a few things. It was priceless. Even now I can't but laugh when I picture Gabriel Byrne and myself on the back of a horse and cart in the middle of New York with a Sinead O'Connor look-a-like at the reigns. When we arrived at Eamon Doran's pub, four lads from the Wolfe Tones were already inside. As Paddy Reilly lives in New York, I'm pretty sure he was there as well. Doran's isn't a B&B but that didn't stop us from staying there for the night. Gabriel and I didn't keep in touch after that but it was still such a lovely experience to meet someone like him and find out that even though he's a regular on the Hollywood scene, he's still one of the lads and a Dubliner through and through.

Another night I enjoyed in New York is one I know Michael Flatley will remember just as vividly. After I had finished performing my show, Michael and I were enjoying a few beers when on the spur of the moment, he decided to introduce me to Prince Albert of Monaco. We made our way to the hotel where the prince was staying, indulging in a singing session as we walked the streets of New York. When we reached the hotel, Michael went to approach Prince Albert, but before Michael could say anything, the prince spotted me and immediately said, "Ah Brendan, how are you? It's great to see you!"

Brian Keane, my manager and constant companion.

In Kilkenny with the Great Cats.

My concert promotion manager, Tom Kelly, smiling at another full house!

The Dubs v Kerry.

To mark my number one hit, Combine Harvester, a pictorial tribute from my friend Ray Kennedy.

Meeting fans in Thurles.

An audience with his Grace in Thurles.

Chatting with a fan in Thurles.

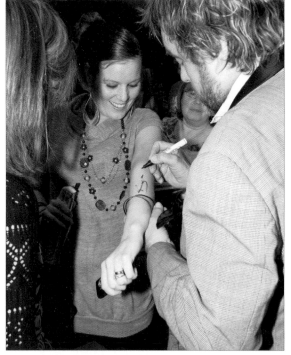

Making my mark in Ballinasloe.

Grace, You're Amazing.

I made him
laugh My Way.

Having a pint of Guinness with the man who brewed it
for forty years – Eileen's dad Paddy Doyle.

A great night out in Kilkenny!

Nun better than me old pal Joe.

With my biographer, the lovely Tara King.

The original Irish film star – Maureen O'Hara – on her birthday, at my show in Killarney. Now there's a real legend.

OIFIG RÚNAÍ AN UACHTARÁIN
BAILE ÁTHA CLIATH 8

OFFICE OF THE SECRETARY TO THE PRESIDENT
DUBLIN 8

27 January, 2003

Brendan & Eileen Grace
17286 SE Galway Ct
Jupiter
Florida 33469
U.S.A.

Dear Mr. & Mrs Grace,

President McAleese has asked me to thank you most sincerely for your Video and for the get well card which were recently presented to her.

The President is recovering well and will be trying to get back to a full work schedule as soon as possible.

The President greatly appreciates your thoughtfulness in writing and sends her good wishes to you both and all the members of the family.

Yours sincerely,

Mary O'Donnell

Mary O'Donnell
Secretariat

My son-in-law, Frank Gillespie, my friend, Ricey Scully, and my political adviser, An Taoiseach Brian Cowen.

He remembered me from when I had performed corporate gigs for his father in Monaco. I think Michael was stunned by our friendship as he wasn't aware that we had previously met. It gave him a good laugh though.

Around the time I released my second record "Liberty Boy" which went on to become a hit, Eileen and I met Eddie and Kay Sweeney. As well as being neighbours, Eddie and Kay were very close friends of ours and while I didn't have many nights off due to working commitments, whenever I did have a night free I always made sure the four of us would hit the town and give it a good lash. We had always wanted to dine in Dublin's famous Mirabeau restaurant, even just the once, so we decided on a date that we would go there and started saving a few months in advance so that we could afford it. This particular restaurant, which was a favourite haunt of Charlie Haughey's, held the reputation of being Ireland's most expensive restaurant. In fact it was known for not having a price list beside the items on the menu. You only found out what your food cost when the bill arrived. On the night in question, we were enjoying our meal when Eddie spotted Charlie Haughey at a nearby table. At the time, I knew of Charlie but didn't know him personally. Some time later, when we received the bill for our meal, it was so expensive that Eddie took one look at it and said, "I think we're after paying for Charlie's meal as well!"

We were aghast by the amount. I think Eileen and Kay nearly cried with the shock they got, but in a way we were expecting it to be the price it was as we had been drinking champagne. It was a huge thrill to be there however, so it was worth every penny.

A Liberty boy like myself, Eddie was extremely fun orientated and he absolutely loved meeting people like Red Hurley, The Wolfe Tones and Joe Dolan. The four of us would also go on trips to America together and during one such holiday in Las Vegas, we met various stars including the singer Neil Sedaka. During this same holiday, we went on a tour of the Hollywood homes. One of the houses we made a point of seeing was that of Eddie's idol, Englebert Humperdink. As we were driving down Hollywood Boulevard we noticed a fabulous looking Rolls Royce Convertible Convertible coming towards us. As it got closer we realised it was actually Englebert himself who was driving and needless to say, we all screamed, "Jaysus it's yer man Englebert."

Immediately I performed a u-turn and drove straight after him. A short distance up the road he was waiting at traffic lights, so we pulled up beside him and Eddie, in a strong Dublin accent, shouted out, "Ingle-bert, we're from Ireland," while putting his hand out the window for a handshake. Naturally Englebert at first seemed very bemused by the whole thing, but was more than delighted to oblige. For Eddie that alone was the equivalent of winning the lottery. For a celebrity of his distinction, he wasn't stand offish in the slightest. In fact, once he heard we were from Ireland, he spoke about how he often played in Dublin. To think, this was all taking place in the middle of the road while we were waiting for the lights to change. Sadly Eddie passed away in 2005 and it goes without saying we all miss him greatly. We are still in contact with Kay and there are several photographs of her and Eddie on the wall of the pub. One such picture is of the four of us standing beside a helicopter.

I was always fascinated by helicopters. I don't know how this interest in aircraft was first inspired but it was always present and no doubt further influenced by my friendship with Ciarán Haughey, who was and still is a major helicopter enthusiast. I am a qualified helicopter pilot. I completed the aviation course in 1980, which at the time was a very unusual thing to do. There was only one training pilot in Ireland at the time and as it transpired, I had to hire a former RAF pilot from the UK to teach me.

I can still remember the first time I flew the helicopter on my own and even more vivid in my memory is that I nearly destroyed myself with the nerves. Each time I had flown, the pilot was always beside me and for some reason it just never occurred to me that I would one day have to go up on my own. On one occasion however, he stepped out of the helicopter, lit up a cigarette, and then looking at me, gestured his hands towards the helicopter as though to say, "Off you go."

I don't know how I didn't collapse there and then. It turned out to be a tremendous experience and afterwards, all I could feel was a great mixture of adrenaline and pure fright. After overcoming that first flight, I was at ease flying on my own and went on to acquire my full flying license. When, in later years, I bought a helicopter, the only person who would never set foot inside it was Eileen's mother Lillie. When we lived in Saggart there was a forest beside us and I used to have her convinced that I would trim the trees by flying the helicopter upside down. Honest to jaysus she actually believed me!

My manager Brian who always had a great interest in aviation subsequently became a qualified helicopter pilot and he, along with the trainer Barry Mooney, were always on hand to accompany me on my air trips around Ireland. It's not that they didn't trust me as a pilot but rather I didn't trust me as a pilot. The apple definitely didn't fall far from the tree as my son Brad also completed his helicopter course. Another man who spent countless hours in the air with me is my long-time friend and helicopter pilot extraordinaire Captain John Barnicle. A former Vietnam pilot, he displayed the most amazing skills, the likes of which I only ever associated with action movies. Funnily enough, even though I have no problem flying a helicopter, I cannot stomach heights. Whenever I visit the Cliffs of Moher I have to stay way back from the edge. If I even see someone standing close to the brink of the cliff, I have to turn away because I just can't bear it. I know another helicopter pilot who also has a fear of heights and gets nervous even climbing a ladder.

For me however, "going up" is no problem, it's the "coming down" part that is another issue altogether. I mentioned earlier in the book how at eight years of age, I climbed up the plinth of the Wellington monument in the Phoenix Park. Of course I thought I was great altogether, until I realised I had to climb back down. Several people, including the fire brigade, had to be called and eventually they managed to coax me down the ladder. I always pinpointed that incident as the start of my descending fear but while I was writing this book, my cousin Shelia informed me that during my holidays in Dunlavin as a child, I would regularly climb up onto the roof of a shed but would be too terrified to make my way back down! I don't know if I still have the fear, because to be honest I haven't climbed up anything to find out. Even though I have this fear of heights, I have absolutely no problem flying a helicopter or sitting in an airplane and looking down thousands of feet. In saying that however, I don't think I could ever endure a paraglide. It's something I would love to do because I can only imagine that it must be the most exhilarating feeling to just run off Dún Aengus on Inis Mór and fly into the air and down into the valleys. In fact charities regularly ask me to participate in parachute jumps but there's just no way I could ever put my nerves through something like that. God knows I already put them through enough. The experts would probably advise that I face my fear, but to be completely honest, I am quite happy keeping my back turned to it. Unless of course the parachute has an engine and a comfortable seat attached, then I might consider facing my fear. My friend Aengus McAnally is in fact an expert in this field as he has admirably clocked up many parachute jumps for charities.

Getting back to the photographs in the pub however, one particular picture which many hone in on is that of me wearing a stetson while standing beside Larry Hagman better known as JR Ewing. He was utterly larger than life. Everything about his persona and image was JR. He completely lived the part and meeting him was a phenomenal experience. I also once met Larry's fellow Dallas actor, Howard Keele. With him I enjoyed a great chat and he gave me a great insight into the show.

Every picture on the wall of the pub has a personal story or memory attached, however one more so than any other carries with it a story capable of inducing as many smiles as it does tears. This black and white photograph, which features me with a smiling friend, is positioned on the wall by the lounge door and every single time I enter the pub, I look towards the corner where this one photograph sits.

At a glance, it looks no different to the other pictures. However, anyone familiar with the events of 7 June 1996 would instantly recognise the man standing beside me in the picture.

It's my wonderful friend, the late Jerry McCabe.

thirteen

When Detective Ben O'Sullivan received his first Scott medal
for bravery, there was a ceremony in Templemore followed by an
after party in the Garda Club in Limerick. As a surprise for Ben,
Jerry arranged for Brendan to be collected from where he had been
performing in Gort. When Brendan walked into the Garda Club that
day, Ben was so incredibly thrilled by the surprise. In fact, you should
have seen the smile on Jerry's face when the surprise guest walked
in. Brendan's joke that day was, "If McCabe had brains he'd be
dangerous!" It became a running joke between the two of them after
that. When Jerry died, Brendan travelled all the way from Florida
to Ireland especially for his funeral. I found out afterwards that he
had decided to walk behind the coffin, but obviously hadn't realised
the length of distance from the church to the graveyard. It was over
an hour's walk and shortly after we began the journey, the sole of his
shoe came off. I'm sure the running joke between himself and Jerry
must have entered his mind when that happened.

Ann McCabe

The Bleakest Day of '96

There is a beautiful quote that goes: "A smile happens in a flash but its memory can last a lifetime."

This is precisely how I remember Detective Garda Jerry McCabe. Always smiling, always laughing, always trying to help someone in whatever way he could.

Both he and his detective partner Ben O'Sullivan were the most good natured men you could meet. I used to call the two of them Laurel and Hardy. Ben was always telling jokes while Jerry might be carrying a minor summons in his pocket which someone had given him to quash. We first came to know each other through a mutual friend from Limerick, Keith Lancaster. He was good buddies with them and whenever I travelled from Dublin to the Greenhills Hotel in Limerick to meet Keith and have a few drinks with him, Jerry and Ben were often among the friends he would bring along.

I had always possessed a huge admiration for the gardaí, so I was delighted to be in their company and we hit it off from the moment we met. We enjoyed several nights out, but for me one night in particular will always stand out.

I had been out drinking with Keith and his friends and on occasion throughout the night Jerry and Ben would drop by for a brief chat as they were on duty.

At the end of the night, I had a hankering for fish and chips so Jerry decided to put me in the back of the squad car and drive me into Limerick to a chipper which was open late. I got my bag of chips and hopped back into the squad car but when we arrived back at the hotel, I had no way of getting in as the front door was locked and the night porter was nowhere to be found. I don't think Ben and I ever laughed as much as when Jerry got on the radio to Henry Street garda station to ask them to phone the Greenhills Hotel and tell them to open the door as we were locked out. In fairness, his plan worked because thirty seconds later, we could hear the phone ringing in the reception area followed by someone running to open the door for us.

I had already made the move to America by this point so Jerry asked me if I would keep an eye out for a particular type of gun holster over there. It was the kind that went under the arm and over the shoulder. The gardaí had different types of holsters but Jerry wanted this particular one so I told him I'd find it for him. A close friend of mine in America, Burt Rubenstein, is a captain of the police, so I explained to him what I was looking for and sure enough he managed to acquire it for me. When I met Jerry in the Greenhills Hotel some weeks later, I surprised him with the exact leather holster he had wanted. I swear to God, he was so thrilled with it that his reaction was akin to a child who had received a dozen Easter eggs along with their Christmas and birthday presents all at once.

Jerry was a character like no other. There was a book in him alone. He was also known for his blessed hands. He was one of those gifted people who could fix anything from an electric shaver to a bus engine. He was so mechanically minded, it was almost unreal.

Whenever I was performing gigs in Dublin, I would usually just stay at our house in Saggart which we had held onto even though we had moved to Florida. One particular Friday morning, I was due to catch a flight back to America so I woke early to get on the road to Shannon. Even though Dublin is closer, I always use Shannon airport. While Dublin is a fine facility, it's too hectic.

That Friday morning, as I was preparing to leave for Shannon, I switched on the news and heard that there had been an incident in Adare, county Limerick. The bulletin revealed that a post office robbery had been foiled and that, in the resulting melée, two gardaí had been shot, one of them fatally. The moment I heard it, I felt physically sick because I knew that, as armed detectives, it was part of Jerry and Ben's duty to accompany the vehicles delivering cash to post offices. No names had been mentioned in the bulletin so I phoned my Limerick friend Keith Lancaster only to discover he was in Spain on holidays. I prayed the bulletin was wrong but something inside me felt hugely uneasy. I began the drive to Shannon with my mind constantly replaying the detail of the news report. When I reached the crossroads in Saggart I spotted two gardaí sitting in an unmarked car. I pulled the car to a halt and figured I would chance asking them about the shooting. After introducing myself, I explained that I had heard about the incident in Adare and was wondering if the garda detectives involved were Ben O'Sullian and Jerry McCabe. They said yes, and when I asked which one of them had been fatally wounded, they told me it was Jerry. They then explained that Ben had also been shot and was being treated in hospital. After thanking them for their help, I returned to the car, completely shattered by the news. I don't know how I drove all the way to Shannon after that, because the shock left me in a daze for the entire journey.

However shocked I was then was nothing compared to how I felt when I learned of the circumstances surrounding the incident. I discovered that Jerry had been shot at point blank range while sitting in the passenger seat of the car. It was a callous act that had been carried out in cold blood and nothing less. I returned to Florida that day but I was absolutely devastated. I couldn't sleep and went through a very hard time. I can't even begin to imagine how Ann and the children coped.

Eileen had also known Jerry very well and was equally as affected as I was by the news. Keith told me about the funeral arrangements which were scheduled to take place the following Monday. From the moment I set foot on the plane that Friday morning, I couldn't relax. I had to get back to Ireland.

I arrived into Shannon airport the following Monday morning at 8.30am in time for the 10.30am mass. I was still very much in shock and to be honest I don't think the impact of the two shootings had fully set in, even at that point. Burt Rubenstein, who had met Jerry once and had given me the gun holster for him, travelled over especially for the funeral. On the day of the funeral, I remember asking Keith if he had seen Ben. That's when he told me that Ben was still in hospital and under armed guard for fear of reprisal. No one was allowed in to see Ben but one of the detectives knew I was friends with him and kindly offered to bring me in. Following the funeral, I accompanied the detective to the hospital. It was absolutely heartbreaking to see Ben that day.

He was built like a tank and as an experienced garda, he had seen it all, but on that particular day, he shed many tears.

He told me how he had emerged from the car to give chase when he was hit with a bullet. Jerry wasn't even out of the car when they suddenly turned the gun on him. His hand was still in his pocket which reveals just how little a threat he posed to the raiders. That day in the hospital, Ben was inconsolable over what had happened. I was hugely concerned about his health. He was on a drip and nowhere near being back to full health and yet he had to somehow deal with the unbearable grief that accompanies the loss of a partner and best friend.

I can't imagine how difficult it must have been for him when a newspaper carried a front page photograph of Jerry sitting in the passenger seat just after he had been shot dead. My first reaction was that of total abhorrence. I felt physically sick by the sight of it and immediately became concerned for Jerry's widow, Ann, and her kids. Fortunately, the McCabe family were already prepared as they had agreed to the release of the photo. They felt it served as a stark reminder of what those IRA raiders did that morning. They were right. What happened in Adare on 7 June 1996 was sheer brutality and should never be forgotten.

I was subsequently told that when Jerry was shot, he hadn't even had time to take out his gun. The holster it was sitting in was the very same one I had surprised him with. Some time after the funeral, his wife Ann gave me the holster and said Jerry would have liked me to have had it, however I told her it had been my present to Jerry and that I now wanted her to keep it as a token of how much he had loved his job.

In 2000, Ben was awarded the Gold Scott Medal for bravery while a posthumous Scott Medal for bravery was presented to Jerry's wife. My own family and I were in attendance at the ceremony that day and it was without doubt one of the saddest occasions I have ever witnessed.

I still keep in touch with Ann McCabe from time to time. Two of her sons are gardaí and are an absolute credit to both Jerry and herself.

Even after all these years, I still find it very difficult when Jerry's anniversary approaches and every single time I walk into the pub, my eyes automatically travel over to the photograph of the two of us together. When someone close to you is murdered, I don't think it's possible to truly comprehend or overcome the loss. For the McCabe family and Ben O'Sullivan, it must have been particularly difficult considering there were times when Jerry's photograph was rarely out of the media. I would say Jerry's smile, now forever stitched in the worn fabric of time, is as recognisable as his name. Every time there was a shoot out, his picture accompanied the article, almost serving as a reminder to people of the dangerous job the gardaí have. Over a decade later, it continues to occur and while I can understand why the media chooses to use his photograph, I do still feel for his family and Ben every time it appears.

Likewise my heart goes out to the Guerin and Turley families every time the photograph of Veronica appears in the pages of a newspaper. She was murdered in her car just a few weeks after Jerry's life was taken from him. I wouldn't say I knew Veronica well. Eileen and I met her on one occasion when we were seated beside her and Graham at a wedding. I remember her being incredibly chatty and overall just one of the lads. We were beyond shocked when news of her death emerged.

Anything to do with crime and violence, whether it be paramilitary or gangland is, in my opinion, one of the greatest pests to society. Families are hit with needless grief and devastation and all because of someone else's actions. Jerry was a good man and a dear friend, and frankly, his life wasn't near long enough.

fourteen

Father Dougal McGuire *(talking about Fr Fintan Stack)*: *"God Ted, I've never met anyone like him. Who would he be like – Hitler or one of those mad fellas?"*
Father Ted Crilly: *"Oh, worse than Hitler. You wouldn't find Hitler playing jungle music at 3 o'clock in the morning."*

Father Ted, Season Two, Episode Nine – New Jack City

Fate Ordained... as Fr Fintan Stack

Over the last four decades I have spent God knows how many thousands of hours touring every inch of the country performing comedy gigs and singing songs, and yet there are still a certain generation of people who know me only from the eight minutes I performed in an episode of Fr Ted.

Fans of the show often quote the character of Fr Fintan Stack line by line to me and have even gone so far as to put me on the phone to one of their friends, not as Brendan Grace mind you, but as Fr Stack. I'm often asked to snarl down the phone the infamous line from the show: "While you were out, I got the keys to your car and drove it into a big wall and if you don't like it, tough! I've had my fun, and that's all that matters."

If there were any passers-by who were not that familiar with Fr Ted quotes then I don't want to even guess what they must have thought of me if they overheard what I was saying.

To sum up Fr Stack for those who are not *au fait* with the show, he's an appalling member of the clergy who is sent to Craggy Island to replace Fr Jack after Jack contracts the hairy hands syndrome and is sent to Saint Clobbert's for treatment. The audition for the role, which was held in Dublin's Burlington Hotel, attracted a large variety of actors, all of whom possessed far more acting experience than I did. There were so many well known faces waiting to audition that it was like a "Who's Who" of the Irish acting industry. It was quite intimidating to see the standard of actors I was up against.

When I walked into the room to read for the part, I was greeted by the creators of Fr Ted, Graham Linehan and Arthur Matthews, as well as a few people from Channel 4. They gave me a verbal rundown of the Fintan Stack character and explained that he was very loud and vociferous by nature. When I heard this description, something told me that all the actors who auditioned before me would probably have shouted and roared their lines. I also figured that they would have delivered a much better impression of loud anger than anything I was capable of, so instead I elected to lower the volume of the character and pump up his level of attitude. Rather than roaring the lines, I just voiced them with an air of gross sarcasm. To top it all off, I accompanied it with a sly, sleazy bastard-esque smile. My line of thinking at the time was that considering how much of a madman Fr Jack is, the character of Fr Stack might have more impact if he was quieter and more sarcastic. Fortunately, it worked.

His voice alone was enough to sour milk, but unfortunately I can't take full credit for his distinctive drawl. When I auditioned for the role, the persona I exhibited was partly that of a teacher I once had in school. The man in question used to talk in a slow sarcastic tone of voice, all while wearing a smile on his face. It often occurred to me afterwards that if he had become a priest instead of a teacher, there would be a real life Fr Stack up on the altar somewhere. Would you believe, however, that Fr Stacks voice was also partially inspired by the great pianist Liberace? When I met him in Las Vegas some years back, the one thing I noticed about him was how he used to talk slowly through a smile and say things like: "I'm the greatest entertainer in the world." It was hilarious, but I knew it would work in a different way for the character of Fr Stack. After I had delivered my lines in the audition room, the reaction was instant. The panel looked at each other, closed the file and said, "That's our Fr Stack."

When it came to recording the episode, I spent a memorable week in London with Dermot Morgan, Ardal O'Hanlon, Pauline McGlynn and Frank Kelly. Part of the storyline with Fr Stack is that he develops the hairy hands syndrome. It took the make up department over an hour to attach the hair to my wrists and hands, and while it was on, it was highly unpleasant. I couldn't do anything while the hair was in place and there was so much glue involved that it felt absolutely horrendous. Apart from that however, my time on the set was amazing. Unfortunately, I never had the opportunity to become acquainted with the real Dermot. I felt like he was always in character and that we never really had the opportunity to meet the man behind the performer.

While Fr Ted without doubt proved very beneficial to my career, at the time I was worried it would result in the opposite effect. An aspect of the Fr Stack character that really bothered me was the level of sleaziness he possessed, which, ironically, was mainly as a result of the tone of voice I had given him. There was also an element of vulgarity which further added to the character's sordid side. For instance, in one of the scenes, Fr Stack implies that three of the priests are thinking lurid thoughts.

While on the one hand it was an incredibly funny line and gave everyone a good laugh, it was also a line that gave me great cause for concern as I felt it wasn't the style I had become known for. I was particularly apprehensive that maybe long-term fans of my comedy would be offended by my use of such vulgarity, particularly while in the character of a priest. Equally as worried was my daughter Melanie. She felt that some of Fr Stack's lines could perhaps damage my reputation as a clean comedian. As an actor herself, she knew that you could spend several years establishing your name and that all it would take was one wrong move to bring about the demise of a career. My colleague Twink on the other hand was delighted I had taken the role. Her view on the whole situation was that a performer should always take the risks and welcome the challenges, and above all, step out of the box in which the public sees him in. She was right. It turned out that the viewers of the episode found it hilarious and as a result of the character's reputation, a return to Craggy Island was imminent.

The writers told me afterwards that they had found the character so different and popular that they were planning to make Fr Stack a regular. Of all the priests that had been on the show, he was the only person ever to scare the bejaysus out of Fr Jack Hackett. Due to this, the writers came up with the idea for future episodes that once word would arrive that Fr Stack was due on the island, Jack would be totally out of sorts beforehand. It would have worked beautifully, but it wasn't to be. Shortly after that particular series of Fr Ted, Dermot Morgan suffered a heart attack and passed away. When Dermot died, the series died with him and rightly so. No one could have played Fr Ted like he did.

Even though my involvement in the series spanned just one episode, there are some people who know me only as Fr Stack. I remember on one occasion in Boston, as I was walking along the street, two guys were walking towards me. They were looking at me as though they recognised me so I just assumed they were Irish. They didn't say anything when we passed but it must have played on their minds because they ended up running all the way back up the street to talk to me. Excusing themselves, they told me my face was very familiar to them and asked me who I was. I explained I was an entertainer from Ireland, and with that came the excited reply, "Jesus, it's that guy Fr Stack."

As it turned out, they weren't Irish, but American born and bred.

The impact of Fr Stack was overwhelming and while it may have been a risky career move, overall I'm quite proud of the character, mostly because he scared the bejaysus out of Fr Jack Hackett.

I have many good friends in the priesthood and fortunately our friendships weren't tainted by my alter ego on Fr Ted. If anything they enjoyed the harmless humour of it.

Likewise, they weren't offended by the comedy routine I created about St Francis, the patron saint of birds and animals. It was a hilarious act but in a way it was connected to my own life. I do believe in reincarnation and, as such, am convinced that some people return in a different life form. While some have to wait and see what they come back as, I think I already know in advance. I genuinely believe I am going to return as a robin. My family on the other hand believe I already was a bleedin' bird. Even though robins are not the friendliest, they will always walk right up to me no matter where I am. Whenever this occurs, I always feed them. Any time I am in a restaurant, be it in America or Ireland, I will take whatever bread is left on the table and place it in a serviette to later throw out to the birds. Crumbs and all. The way I see it, a crumb is a meal to a robin. Half a nut is probably food for three days. The kids tease me relentlessly about it but we'll see who's laughing when I return as a bird and the droppings start landing.

You don't see stray dogs or cats these days, but years ago I couldn't pass a stray without bringing it home. We only lived in a flat at the time and I would often arrive home with a dog. These days however, if I see a stray, I immediately look for a shop where I can buy a tin of dog food for it. There was one occasion when I was travelling through Waterford and spotted two donkeys looking out over a gate, so I went into the town and bought a bag of carrots and then returned to feed them.

Given how I used this interest in animals as part of a St Francis comedy routine, more often than not, when I listen to a joke, I find myself wondering just how much of it came from a real incident experienced by the person behind the comedian persona. Most of the stories I tell on stage are based on exaggerated versions of real life. Anyone who knows my show is aware that I slag the absolute bejaysus out of the mother-in-law. I tell the crowd that if she were in India she'd be sacred, at which point I would then pretend to look over at her and shout, 'go on ya aul cow ya'. The reality however is that my late mother-in-law Lillie had an incredibly sweet nature and was the complete opposite to the person I had described on stage. What's more, Lillie was often in the audience while I regaled them with such elaborate stories about her. Likewise, on stage I would often speak about my missus Eileen as though she were a sumo wrestler. I would also go on about how she has damn all teeth and if you were to believe my description of her, you would think she was so ugly that she couldn't walk outside the front door. Of course, when I introduce them both to the audience at the end of the show, they see they are the complete opposite of what I described.

I'll never forget one particular gig I was playing in Dunmanway, county Cork during which I gave the mother-in-law the usual abuse. After the show, I introduced the crowd to both my wife and my mother-in-law. A short while later, a group of women approached Lillie, sat her down, and more or less apologised for the jokes I had told about her.

Eileen is often asked how she puts up with me and the jokes I make about her on stage but the truth is that she takes it all with a grain of salt. There is little I can say or do that will shock her these days. After all, when we first started going out together, I arrived to pick her up in a hired car because my own one was in the garage being painted a bright orange with flowers on the back. My brightly coloured chick magnet also had a phone. Unfortunately, however, the phone had no dial tone. When Eileen was in the car, I would press the buttons as though I were making a call to my sister Marie, however I would already have her side of the conversation taped beforehand. On the tape Marie would ask a question and then pause for a few seconds during which time I would answer. I would always have my answer rehearsed and it genuinely looked like a two way conversation was taking place when in fact I was just talking back to a hidden tape recorder.

When she introduced me to her parents, I was wearing a dark brown suede jacket and mustard bell bottoms with buttons all the way down. Eileen thought they were going to freak. Fortunately, they overlooked the dress sense and we developed a close friendship.

It's a good thing too, otherwise the stories behind those in-law gags may have had their very own real life origins.

fifteen

Brendan likes to borrow things. He buys his clothes from Louis Copeland and with great pride he would often open up the jacket to show the label "Tailored by Louis Copeland". There is a story however that Brendan was in Louis' shop one day and saw a box of "Louis Copeland" labels on the desk. It's reputed that he "borrowed" a few of the labels and had them sewn onto the clothes he bought in America – "Exclusively tailored by Louis Copeland". Brendan has a great sense of devilment like that.

I don't think many people realise that he is a wonderful singer and can pull off a great Elvis impression. The thing is, he will start off serious but by the end of the song everyone is rolling around laughing because it always turns into a parody or a skit. I may have seen Brendan perform over a hundred times in the last twenty years but there was never an occasion where I have not laughed. He is never the same; he's always different. I love the Father of the Bride act, particularly when he calls on the chef to come out and face them, and in reference to the brussels sprouts, adds, "I thought he had made a balls of the cabbage."

I know Brendan very well, but to this day, when he performs his drunk act, I cannot tell if it's just an act or whether he really has had a few jars. He does that act too bloody well.

Ronan Collins

Men, Check Yer Prostitute

Picture the scene. It's 1983 and spotlight night in the Stillorgan Park Hotel. Centre stage is Joe Dolan, belting out the tunes as only Joe could do. As far as he's concerned, the schedule for the night is straightforward; nothing he hasn't seen or done before. That is, of course, until two rather masculine looking nuns arrive into the dance room on the back of a 1300cc Kawasaki motorbike. Tearing up the dance floor, their next stop is centre stage beside the man himself.

When I look back on that night, the first thing that comes to mind is the comical look on Joe's face. He was speechless. After all, the roar of the Kawasaki as it entered the room was the first he knew of the surprise appearance of these two, incredibly ugly, butch looking nuns, aka Kevin Hough and yours truly. It was worth it, though, as I distinctly remember the crowd roaring louder than the Kawasaki itself when we decided to join "their Joe" for a quick song.

As part of the joke, I was wearing the most ridiculous looking set of teeth. They were custom-made dentures and looked as though they were too big for my mouth. I still use them in my act today and their origins do not stem from a joke shop but rather a dentist's surgery. Those teeth had to be specially made for me. Not many people know this but they were inspired by RTÉ's Mike Murphy. I've always had great admiration for Mike as a broadcaster but I never thought that the one time I would go to ask him for advice, it would be with regard to the kind of teeth he was wearing. Mike, as part of his hugely popular series, The Live Mike, would perform a variety of acts in which he sometimes wore false teeth as part of a disguise. These had been specially made for him and when I enquired, he graciously gave me the number of the man who had created them. I still often wonder if anyone overheard us discussing the pros and cons of dentures that night and what on earth they must have thought.

Anyway, I followed up Mike's contact and had the teeth made for use as part of my comedy priest act and later as part of my nun act: Sister Kawasaki and Sister Hairy O'Mara. I have even worn those big ridiculous looking teeth when out in public purely for the pleasure of witnessing the various reactions from people. I would wear a hat so no one would recognise me as "yer man from the television" but rather instead see me as a dentally challenged individual. I carried out a similar trick in several television interviews. During an interview with Bibi Baskin for example, she went to read her notes and as she was looking away, I threw the teeth in. When she looked up, she almost lost it she was laughing so much.

Gráinne Seoige encountered a similar fate when filming a live preview for her show early in the evening. As she was talking to the camera about what was coming up, I slipped in the teeth. When she looked over and saw me with a mouth full of enormous teeth staring back at her, the poor woman corpsed. In the theatre business, when one person deliberately does something to make the other person laugh, it's called "corpsing". Jack Benny, Bob Hope and Bing Cosby were past masters at corpsing. There were times during their television shows where you could tell the script had stopped and they had gone into auto-pilot, just setting each other up with a joke. Some actors despise it.

Personally, however, if someone makes me laugh, so be it. The way I see it, there are worse things that can happen to a person, like having the actor Colm Meaney beat you in auditions. I auditioned for Alan Parker's film *The Commitments* as well as the movie *Far and Away* which starred Tom Cruise and Nicole Kidman only to be beaten to the roles on both counts by Meaney. Any time I say his name now, I jokingly follow it with the words "the bastard", but to be honest he seems to be great craic. If he wasn't such a bloody good actor as well, I might have stood a chance at winning those two roles. One film role I did manage to keep from him was that of Murphy in *Moondance*.

Nuala Moiselle was the casting director who recommended me for the part and to this day I am grateful to her for giving me my first role in a movie. Having lived on a diet of Darby O'Gill for many years, it's fair to say I know every word of the script. As such, I want to make it clear in this book that if there is ever a remake of the film, I want an audition for the part of the leprechaun. I will even arrive with a fleet of understudies as my kids know the film line from line having each had childhoods in which their dad made them watch it repeatedly.

Regardless of how big a leap I make into the acting industry, my association will always lie with comedy. It's my trademark, although if my good friend, the broadcaster Ronan Collins, is to be believed, my trademark is in fact one I share with Louis Copeland – funeral attendance. Ronan, along with a number of other friends, is convinced that Louis and I are the two people most spotted at funerals. Christy Moore's trademark on the other hand is his t-shirt, so much so that we always call him "a storm in a t-shirt".

Dickie Rock's trademark is now the stuff of industry legend. Once you get a name in showbiz it sticks as nicely as the proverbial to a cow's backside, and poor Dickie knows this only too well. Back in 2002, I, along with a number of other Irish entertainers, participated in a charity golf function. Some of the names that took to the course that day included Ronan Collins, Finbar Furey, Red Hurley, and Paddy Cole. I was to be on a team with Ronan, Paddy, and Dickie Rock but Dickie never showed up on the day. He has a reputation in the business for being as tight as tuppence and because of this, a joke made its way around the group that he hadn't bothered turning up because he had heard he would have to buy a drink.

There's a funny story that when Dickie's kids were small, he managed to get his hands on triple glazing even though double glazing itself had only just been introduced to the market. The joke goes that he hadn't bought it for its insulation value, but rather so that his kids wouldn't be able to hear the Mr Whippy van when it would pull up outside. The great thing about Dickie is that he has a wonderful sense of humour. Admittedly, it doesn't help the poor man's case when his own friends tell the Mr Whippy story, and believe me when I say we *continuously* give him a hard time about his reputation, but true to form, he always takes it on the chin. To be honest, Dickie was wise with his money, it's just unfortunate that his financial approach has landed him with an undesirable reputation.

Dickie and I were both managed at one stage by Connie Lynch. During his career, Connie managed major entertainment acts and was responsible for bringing about the legendary "B&L". Everyone has heard of B&B's but Connie introduced the concept of B&L's. The "Bed and Breakfast" deal never worked for showband musicians because their shows finished so late that they would never be up on time the following morning. With this in mind, Connie managed to convince the hotels to agree to a "Bed and Lunch" deal. As well as being a remarkable manager, Connie, who is a very good friend of mine, also possessed a wacky sense of humour which is something I absolutely love in people. Another character who had it was a Tralee man by the name of Nedeen Kelleher. Just like Brendan Coffey in Galway, Nedeen was a loyal fan who would always come along to see me perform whenever I was playing locally. Nedeen was known and loved by The Dubliners, Red Hurley, The Wolfe Tones, Joe Dolan, Brendan Shine, The Fureys as well as myself. Any time we were in Tralee, he would take us out for a jaunt on his horse and cart. We used to get great fun out of him by winding him up with our questions about the difference between a ginnit, an ass and a donkey. There were hundreds of jarvies in Killarney but Nedeen was the only one in Tralee which was probably why so many tourists remember him so fondly. I could almost bet that those tourists were all brought by Nedeen to the same pub in Blennerville. What they probably didn't know was that Nedeen somehow had his ginnit trained never to pass this particular pub. No matter who was on the cart, once the ginnit was outside this pub, it would stop. It was like the scene from *The Quiet Man* when Barry Fitzgerald was on the pony and trap and when he would arrive at Cohen's Bar, the pony would stop. He would then turn around and say to his passenger, "Jaysus I've a shocking thirst."

Nedeen used to say this exact same line and straight away the lads and I would all hop off and go inside for a drink.

One day, after enjoying a few drinks with Nedeen, we went back outside where the ginnit was waiting. Nedeen was in the bathroom, so the drummer, Joe McCarthy, who is better known as Joe Mac, decided to detach the cart from the ginnit. Opening a nearby gate into a field, Joe led the ginnit into the field before reattaching the cart to the ginnit through the bars of the gate. When he was finished, it looked like the ginnit had climbed through the gate but was now stuck because of the cart. When Nedeen arrived out and saw the ginnit on one side of the gate and the cart on the other, the poor man hadn't a clue what was going on. Of course, Joe tried his best to convince him that the ginnit had climbed though the bars of the gate. Nedeen had a few drinks on him at this stage so he was almost beginning to believe Joe. We were falling around the place laughing and even just writing this, it brings a smile to my face when I think of Nedeen standing there trying to figure out how the bloody hell his ginnit had made its way through the bars of the gate.

Nedeen was an unforgettable character. He was funny even when he wasn't trying to be. For instance, there was one occasion when, during a show I was performing in the Brandon Hotel in Tralee, I could hear a strange noise. It got to the point where I actually had to stop the show to see what it was and that's when I realised it was Nedeen snoring, asleep in the front row.

Anyone familiar with my comedy routines will know that I often perform a *seanchaí* act. This I learned from the original of the species, the late Eamon Kelly, and the act met with his approval too. For this, I dress up in an old hat and coat with bailing twine in place of a belt. When it comes to adopting the country accent, I always base it on Nedeen Kelleher. In fact, whenever I perform an act in which I have to speak in a strong country accent, it's Nedeen's voice I'm mimicking.

This was a technique I learned and developed from the great Irish actor and singer/songwriter Joe Lynch, who played Dinny in Glenroe. He and I first met through Eddie Downey's clinic in the Montrose Hotel. Jesus, Joe could talk for Ireland. Whenever we were in the sauna for instance, he would be regaling us with the most unbelievable stories. Even though he is best remembered for his role in Glenroe, Joe had been involved in a large variety of productions, some of which required very different accents from him. I have seen Joe converse in a variety of dialects and it always seemed effortless. It was as though he could take off any brogue with the greatest of ease. Even when he was playing the role of Dinny, you only ever heard the Wicklow accent in his voice and never his natural Cork tone.

Adopting an accent for a role may appear relatively simple but it is actually quite difficult. We have all watched films where a Hollywood actor is performing a role in an Irish accent but yet, despite his or her past blockbuster successes, they can't seem to grasp something seemingly as straightforward as an accent. In order for it to be convincing, certain words have to be delivered differently and then of course there is the whole area of diction. However, while all these details are important in their own right, there is one particular trick I learned from Joe that rarely fails. He and I started discussing accents one day when I asked him how he managed to always remember the exact accent to use. That's when he told me that the only way he could do it was to think of someone else who spoke in that particular accent. He would simply imitate them. Joe's character in Glenroe also had to walk with a limp, which is harder than it sounds when you don't physically have a limp. Joe would think of someone he knew who had a limp and he would imitate them. He would channel a particular person through whatever character he was playing. I did the same with my *seanchaí* character. I would think of Nedeen and channel the accent and gestures he had. Likewise, whenever I perform my routine of the Yank coming home to Ireland, I use the voice of either my American friend Bert Rubenstein or my Aunt Wyn's husband, Uncle Bud. My Father of the Bride skit is a combination of the actor Brendan Caldwell, the comedian Bob Newhart and my father. There are traits they possessed which I incorporated into the act.

Sadly, Nedeen passed away around 15 years ago. On the day of his funeral, a large contingent of well known singers and performers travelled to say their last goodbyes. His wake was the way he would have wanted it – an absolute hooley. When the mass was over, we all carried his coffin out to the hearse. This particular hearse had two seats each side of the coffin and was like nothing I had seen before or since. Myself, Ronnie Drew, Paddy Reilly and Finbar Furey sat into the four seats beside the coffin. We felt it was an honour to have been asked to walk behind the coffin however it was an even greater honour to have been asked to accompany the coffin in the hearse. After all, there was many a time when we enjoyed a journey with Nedeen on the ginnit and cart, so it was very moving that here we were with him on his final journey. On our way to the graveyard, we spoke to Nedeen and told jokes. While we were deeply saddened that he was no longer with us, we were determined his funeral wouldn't be a glum occasion because Nedeen was never once in his life a glum character. In the graveyard, we all participated in song. Finbar Furey played a beautiful tune on the tin whistle while I sang the Rose of Tralee. It was evident from the funeral alone that Nedeen was highly thought of in his home town and beyond. I still see his family every so often and I believe a memorial dedicated to Nedeen is soon to be constructed in the town of Tralee. Regardless of where in the world I may be at that time, I have every intention of flying home for the unveiling.

A good friend of mine who I mentioned earlier in the chapter is the drummer Joe Mac. Joe is the clown of showbusiness and someone I always thought should have been in comedy. I can honestly say he would definitely have made it as a comedian. Everyone knew him for his great sense of humour not to mention his legendary pranks. Some years back, a number of bands ended up staying in the same hotel in Bundoran and needless to say, we all got together for a session. At the time, Joe had a can of Andrew's Liver Salts with him which he emptied into the urinals so that when one of the lads would go to take a leak, the salts would start to bubble and froth. After a while, when one of the gang went to the jacks, Joe followed him out. I'm sure the lad in question was fretting by the sight of the fizzing until he looked over and saw Joe holding a can of Andrews and laughing hysterically. He would pull pranks like that which were hilarious. He had a similar sense of humour to my father, only Joe's was more madcap, particularly when we were all on the tear.

Whatever about alcohol poisoning, it never fails to amaze me that people in showbusiness back in those days haven't since died from cholesterol poisoning. We used to eat the greasiest food that we could possibly get our hands on. One of the places we would frequent was called Molly's on Richmond St in Dublin. You could go into Molly's late at night for a few drinks and more often than not you would see someone in there having a mixed grill. It definitely wasn't unusual to see someone falling asleep in the middle of cutting their chop or rasher. Even though their hands would have fallen away from the knife and fork, the cutlery would never fall as the amount of grease in the meat would hold them up. Today, however, I am incredibly conscious of my overall health.

Prostate cancer in particular is something that I try to remind men about whenever I can. I usually get the message across through a comedy routine in which I jokingly tell them to check their prostitute. It seems to work as several people have approached me about it, saying how they found it to be a novel way of getting the point across.

From what I'm told, prostate cancer is now more rampant in men than breast cancer is in women, however it's a very treatable disease if caught early. I have no qualms over admitting that I keep my "prostitute" checked. Every so often, I have the relevant tests carried out to ensure everything is as it should be.

For me the message really hit home when I heard Derek Mooney interview the RTÉ newsreader Michael Murphy on his radio show. As I was listening, what struck me most was how frank and honest Michael was about every aspect of his experience with prostate cancer. He exhibited a tremendous sense of courage and didn't shy away from discussing the process and what he went through. I was so moved by his words that I felt compelled to write to both Derek and Michael simply to thank them for highlighting the subject to the level in which they did. Derek later told me that he had been inundated with letters about the interview. Another man whose words stand out in my mind are those of Sonny Knowles. Sonny appeared on The Late Late Show about 15 years ago and spoke candidly to Gay about his time undergoing treatment for prostate cancer. I firmly believe that men like Sonny and Michael saved lives by speaking out about their experience. After all, their stories couldn't but have encouraged men to go for a check-up. I was already mindful of having health checks but it was refreshing to hear such well known personalities speak out about it. Men by their nature don't like talking about health problems, so interviews such as those really helped shed the taboo attached to conditions like prostate cancer.

As a broadcaster Michael Murphy had a wonderful personality and wit as did his fellow newsreader Maurice O'Doherty. During one bulletin, Maurice had to excuse himself as he couldn't stop laughing at the previous news item he had just reported. I think they went straight to the weather segment while Maurice tried to compose himself. I have heard many stories of the hilarious antics that go on during the ad breaks of news bulletins and how the anchors return with straight faces is something I will never figure out.

While our newsreaders may have to adopt a firm poker face for when they appear on our screens, one well-known personality whose face is rarely devoid of a smile is that of the famous tailor Louis Copeland. Having known his father, Louis Copeland Sr, I can say with full confidence that Louis inherited from his father not just that famous surname but his sense of humour as well. I often used to joke with Louis Sr about where he bought the suits that he himself wore. His reply was always: "Burtons". When I would ask why, he'd always shoot back with a smile, "Because I can't afford my own."

Ben Dunne is another man who always enjoyed a good joke, whether it be at his own expense or otherwise. I performed a number of corporate shows for him in the immediate weeks following the incident in Orlando where he was arrested after being found in a hotel room with a large quantity of cocaine. In one of the routines, I told the waiters from the stage to clear the white sugar from the tables along with anything that resembled a straw as Ben was in the room. Needless to say, my gag was greeted by a pregnant silence from the audience until they looked over at Ben's table and saw him almost breaking himself laughing at the gag. It's probably hard to believe but in 1991 I had Ben Dunne and Charlie Haughey at the same party in our house in Saggart. It wasn't intentional by any means, they were two good friends of mine so they were both on the invite list as it was a joint celebration for my daughter's confirmation, my nephew's baptism and my fortieth birthday.

A year later, Ben appeared in my house again, only this time he was on the television in my living room compliments of RTÉ news who were broadcasting scenes of him arriving into the airport from Orlando. The one thing that struck me about him was how he dealt with the situation. There were no crocodile tears, just genuine honesty. When he admitted his actions on television that evening, he gained so much respect that I'd say he could have run for the Irish presidency that year and would have won by a landslide.

About twenty years ago, my family and I were in Spain when we met Ben and his family who were staying in the same hotel as us. While our two families were at dinner together one evening, a number of Spanish musicians arrived in with guitars and began serenading the crowd. When they had finished their song, Ben got up and introduced me to the musicians as the Pavarotti of Ireland. They had broken English so Lord only knows what they thought he had said. Ben went on to ask them if they would give "Pavarotti" the guitar to play a song but I think they picked him up wrong as they responded by giving him directions to a karaoke bar. Ben, mad for some fun, took out a few hundred quid and asked them if they would sell the guitar to him. He ended up buying the guitar for me and as a result we enjoyed a memorable session of Irish ballads for the rest of the night. I didn't want to keep the guitar as I already had my own, so when we were finished, I gave it back to Ben who in turn gave it to the *maître d'* with the request that he return it to the musicians. He basically bought it for the night. Ben was always a good natured generous rogue like that, which is precisely why I don't believe him when he denies any involvement in the following incident.

There's a story about Ben that has never been confirmed but is widely accepted as fact. Seemingly, some years back, he was being driven to a meeting when a puncture occurred. Not only was his driver short of a wheel brace, but no one bothered to stop and help until some time later when a man pulled up alongside and offered his assistance. The driver of Ben's car explained their situation so the man took the wheel brace from his boot and changed the wheel for them. Ben went to give him a £50 note for his trouble, however the man, recognising Ben, refused to take it saying that it was an honour to have been of help to him. When that man woke up on Monday morning, he was informed that his mortgage had been paid. Ben never admitted it but to this day the man is convinced that Ben took note of his number plate, found out where he lived and cleared the man's mortgage. Ben still maintains a plea of no involvement but none of us believe him as it is very typical of him to be so modest.

Another man with a great sense of humour and a penchant for pranks was the late Ronnie Drew. One day, back in the seventies, Ronnie was sitting in the passenger seat of my car while I was driving along the South Circular Road.

As we were approaching the traffic lights on Leonard's Corner, he turned to me and asked me to slow down at the bus stop where there were a number of people waiting. Not passing any remark, I did as I was asked and brought the car to a halt. Next thing, Ronnie rolled down the window and of course everyone at the bus stop was staring at him because Ronnie quite possibly had the most recognisable face in Ireland. He honed in on one lady and in his distinctive Dublin brogue, asked her, "Do you know where Donore Avenue is?" The woman appeared to be so fascinated to be talking to Ronnie Drew that she only just about managed to get the words out of her mouth to explain that she wasn't familiar with the area and therefore didn't know where Donore Avenue was. At this point, Ronnie says back to her, "Well missus, you go up to the third turn on the right and that should take you to Donore Avenue." After we pulled off, Ronnie was breaking himself laughing in the passenger seat. His wit was as priceless as it was unpredictable.

A colleague of mine who shares my appreication of unpredictable wit is Adele King aka Twink. She and I are showbusiness's brother and sister. The first time we performed together was in a sketch for the Twink series many years back. The story behind the skit centered around me taking her to the debs but getting floored drunk as the night progressed. As part of the act, another character came over and asked if I would mind him dancing with Adele. At this point however, I decided to go off-script and replied, in the drunken state of my character, "no I wouldn't mind... provided you don't mind going home with a broken nose and your teeth in your arse pocket." Adele tried her best to keep in the laughter, however the face on the poor actor nearly dropped. My heart went out to him because the line wasn't scripted and so naturally he wasn't expecting it. The audience got agreat laugh out of it and to this day Adele and I still share a laugh over that one particular incident.

The amazing thing about comedy is that it can reveal a side to someone you never knew existed. If ever an incident exemplified this, it was the night I appeared on a talk show alongside Reverend Ian Paisley.

Prior to meeting him, I had conjured an image in my head as to the type of man I would be greeted by. I envisioned him to be a dominant individual and staunchly anti-Catholic. The reality couldn't have been more different as, upon introduction, I received from him a firm handshake followed by a few jokes and a laugh. At first, though, it seemed as though the atmosphere was going to be that of an entirely different nature. When Reverend Paisley entered the studio the first thing he said in his strong Northern drawl was, "I'm very, very disappointed." At this point, a few people nervously held their breath, wracking their brains trying to think what could possibly have gone wrong. The Reverend went on: "I really am very disappointed ... that there are no protesters."

There was a unanimous sigh of relief that the big man was joking.

The whole experience was phenomenal for me because I had always wanted to meet him. When it came to Reverend Paisley, my inquisitive nature always went into overdrive. He was a larger than life character and even though I didn't know a lot about the man behind the public persona, I was convinced he would be hugely interesting to talk to. My mother, on the other hand, was genuinely convinced he was the devil. In saying that, however, she could see the humour in him. Ma herself had a natural flair for comedy which often arose in the most unlikely of situations. For instance, when my mother couldn't find a shirt for my father one morning she placed a little white button into my hand and told me to run downstairs to ask Mrs O'Reilly if she would sew a white shirt onto the button. There were countless incidents where most would choose to moan, but that was not Ma's style. She preferred to smile than sulk and as such her quick wit always governed the way in which she responded to the slightly more difficult times.

The day I told Ma that I was going to be appearing on a live television show with Reverend Paisley, the first thing she asked me was if I felt I was doing the right thing. She was basically asking me that if an argument developed, did I feel I could emerge on the right side of it. Overall, my perception of what lay ahead was a positive one and as it turned out, I was right. The show, which was being hosted by the Reverend's daughter Rhonda Paisley, was a tremendous success. I managed to make Reverend Paisley laugh which back then was not an occurrence people witnessed too often. I don't know if my religion was immaterial that night but I certainly wasn't made feel uncomfortable for being of a different faith. If anything, I look upon that show as one of the highlights of my professional career.

Another highlight was the wonderful friendship I struck up with the late Joe Dolan. It could easily be said that Joe was as known for his charismatic quick wit as he was for his music. Every time I met him he would always tell me a joke I had never heard before. I don't know where he got them, but they were always hilarious. One night, he was telling me a story about a dog that belonged to a Dublin woman, but he told the gag as though it had genuinely happened. According to Joe, the dog had caught sight of the new postman on duty in the area and immediately darted after him. Naturally, the postman starts running like the hammers of hell when next thing he hears the owner of the dog shouting after him in her strong Dublin accent. She roars, "There's no need to be runnin', the dog has no teeth." To which the postman shouts back, "I know that missus, but he could give a nasty suck!"

Back in the days before I developed a friendship with Joe, I was an avid fan of his work. However Joe was the kind of individual who could charm the bejaysus out of you, so even if you didn't like his work as a performer, you couldn't but like him as a person. When I first spoke to him as a youngster, I referred to him as "Mr Dolan" to which he replied, "Mr Dolan was my father's name, call me Joe."

That alone was enough to immediately render me at ease and as such, it's a line that I myself use to this day whenever I meet a nervous fan who refers to me with a formal greeting. In the relatively early stages of my career, I decided to introduce myself to Joe after spotting him in the lounge of The Hitching Post in Leixlip. By this time, I had a record in the charts and had appeared on The Late Late Show which was probably why, when I introduced myself to him, his first words back to me were: "Ah ya bollocks ya, you don't have to tell me who you are!"

From that night onwards, we became great friends. We would go to each other's shows and enjoy a few pints afterwards. We had many memorable mad nights out and to be honest the only thing I didn't have in common with him was a penchant for golf.

I spoke to Joe about a week before he died but I didn't realise how sick he was at the time. He was his usual self but I knew by him he was tired and drained. When my good friend Ronan Collins phoned me in America to tell me that Joe had died, I had to be held up I was so grief-stricken and shocked. I had known Joe was ill, but I simply thought he would be out of hospital within a week and cracking jokes as usual.

Never did I imagine I would hear those heartbreaking words, "Joe is gone."

sixteen

Brendan was always so spontaneous in a performance. Even though we would have had a script, he would sometimes throw in a hilarious line at a moment when you would least expect it. In the middle of a performance, it wouldn't be unusual for him to suddenly say something like "Ah Jaysus I thought the bar was closing, it was only me eyes."

My dad often said "Some people say funny things, other people say things funny." Brendan says things funny. I admire him both as a person and as a performer and I am adamant that we haven't seen everything he has to offer yet. There is so much more he has yet to surprise us with. Brendan is a marvellous actor and I think it would be a sad day if we thought we had seen everything there is to see from him. I want to see him broaden his range and break into something like drama. And you know what, being asked to contribute to this book might just be the stick of dynamite I need to shove it you-know-where in order to get him to do it.

Twink

Wedding day smiles with our friend Fr Seán Breen.

Up, up and away.

Me and me mot!

Quality time
with the family.

With Eileen and my infamous mother-in-law Lillie.

Not the pope but Fr Seán Breen at the renewal of our wedding vows on the occasion of our 25th wedding anniversary at our home in Florida.

Me and Eilo on our 35th wedding anniversary in Charleston, South Carolina.

The three Graces.

Miami Voice.

Whoo seddah?

Three generations – me with my
aunt Wyn and sweet baby James.

My son Brendan holding newborn Patrick. Sitting beside
him is his son Aidan, and Mel and Frank's son, James.

Me with my sister Maria

The second daughter to wed! The new bride Melanie with her sister Amanda and their respective husbands, Frank Gillespie and Martin Lynch.

Brendan, the famous Aunt Wyn, Eileen and Uncle Bud enjoying Melanie and Frank's big day

The late Johnny Burke, whose portrait can clearly be seen on the wall, was considered "one of the guests" on the day of Melanie and Frank's wedding in Spanish Point, county Clare.

A trouserless father of the bride!

My girls. Eileen, Melanie and Amanda.

Amanda and Martin's wedding.

I'm warnin' ya Gillespie – take good care of her.

Grandson James, a tuxedo toddler.

It Started On The Late Late Show

I t's not uncommon for me to receive a letter in the post addressed to: "Brendan Grace, Dublin". A number of years ago, a letter somehow managed to reach me despite it being only addressed to: "Brendan Grace, Comedian, Ireland".

Even after all these years, the one thing that continues to fascinate me about television is the aspect of recognition. It can be somewhat unnerving to think that absolute strangers know who I am, but for the most part it's a lovely feeling because I am often treated as a friend.

I can still remember the excitement of my family over my first television appearance with The Gingermen on Shay Healy's weekly programme, The Ballad Sheet. As a solo performer, however, my big break greeted me in the form of The Late Late Show. While I had been doing well for myself prior to my first appearance on the show, my situation couldn't possibly have been better afterwards.

I remember back when the closing song for the show was Nat King Cole's "It Started on the Late Late Show", and in a way that's a theme tune that could most definitely be applied to my own life. Its effect on my career was profound. Testament to this was that on the Monday morning following my appearance on the show, my diary for the year was jammed full with bookings.

I owe a lot to RTÉ and Gay Byrne for the amount of opportunities and shows they sent my way. They gave my acts airtime for which I will always be incredibly grateful. It had such a significant impact on my career, the extent of which I cannot even begin to describe.

For me there have been many memorable Late Late Show moments. Following the incident in which Sinéad O'Connor ripped up a picture of the pope, I appeared on stage dressed like a pope and tore in half a picture of Sinéad O'Connor. I then walked off. It was a visual gag; there was no beginning or ending, I just walked on, ripped up the picture and walked off. Brief and all as it was, it received a hell of a laugh.

On another occasion, I appeared on The Late Late Show with Maureen O'Hara which for me was an unforgettable experience. Maureen is one person for whom I have always had tremendous admiration and for years it was my ambition to meet her. I once sent her a letter accompanied by my video, to which she replied with a note saying how much she had enjoyed it. This letter is now framed in my pub and sitting near it on the wall is a photograph I cherish just as much. The circumstances in which the picture was taken were surreal to say the least. On the day in question, I had been enjoying a drink in Harrington's pub in Glengarriff in west Cork along with Eileen and Melanie, when a woman approached me and asked if I was Brendan Grace. Her next words to me were: "I heard you would like to meet my mother."

For some reason I thought she had said her mother would like to meet me. She then told me that her mother lived in a house nearby, so I gladly agreed to meet her. It was only when the woman mentioned the name Maureen O'Hara that I realised who I was on my way to meet. The nerves almost enveloped me. I actually could not get my head around the fact that I was about to meet the legend herself. Sure enough, when Eileen, Melanie and I walked into the hallway of this very elegant house, standing in front of us was Maureen. I mentioned earlier how I cry whenever I hear the song "My Son", well that song might as well have been on full blast for all the tears I cried that day, I was so moved. When we sat down, I spotted the video I had sent her sitting at the top of the pile beside the television. It was an incredibly nostalgic moment because Maureen was a childhood icon of mine.

A few years later, her 80th birthday was held in the Dun Raven Arms Hotel in Adare, county Limerick. As there was a big civic reception to be held in her honour, she asked me if I would present her with her birthday cake. Naturally, I was honoured by her request and fulfilled it while serenading her with the song

"The Isle of Inisfree" from *The Quiet Man*. We formed a lovely friendship and I later presented her with cakes for three subsequent birthdays.

When you meet your heroes, you are usually so stunned by being in their presence that the first words out of your mouth are ones you come to later regret. This was certainly the case with me on more than one occasion.

In 1987 I was on a plane from New York to Chicago when I saw this person of small stature in a tracksuit and a cap. I didn't take much notice until he turned around and I realised it was Elton John. I was standing right next to him and when I realised who he was I was so shocked that I blurted out, "Hello Mr John." I said it so fast that all he could do was laugh.

He then said to me, "That's an Irish accent I hear."

On another occasion, I was introduced to Prince Albert of Monaco by Dr Michael Smurfit. I wasn't *au fait* with how he should be addressed so instead I verbalised the first thing that came into my head: "Howya prince!"

Later that night, when I stepped up on stage to begin my act for the gala at which the prince was in attendance, I greeted the crowd and said "I'd like to give a special welcome to his highness who is here tonight, although I'm told he prefers to be called Dr Smurfit, or Michael to his friends."

Prince Albert got a great kick out of that joke. Not only is he a man of a lovely placid nature, he also has a wonderful sense of humour so I knew he would appreciate the comedy of it. A similar incident occurred with Lord Henry Mountcharles in 1999. I was on a plane packing my bags into the overhead compartment. A very courteous and polite man was waiting to pass me and when I turned around, I realised it was none other than Lord Mountcharles. I should have said "Hello Henry" but I was so surprised to see him that instead my immediate remark was: "Ah howya lord!"

It was only when I said it that I realised how stupid it sounded. He laughed at my reaction, so I think he assumed I was joking.

I appeared on The Late Late Show many times and there is a story I told on one particular occasion that people still mention to me. I was recalling for

Gaybo a nostalgic story about the happenings of one Christmas Eve during my childhood and for it, I adopted a very serious tone of voice. I explained how I had heard a noise emanating from the attic of our Echlin Street flat one night and how it progressed into a strange thumping sound. I then went on to recall how my father stood up on a chair and slowly pushed open the attic door to see what could be causing such an unusual noise. By this point, the crowd was in complete silence and a number of people who watched it on television have since told me they were on the edge of their seats. I went on to describe how my father nearly died with shock when he saw what was there in front of him.

"What was it?" asked Gaybo, enthralled.

Pausing slightly, I replied, "A turkey running around in a pair of hobnail boots."

I caught out Gay hook, line and sinker and I don't think I will ever forget the look on his face when he said back to me, "You eejit!" His reaction was as funny as the story itself at the time. There are people reading this book who will remember that night and I'm sure some of them were absolutely disgusted that it was a joke and not the serious tale I had initially led them to believe.

Gay always called me "son" and he treated me like one as well.

Coincidentally, his daughter Crona lives in my adopted home village of Killaloe and is a good friend of my daughter Amanda, as well as being pals with Eileen and me. Another pal of mine from RTÉ is the tremendously talented Adele King, aka Twink, with whom I performed on Play the Game for just over three years. In 1996, the year she and I turned 45, Adele phoned me with a great idea for a theatre show in which the two of us would star, entitled The Craic is Ninety. Unfortunately, it never came to fruition but I do harbour ambitions of us working together again sometime in the future.

Ronan Collins, with whom I have been good friends for many years, was another Play the Game colleague of mine. I can remember Ronan back when he wore large bellbottoms with a packet of Benson & Hedges under his belt. In his defence though, bellbottoms were all the rage back then.

In 1984, I left Play the Game to take up the job of hosting Sunday Night at the Olympia. Even after landing these shows, I continued gigging full time. From community halls to Carnegie Hall, I played wherever I was asked. Carmel Quinn, wife of Bill Fuller who I mentioned earlier, was a well known Irish entertainer who became America's sweetheart during the fifties and sixties. Her nickname was Brown Bread because every time she appeared on The Late Late Show she would always talk about Irish brown bread. In 1975 and 1976, she invited me to appear on the stage of Carnegie Hall with her which, needless to say, was a huge deal for me. After all, to tread the stage of that particular venue was the ultimate achievement for an entertainer. 1975 was also the year I performed in New York's Madison Square Garden. The concert was called The Three Brendans and consisted of myself, Brendan Shine and the late Brendan O'Dowda. Despite entertaining the crowds of these two world famous venues, I never received an invite from a particular folk club that was based on the Navan Road back in the seventies and whose singer was my good friend and RTÉ broadcaster, Pat Kenny.

There is an assumption that people in entertainment take no notice of when their name is mentioned on television because they are so accustomed to it. That's not necessarily the case. I don't know about other personalities, but even after a few decades on the scene, I am still always pleasantly surprised by a mention. I remember being extremely chuffed when Christy Moore, following his hit "Lisdoonvarna", recorded a song called "Come to the Cabaret" in which he mentioned my name. In the song, he talks about a trucker who pulls into the car park of a Mother Hubbard's restaurant and says to him, "Hey there I know your face, are you Bono or Brendan Grace?"

Bill Cullen on his series The Apprentice also used my name in rhyming slang. I think it's more commonly used in Dublin, but for those who don't know, rhyming slang is is the use of a rhyming phrase instead of the actual word itself. For example, if someone refers to "apples and pears", they are actually talking about the "stairs". Likewise, if someone says they want to hail a "Joe Maxi", they are talking about a "taxi". On The Apprentice however, Bill would use "Brendan Grace" as rhyming slang for the word "face". He was talking about one of the candidates at the time and I think the way he put it was: "I didn't like the look on his Brendan Grace."

Recognition is something that always surprises me. I find it incredibly charming when people take me by the hand and bring me over to meet their mother, father or grandparents. It's so endearing because there is nothing nicer than being able to bring about a smile in someone. Giving back is hugely important to me. I have always been active in children's charities. In fact, my very first solo gig was a children's charity show. I was the patron of the Bubblegum Club for ten years, however I have since gone on to champion other causes, particularly those related to hospices and charities for the elderly. Charity work remains close to my heart and if playing a gig will bring in the funds that will make a difference to someone's life, then I am more than happy to do what I can.

I have seen people in the business, people I won't name, being incredibly rude towards fans. It's the exception, but it does happen. I can never understand people who complain about being recognised because I believe that anyone who has chosen this particular medium from which to make a living, and in most cases a good living, has quite the cheek to complain and be pissed off with their fans. It never bothers me when people ask for autographs and photographs but there have been occasions when I have been approached at a funeral. Usually the person who asks doesn't really consider the implications of signing an autograph while standing in the middle of a crowd of mourners, so usually I would just quietly tell them to email me their address or write to me at the pub and I will send them an autograph that way. I would never feel comfortable signing an autograph at a funeral simply because it is an event that is meant to be treated as sacrosanct, but people do ask.

In showbusiness, there has always been a certain romanticism attached to dying on stage. Possibly the most famous example of a stage death was that of the entertainer Tommy Cooper. I was watching his show on television that fateful night in April 1984 when he collapsed midway through his act. He just fell to the ground and at the time I immediately sensed there was something wrong as he had fallen far too smoothly for it to have been an act. It was too realistic. For what seemed like a lifetime, nothing happened. Suddenly, the curtain went down and the host, Jimmy Tarbuck, appeared on stage to introduce an ad break. I phoned a magician friend of mine, Tony Sadar, and he too was of the opinion that what we had witnessed wasn't an act. Sure enough, at the end of the show Jimmy Tarbuck appeared on stage and announced that Tommy had passed away.

In 1998, my good friend Chris Casey left us in exactly the same manner. He was on stage in a Dublin venue and as he was delivering his lines, he simply fell to the floor. It's heartbreaking to lose someone so well liked in such an abrupt fashion, but in some way there's a comfort to be had from knowing that the person died doing what they loved best, performing.

My manager Brian always tells me that I'm worth more to him financially dead. As if that wasn't bad enough, my wife tells me the exact same thing. It has long been a private joke amongst us simply because when a performer dies, sales of their merchandise shoot up. Even though I argue I'm better value alive, I still hear back, "Yeah, but Bren, you're worth more to us dead."

Personally I don't want to die on stage; I would rather be with my family. However, if my mother was right all along and reincarnation really does happen then when I go to die a second time around, I might give the stage a bit of thought.

Acknowledgements

Even though this is not a cookbook, there are many fine ingredients to be found within, the suppliers of which I would like to sincerely thank. So here's the menu.

For starters, I would like to address the many friends and colleagues who contributed wonderful quotes and stories regarding their memories of me. Thank you also to my dear friend Pete Saint John. Your magnificent songs will remain forever etched in our minds and I am truly honoured by those noble words you penned for the foreword of this book.

Now for the main course. I realised from the start that my chosen career was not just a dream fulfilled, but also an actual business. As such I maintained a professional attitude and always surrounded myself with individuals who I felt would be of similar mindset. In this regard, my cast and crew are simply the finest. My booking manager Tom Kelly is the very best and a true professional, while my own personal manager, Brian Keane, is my right hand man. Brian, aka captain, wears many hats from personal manager and scriptwriter, to tour manager and product manager. More than anything else however, he is my constant and loyal companion.

Thank you sincerely to my publisher and friend John O'Connor of Blackwater Press who introduced me to the lovely and talented Tara King. She commuted between Ireland and Florida in order to get the book right and in doing so, became part of my family. Her skill and professional ways drew every tale and yarn out of me with dedication and care and presented them in the form of a novel. Thank you Tara.

For the dessert course, I would like to thank my wonderful family, each of whom played a pivotal role in this book by enthusiastically helping me recall all those lovely events from throughout my life. For that I am very grateful. To my children Amanda, Melanie, Bradley and Brendan Patrick, I often scared the bejaysus out of you with the pranks I played but thanks all the same for being such good sports and for the many wonderful laughs we enjoyed over the years. To my grandchildren, I do hope that when you're older you will enjoy reading about your grandad's life and travels. I also hope that the stories of my own childhood will amuse and delight you.

GALWAY COUNTY LIBRARIES

Above all, I want to acknowledge the lady who came into my world 37 years ago and made it all happen in living colour, a beautiful lady and soulmate, Eileen Doyle. This wonderful woman has remained by my side from the start, shared with me many laughs and created many memories. From girlfriend to wife, from mother to grandmother, the love of my life and my forever friend, she still closes her eyes when we kiss ... she hates to see me enjoying meself!

Finally, a big thank you to you the reader for inviting me into your library. I hope you'll enjoy the journey, the stories and above all, the many many laughs.

Brendan Grace